Connected Parenting

*Set Loving Limits and
Build Strong Bonds with
Your Child for Life*

Jennifer Kolari, MSW, RSW

Avery
a member of PENGUIN GROUP (USA) INC. *New York*

Published by the Penguin Group
Penguin Group (USA) Inc., 375 Hudson Street, New York, New York 10014, USA • Penguin
Group (Canada), 90 Eglinton Avenue East, Suite 700, Toronto, Ontario M4P 2Y3, Canada
(a division of Pearson Penguin Canada Inc.) • Penguin Books Ltd, 80 Strand, London WC2R 0RL,
England • Penguin Ireland, 25 St Stephen's Green, Dublin 2, Ireland (a division of Penguin
Books Ltd) • Penguin Group (Australia), 250 Camberwell Road, Camberwell, Victoria 3124,
Australia (a division of Pearson Australia Group Pty Ltd) • Penguin Books India Pvt Ltd,
11 Community Centre, Panchsheel Park, New Delhi–110 017, India • Penguin Group (NZ),
67 Apollo Drive, Rosedale, North Shore 0632, New Zealand (a division of Pearson New
Zealand Ltd) • Penguin Books (South Africa) (Pty) Ltd, 24 Sturdee Avenue, Rosebank,
Johannesburg 2196, South Africa

Penguin Books Ltd, Registered Offices: 80 Strand, London WC2R 0RL, England

First paperback edition 2010
Copyright © 2009 by Connected Parenting Inc.

Most Avery books are available at special quantity discounts for bulk purchase for sales
promotions, premiums, fund-raising, and educational needs. Special books or book excerpts
also can be created to fit specific needs. For details, write Penguin Group (USA) Inc. Special
Markets, 375 Hudson Street, New York, NY 10014.

ISBN: 978-1-58333-394-5 (paperback edition)

Printed in the United States of America
10 9 8 7 6 5 4 3 2 1

Book design by Jennifer Ann Daddio/Bookmark Design & Media Inc.

Neither the publisher nor the author is engaged in rendering professional advice or services to
the individual reader. The ideas, procedures, and suggestions contained in this book are not
intended as a substitute for consulting with a physician. All matters regarding health require
medical supervision. Neither the author nor the publisher shall be liable or responsible for any
loss or damage allegedly arising from any information or suggestion in this book.

All the patients described in this book are composites. Extensive details have been changed to
protect the confidentiality and privacy of patients and research participants. The patient cases
in the book are emotionally real, but no case corresponds to any actual person, living or dead.

While the author has made every effort to provide accurate telephone numbers and Internet
addresses at publication time, the publisher and the author assume no responsibility for errors,
or for changes that occur after publication. Further, the publisher has no control over and
assumes no responsibility for author or third-party websites or their content.

*To my children
and children everywhere*

Contents

Part One.
Making or Repairing the Connection

Part Two.
Setting Appropriate Limits

Part Three.
Connecting and Containing in Special Situations

Acknowledgments

I am thankful to so many people who supported me and have been a constant inspiration to me. To my agent, Rick Broadhead, thank you so much for believing in this project and its message. Thank you for all the time you put into it, for all your support, and for all your long conversations with me. To my editor Lucia Watson in New York, thank you for your clear understanding of the vision of this book and for your commitment and belief in the philosophy behind Connected Parenting. You brought clarity, power, and organization to the work. Thank you to my Canadian editor, Alex Shultz, for inheriting this project and getting behind it midway through. To Barbara Berson, for loving and "getting" this book, for your support and excitement. I will never forget the day I got that phone call from you. I am forever grateful. To Judy Kern, I couldn't have written this without you . . . no, really! Thank you for all your help, for your wit, for your wisdom, and for your fantastic laugh. It was a great journey.

Faye Mishna, for being a truly unforgettable teacher whose lessons helped me to be a better clinician, person, and mother. So much of this book and the philosophy behind it were inspired by your wisdom and your teaching; thank you.

Tish Cohen, together we are one person. You are my best friend, and I am thankful for that every day of my life. Thank you for the continuous conversation we have been having since we were twelve years old and . . . Mammoth really is as high as the Rockies. Thank you for all your help with editing, for being my Houston, and for editing this acknowledgment section.

Alisa Kenny Bridgeman, thank you for the hours you spent on this book combing over every word and for listening to me whine. You are brilliant. Thank you for your support, your friendship, and your brain. Cindy Smolkin, my right hand, I love that you are working with me at Connected Parenting. You are a spectacular therapist and even better friend. I am looking forward to growing Connected Parenting with you. Thank you for your enthusiasm and endless support. Janis Beach, you are the other primary teacher in my life who has taught me so much. I can't thank you enough for everything you do and have done for me and for being astonishingly smart. I am still pinching myself that you are working with me at Connected Parenting; I am so honored. Marsha Gallinger and Daniela Kozlov, the other members of my dream team, thank you for being part of it all, for lending me your talent. I am so grateful to you both. Beverly Kavanagh, thank you for your unending belief in Connected Parenting, for your trust, and for your support. Your point of view was more helpful than you will ever know. Robin Stone—you rock, thank you for your opinions, your support, and your incredible sense of humor. Sarah Hall at Blue Sky Communications Inc., you are wonderful. Thank you for your energy and for everything you have done for me. I would also like to thank all the families I have worked with for letting me into your lives and for trusting me with your children. You are all very special to me; thank you. To the kids whom I have worked with, thank you for all that you have taught me. Thank you for working hard, being honest, and being so real. You are all treasures, each and every one of you.

Most of all, I would like to thank my family. My husband, Barry, what can I say except thank you for being the love of my life. Thanks for holding down the fort while I wrote, worried, and stressed. To Jacob, Zoë, and Olivia, thank you for allowing people to know your names and share your stories. You are spectacular kids. I love you all so very much and I am so deeply proud of all three of you. You are my true teachers, and you continue to teach me every day. Thank you, my babies.

Mom and Dad, you are the best parents and, as far as I'm concerned, the original Connected Parents. I knew every day as a child how loved I was. It was a part of me and still is.

To my sister, Rebecca, the rock of Connected Parenting, I could not do it without you. You are so smart, so supportive, so proud of me, it fills me up. It makes me sad for all the people who don't know what it's like to have a sister.

Author's Note

I invite you to think of this book as a recipe with many ingredients, some common and familiar, others new and original. Just as there are many recipes for a great cake, there are many great parenting books and models; this one is my recipe. Much of what I've learned and write about comes from twenty years of families letting me into their lives and sharing their experiences, from my work, my observations, and the repeating patterns I have seen. Much comes from being a mother of three beautiful children, from paying attention to those patterns and recognizing them in my own parenting and in my husband's. The rest comes from many sources: professors, colleagues, supervisors, conferences, and courses I've attended. I have made an effort to be sure all those professionals and studies are properly cited. I do not claim that no other professionals are saying at least some of what I am, but I've put it all together in the unique way that works best for me, for my children, and for the families I have had the privilege of working with. Please remember that the advice given in this book is not meant to replace medical advice or the direct advice of a mental health care professional. I hope this recipe will work for you and supplement the knowledge you have gathered over your own years as a parent.

The Keys to Connection

Because you have picked up this book, chances are you have experienced moments when you have been totally exasperated, frustrated, and exhausted by your child's behavior. You have lived through meltdowns and flailing legs as you try to put on your child's shoes; you've fought battles every day over the smallest things, and heard the word "no" more than you would care to imagine.

You may be the parent of an anxious child who is crying and stuck to your leg, refusing to go into the birthday party with all the other happy, enthusiastic kids. Maybe you are the one whose child is rambunctious and aggressive and who feels the judgmental glances of other parents dropping off or picking up their kids at school. Maybe your child is usually pretty good, but when he's bad he takes everyone down with him. There are many parents who feel the way you do. All parents feel that way from time to time, and all children can be challenging at times, but some children are different. The sensible consequences and strategies that sound great and work with other children—even your own other children—don't always work on them. If any of the above sounds familiar to you, you already know you are the parent of a challenging child—or a gladiator child, as I affectionately call such children.

Children's behavior can be challenging for many reasons. Most often it's as simple as temperament and personality; sometimes it's caused by family issues and stressors; sometimes it's caused by anxiety; and at times there is an underlying issue such as attention-deficit/hyperactivity disorder (ADHD). Whatever the reason, like all children, challenging children have many wonderful traits. They can be funny, smart, loving, energetic, and sensitive. They can, however, also be intense, defiant, and hard on their siblings. They can fixate on the smallest things and excel at wearing you down. They can get wound up and overexcited and have a hard time calming themselves. They can argue like the best of lawyers, ruin great moments, and embarrass you in public. They can make you sadder and angrier than you ever thought possible, and cause you to question every parenting decision you make. You love them with all your heart, but at times you can't stand to be around them. Maybe you question yourself, have terrible guilt, fear for your child, and wonder why no one else seems to have a child quite like yours. Parenting can be extremely difficult, as well as extremely rewarding, but parenting a challenging child is a job that truly requires support, guidance, and a really good plan.

This book is but one in a sea of parenting books, each promising to make parenting easier. There are many great parenting books with great insights and strategies to offer; all of them have something important to say. So what on earth could be different about this one? This book will offer you a unique and powerful perspective. These pages are filled with a host of specific strategies that I suspect will be different from others you have tried and that work with all children. If your child is not particularly challenging, these strategies will work like a dream, helping you and your child stay close as they help your child develop confidence and a strong sense of self. And if your child is a gladiator, this book becomes even more crucial because it will provide you with new and incredibly effective ways to build or re-build loving bonds, and help him or her develop better emotional regulation, impulse control, social health, and resilience.

What makes this program so different is the fact that the Connected Parenting method is primarily based on therapy techniques, not parenting techniques. It helps you to bond with and soothe your kids, as well as to model compassion, empathy, responsibility, and a commitment to deep understanding. It gives you a way to effectively contain—that is, to set boundaries—and to guide and correct behavior that comes from a place of love rather than from anger or frustration. By doing that, it brings out the best in both you and your child. Following the program won't be easy—nothing worthwhile ever is. But in the end, your child will be more compliant, more relaxed, and—most important—happier, and you will feel proud of your parenting and closer to your child.

More often than not, when the phone rings in my office, the person on the other end is the frightened or desperate parent of a child who may be very much like yours. These parents describe their children as anxious or defiant or emotionally volatile or as little warriors with whom they engage in endless battles. They are likely to tell me that although they love their child, at times they also hate him. They say that this is not what they signed up for, not what they thought their child would be, and not how they had pictured themselves as parents. They may describe their home as a war zone or themselves as tiptoeing around, trying to avoid the next skirmish. They confess that they don't know how they're going to get through the next ten or fifteen minutes with their child, let alone the next fifteen years, and, most often, they feel terribly guilty not only about their feelings but also because they think they may be the cause of the problem.

Again and again these beleaguered moms and dads promise themselves that they're not going to yell anymore, that they will be more patient, that they will no longer say things they really don't mean, such as, "If you can't behave I'm going to have to give you away." And then, two or three days later, their child will do something that makes them crazy and they'll just snap and say or do the same thing all over again. On a good day, they love their child so much that it hurts and desperately want her to be happy and understood by others. On a bad day, they want to be anywhere but near this child and can feel resentful, hurt, and angry at the toll his behavior takes on them and everyone else in the family. Most of all, these parents are overwhelmed by how much time their challenging child demands, often at the expense of other children in the family.

If you share these feelings, I want to assure you, as I do them, that it's not your fault. Most of us could not do any better, and those who have relaxed, easygoing children have no idea what it takes to keep your patience day after day and love a child who is sometimes so hard to love. It can be heartbreaking and tremendously stressful, not only for the child and his or her parents, but also for siblings and extended family. What develops in these situations is a dynamic between you and your child that brings out the worst in each of you—but you do have the power to create amazing change.

Most of the children I work with have more than the average share of emotional problems, and they may or may not also have an underlying condition that exacerbates their behavior. The extreme satisfaction I get from my job is that I can offer hope and a plan that will help *all* parents to strengthen and enhance the connection between them and their children and, at the same time, bring out the best in their children. I can help to bring the experience of parenting even the most challenging child in line with the best of what parenting holds.

Empathy is the most important part of being a parent; in truth, it is the most important part of being human. It is what connects us to one another, what holds relationships together, and what allows us to experience mutual respect and deep caring. We know that children respond well to empathy from birth, that it is critical for healthy development in general, and, in particular, for the development of a cohesive and organized sense of self. For that reason alone, empathy is an essential parenting tool, and while we do not always feel like being empathic, it is critical in many, many ways to our child's happiness and success.

Understanding how to use empathy as the first step toward repairing frayed bonds and changing behavior will enhance and integrate all the techniques you already use and all the knowledge you have already derived from your own experience, from other parenting books, or from other resources you have accessed. It is a beautiful gift to your children and a lovely way to parent. The empathic method I teach takes commitment and a willingness to try whenever possible to be nondefensive, to choose your words carefully, and to stay confident and consistent in the face of negative behavior. The rewards it offers are many, and the results last a lifetime.

Many parenting books discuss how important it is to listen to your children and to be empathic. What many books don't tell you, however, is *how* to be empathic and how to move beyond empathy to control and correct difficult or unacceptable behaviors. The whole point of connected parenting and the method I teach is to empathize not only so that your child will feel safe and understood, but also so that you, the parent, will be better able to correct and guide his or her behavior.

Many of us think we already know how to be empathic, but, as easy as it sounds, being empathic and listening well are very difficult skills, requiring practice, patience, thoughtfulness, and a nondefensive stance that is extremely difficult to maintain when you are hurt or angry. In addition, empathy, in and of itself, isn't enough. We also need to know what to do next. Once we've empathized with a child's anger, frustration, or anxiety, how do we go on to make him understand that the coping behaviors he is using are not acceptable and will not serve him well? In short, how do we get him to change?

This guide takes you that crucial extra step and provides you with a blueprint for creating positive change. The skills I teach sometimes seem counterintuitive, but you can acquire them, just as my clients do, with the help, support, and insight this book will provide. In the beginning you may just have to trust that what you're doing will work, but when it does, it will be life-altering for both you and your child.

I am a social worker and a child and family therapist, and one of my major influences comes from a particular kind of therapy called self-psychology, which is based on the premise that, as a therapist, you work very hard to be attuned to your client's feelings and experiences and to be aware of your own agenda and intent. Over the years, I have developed a rather eclectic approach to therapy that combines compassion and deep caring with consistency and limit-setting. Learning these techniques has been exciting and challenging. It has taken a lot of practice, but my reward has been to see wonderful changes in both the children I work with and their parents. The tools I use and teach enhance closeness between parent and child, lower anxiety, reduce power struggles, and, most important, build resilience in the child, while at the same time bringing out the best in us as parents. My therapeutic model helps us to treat our children with compassion and dignity, and to support behavioral change from the inside out.

What is also important about this model is that it recognizes that we all make mistakes and offers ways to repair and "redo" when necessary. As a mother, I know how frustrating parenting can be and that we all lose our temper and blow it sometimes. Even though I teach connected parenting and believe in it fully, I still get angry and don't always do what I know is right.

To illustrate the power of the forgiving nature of this model, I would like to share the story of Mollie, the client who first helped me to understand how important empathy is.

At ten years old, Mollie had already cultivated such a negative personality for herself that I found it extremely difficult just to be in the room and remain positive with her. I was green as grass and ready to save the world, I was ready to be caring and understanding and supportive to this client, but Mollie was more of a challenge than I could have anticipated.

She was the product of a rape, and because of the way she came into the world, her mother, Kate, had great difficulty loving her. In fact, Mollie used to throw herself down the stairs as a young child just to get some kind of affection from her mother. When I spoke with Kate, she told me that even in the hospital nursery Mollie had screamed and cried *in order to* wake the other babies, and that when she nursed, Mollie had bitten her on purpose. In other words, Mollie's mother was projecting purposeful malevolence onto what was, in reality, normal infant behavior. It was clear to me that the child just couldn't win, but that didn't really help me when I was in her presence.

Because she'd been so consistently rejected from birth, Mollie seemed determined to keep people at arm's length so that they would never get close enough for her to risk another rejection. Her unconscious thought process appeared to say: "If I try to get close to someone he or she will wind up hurting me, so I won't give anyone any reason to do that."

By the time I met her, this young girl was incredibly rude and offensive, and had the habit of picking on every little thing anyone did. I knew what was going on, and I tried my best to be professional and to not be affected by what she said, but after a few weeks it was becoming very difficult. Being with her was exhausting. She was pushing buttons I didn't even know I had, commenting on every aspect of my appearance, every mispronounced word that came out of my mouth.

It made for a very long therapy hour, and at some point I went to my supervisor and said, "You know, I think I have a problem. I'm not sure I can do this. I don't think I'm cut out to be a therapist after all. I find it difficult just to sit in the room with this child. What am I going to do?"

Her response was, "That tells you a great deal about this little girl. This is how *everyone* reacts to her. Imagine walking through life and having everybody feel about you the way you do—even your therapist can't stand being in a room with you. You have to go back in there and tolerate that negativity. Don't respond the way others do, and show ruthless compassion." By that she meant that I had to do nothing but remain unfailingly compassionate no matter how Mollie responded. It was my introduction to self-psychology.

One of the ways I'd been coping with this difficult child was to be a few minutes late entering the room. It was only three or four minutes but, to be entirely honest, I really needed to gather myself up to face her, and wasting a few minutes seemed the only thing to do. So, I would walk in late to our session and Mollie would verbally attack me, saying I was stupid, I was the worst therapist in the world, and I should be fired. I would then respond in what I thought was a very empathic, professional way, saying things like, "It must make you very angry when I come into the room late," to which she would answer, "Of course I'm angry, you idiot."

After I had spoken with my supervisor, and again walked into the room a minute or two late, Mollie, predictably, attacked me. This time, however, I was ready with a new attitude and a new response. In a very understanding voice with not an ounce of defensiveness I said, "You are absolutely right. This is your hour. It belongs to you. You're never late. It's your time and I chose to do something else with it. This isn't the first time I've done that either."

That was all I had a chance to say before tears welled up in her eyes and she said, "People always do that to me! They never care about what I want . . ." And there it was. For the first time in the four months I'd been working with her I saw a real little person in there who was suffering and hurting, and *that* was something I could connect with.

What I had done was to let Mollie know that I understood what she was feeling without defending and explaining myself. I had reflected her experience back to her without judgment. This is mirroring, a technique developed by Heinz Kohut, the father of self-psychology. My own version and interpretation of this technique is at the core of what I'll be teaching you in this book. What I *didn't* do—and this is extremely important—was to try to *tell* her what she was feeling or to "fix" those feelings. If I had said, "You must feel . . ." I would have broken the connection by letting her know that I was observing her and trying to figure her out. Instead I had responded, with words, expression, and body language, *as if* I were joining with her in the experience. I was letting her know that I felt her feelings without ever having to state them and, at the same time, I was letting her know that she had a right to those feelings. I continued to mirror, and week by week something wonderful happened. Mollie stopped insulting me, she asked for help, and she became more pleasant, even warm. It wasn't long before I began to enjoy rather than dread our sessions. Within a couple of months others in the office also noticed the change in her, began to comment on this, and changed their own responses to her. It was a powerful therapeutic experience that would affect us both forever.

To this day I am grateful to that supervisor and to that child for teaching me about empathy. It was a lesson that has had a profound impact on me as a therapist, as a person, and, ultimately, as a mother. It made me understand on the deepest level that the most effective way to change behavior is through nondefensiveness and unfailing compassion.

Before you begin to practice connected parenting it is important to understand why it works and how it affects your behavior as a parent. What does it mean to take a nondefensive stance? What it means for me as a therapist is that I must never assume my actions have been understood the way I intended. As human beings we filter our experiences of one another through our own history of successes and failures. This is called intersubjectivity, which essentially means that reality generally lies somewhere in the middle of how a communication or action is intended and how it is perceived by each individual. Let's say, for example, that I am in a session with a client who begins to tell a particularly intense story toward the end of the hour. I might reflexively glance up at the clock because I'm worried that she may not have enough time to finish. If I did this with five different clients, they might experience that one action five different ways. One client could interpret it to mean that he's boring me and I can't wait until the session is over. Another might think I just wanted to finish so I could make more money off my next client; a third might not even care that I looked at the clock, and so on. Therefore, I need to be acutely aware at all times of how anything I do or say might affect my client. And, furthermore, if he or she is adversely affected by something I say or do, I have to be prepared to make what Kohut called an "empathic repair." So if I noticed that my client seemed upset I might say, "You were telling me something very meaningful and important and I looked at the time right in the middle of your story." The client might then say something like, "Don't worry, it didn't bother me," or "That's what always happens to me. I feel like no one ever listens!" I might or might not then explain my reasons for glancing at the time, depending on the client and what she might need in order to move on.

As parents, we often assume that our children understand our intent, when in fact they often do not. This book will help you to become more attuned to what your children are experiencing when they act out, and then let them know that you do understand and empathize with their feelings, which is a kind of therapeutic parenting. You won't be able to do that every moment of every day. I talk about it, teach it, and try to integrate it into every part of my own parenting, and yet I too sometimes find it hard to remember to do it.

That's why it's so important to be aware of our own agenda and the impact it has on our ability to be empathic. Often, when our children are unhappy or in pain, we just want to fix it for them. We want them to stop hurting and be happy. When they're angry or acting out, we want them to calm down and behave. But that's *our* agenda. What we forget at these times is that it's important for us to hear what *they're* thinking and feeling before we try to fix the problem. Even though our intention is to help, it can be experienced as invalidating when our child is upset. Just as in the example I gave about glancing at the clock, we have to wait for the right moment to introduce our agenda into the conversation.

Imagine that you have had a very upsetting day. Let's say someone stole a great idea you had at work. You go home to tell your spouse about it, and he responds with his own agenda. He might say, "Well, why do you let people treat you that way? You should . . ." or "That happened to me once, and I . . ." That kind of response might leave you with an empty feeling because you really just needed to vent and to feel that you were being listened to. What we all want is to be understood. What you really wanted to hear is something like, "Someone stole that amazing idea about the . . . I saw you working on that! How does someone think they can get away with that . . . You mean he just presented it as his own?" The validation comes from having someone mirror and articulate exactly what we are feeling. That comes from paying careful attention to what the person said, her body language and tone of voice when she said it, and how it fits in with what you know about her or what you yourself would feel in those circumstances.

I know that when your child is behaving badly, the last thing you want to do is to let him think that's okay—and it isn't. But children are so reactive that to them, their thoughts, feelings, and behaviors are all one and the same. Therefore, if we get mad at them for their behaviors, they automatically think we're also mad at them for their thoughts and feelings. Therefore, letting your child know that you understand—or are at least trying to understand— what he's experiencing that caused his behavior is the first step you need to take in order to change that behavior. Until you do that,

you won't be able to take the next steps, which are to let the child
know that the behavior is problematic and that you'll be expecting
different behavior in the future.

The strategies I discuss in this book are, as I've said, counterintuitive,
and you may not fully appreciate their power until you experience
their effect firsthand, as I have done hundreds if not thousands of
times with my clients. I remember, for example, a little nine-year-old
boy named David. He was very bright and socially successful, but he
was extremely sensitive and reacted emotionally to events or frustra-
tions a less emotional child would handle quite easily. He could be
happy and laughing one moment, and sullen, sad, or furious the
next. Some children seem hardwired to react more emotionally than
others, but David's mother had become so frustrated by his unpre-
dictable and, in her view, extreme reactions and mood swings that
the bond between her and her son had become frayed almost to the
breaking point. By the time she was referred to me by her pediatrician things had gotten to the point where, as she tearfully explained,
she could hardly bear the thought of his getting off the school bus
each afternoon.

I met with David's mother, Sarah, for a several weeks before ever
meeting her son. She told me that she loved her child but was getting to the point where she cringed each time David walked into the
room, wondering what kind of mood he'd be in. As a mother, she
was devastated by this state of affairs, sad, and very angry with herself. I explained that the situation wasn't her fault. They had come
to this place together because of a push/pull dynamic that had
strained the parent/child relationship, and it was David's own frustration that had led to his difficult behavior.

Despite feeling hurt and exhausted, Sarah threw herself wholeheartedly into the program and worked incredibly hard at mirroring and connecting with her child. I coached her every step of the way as she rebuilt the frayed bond and got closer and closer to David. Before too long, David was in a good mood far more often, his sullen moods decreased, and things that previously would have sent him into a rage began to roll off his back. At that point, Sarah and I felt it was time for David and me to meet.

His mother drove him to my home office, and since he refused even to get out of the car, our first meeting took place in the back-seat. I sat there with him and mirrored what he was feeling. "You know what?" I said. "You don't want to be here. You don't want to speak to me. You've been dragged here and you don't want to be here, and my job is to advocate for you. So if you really don't want to be here, I'll advocate for you not to be here, but you have to know what you're saying no to. I promise that I won't ask you anything personal. You don't have to worry. For this session I won't ask you a single thing other than what you want to talk about."

His mother had already told me how much David loved dogs, so I went back into the house and got our dog. That was enough incentive for him to get out of the car, and we sat on the grass together petting the dog. He then began to talk about how much he loved riding horses, and I started to mirror and engage with him about that. From there, he was willing to come inside, and we played a board game together.

By the second session, David began to open up, and before long he began to tell me about his feelings. "My mother's mean and she hates me and she's always yelling at me to stop crying or that there's nothing to be mad about . . ." That is, everything Sarah and I had discussed but that David had previously refused to talk about.

After three or four months, I received one of the most gratifying and moving phone calls of my career from Sarah, who said, "I can't thank you enough. I have my son back." This didn't happen because I am such a brilliant therapist; it comes from tapping into the power of empathy and compassion, which is why people let me into their lives every day.

Mollie, David, and the many other children whose stories you'll be reading have made me realize that the way to begin changing behavior is not by threatening, lecturing, or reprimanding, but by listening and caring. Discussing the problem, voicing your concerns, and offering guidance and limits also have a very important place in creating behavioral change, but only when they come after empathy.

When you yell at your child, he will feel threatened, and because he feels threatened he will defend himself with all his might. Personally, I cannot think of a single time when someone has yelled or screamed at me and I've said, "You are so right . . . I don't know what I was thinking. I am completely wrong here. Let me see what I can do." Even if I agree deep down, when I'm spoken to that way, I feel angry and humiliated, and I need to protect myself. It is no different for children. Just because they are younger doesn't mean they feel things any less. When you reflect your child's feelings or his experience to him with understanding, however, you leave him nothing to defend against. You create safety in the conversation and he is completely disarmed. This may seem like a simple concept, but as you'll see, practicing it isn't always as simple as it sounds.

At the heart of what I teach is kindness. Deep listening, caring, and compassion build strong, emotionally healthy children equipped with the neurological hardware to weather whatever life throws their way. Maintaining that kind of empathy is very hard when your child screams at you, throws tantrums, and says no to almost everything you ask, but it is the surest, most effective way to change behavior.

And on a broader scale, it is also an ideal way for humans to interact, and helps build a better world one family at a time. Somehow, as a society, we seem to have decided that we need to make people feel bad in order for them to do the right thing. Approaching our children with compassion, setting reasonable limits, and supporting them as they make good decisions is a much better way to parent. That's what connected parenting is all about.

Part One

Making or Repairing the Connection

ONE

The Power of
Connection

From the moment your baby is born, you and he begin to form an attachment to each other that will, ultimately, become the foundation for his being able to separate from you and thrive in the world. It is, in fact, from that initial attachment that he learns not only how to connect with others, but also how to understand himself and how to organize and express his feelings in appropriate ways. In short, it's through connecting with you that your baby learns how to connect with the world—how to become a social creature and a human being.

Making the Initial Connection

While your baby is still in utero, the rough road map for his brain is being laid out, and when he is born, whatever potential he has is already there. From that point on, assuming he is protected from the elements and has enough to eat and drink, the most important aspects of his development come from his interactions with you, his parent. When you coo at him, make giggling or gurgling sounds that echo his own, stick out your tongue, or screw up your face and mimic his facial expressions, you are doing something that is vitally important: *you are mirroring your baby*. It seems that these moments of mirroring connect you with your infant and actually help build the neuropathways that determine how his brain will develop. This ability of the brain to learn, adapt, and change is what is known as neuroplasticity.

The human brain contains what is called a mirror neuron system. Our mirror neurons fire both when we perform an action and when we observe that same action performed by others. Scientific research suggests that the mirror neuron system in humans develops well before twelve months of age and that it may be responsible not only for the acquisition of language, but also for the development of other cognitive functions, including the infant's ability to understand and make inferences and predictions about other people's behavior.

Your baby's brain actually seems to crave the connections that occur when you mirror. Through his interactions with you, he begins to organize unfamiliar stimuli into meaningful and predictable patterns, and by doing that he starts to feel, *Okay, this world is a little strange and frightening. I don't know what all these things are, but this person seems to show up and seems to soothe me, and when I make this noise, that happens*. And, fairly quickly, his understanding of these connections—cause and effect—becomes more detailed and consistent, which allows him to relax, predict events, and eventually figure out who he is. Scientists believe this is how humans develop social cognition.

Over the first few years the brain grows rapidly, and although this growth continues to some degree throughout our life, it is the most accelerated from birth until age five. As Alison Gopnik and her colleagues point out in *The Scientist in the Crib,* these are the years when the brain builds itself and connections are made most rapidly—at almost twice the rate of the adult brain—which is why mirroring with babies and young children is so important.

As babies interact with their parents, their brain is learning, pruning, and specializing, figuring out what information is important and what isn't. The more time you spend communicating with your baby and the more you accurately interpret your baby, the more likely it is that the synapses that promote emotion, thought, physical movement, and empathy will develop. The more pleasant experiences a baby has, the more the brain specializes for positive emotion. According to psychologist Gerald Dawson, this may mean that later in life he or she may cope better with stress, become more resilient, and be more positive in general. On the other hand, if an infant is constantly upset and his feelings aren't being soothed, his brain will be built to deal with negative experiences, and will adapt and prepare for stress and disappointment—which can make it more than likely he will be prepared for the worst and ready for disappointment and stress.

What all this means is that we, as parents, are intimately involved in building our babies' brains. Beyond that, seeing them respond so positively also feels wonderful for us, and the bond we develop with our babies through these interactions is, in effect, the ultimate connection. As you'll be learning, however, even if your child spent his early years crying, being upset, and throwing tantrums, his brain can still form new connections through having new experiences that you can provide by mirroring and reacting consistently.

The Importance of Parental Bonding

Back in the 1950s and 1960s, psychologist Harry Harlow, a pioneer in the field of human behavior, did a series of experiments with infant rhesus monkeys that had been separated from their mothers almost immediately after birth. In one study the baby monkeys were given two surrogate mothers, one made of wire mesh equipped with a nipple for nourishment and a light for warmth, and the other covered in cloth but without the nipple or the light. Although the researchers found that the infants spent significantly more time clinging to the "mother" that was covered with cloth, follow-up studies showed that even the cloth surrogates were ultimately inadequate as substitute mothers and that the infants developed "autistic-like" behaviors including self-clasping, social withdrawal, and rocking.

Studies have also shown that when babies are completely deprived of early maternal interactions, where their physical needs are taken care of but there is little time for anything more than changing diapers and handing out bottles, the babies don't make eye contact, tend to rock and scream, and have difficulty developing an attachment bond. In other words, they appear to develop autistic-like symptoms.

Mirroring seems to be about much more than simply copying. I believe it may help babies organize themselves emotionally. The newborn brain is flooded with an incredible amount of new information it needs to organize and process, and we, as parents, are an important part of that neural process. As we accurately reflect the baby's sounds and facial expressions, he or she will begin to think, *Mom seems to understand me, so I think I will be all right.* He is constantly analyzing and processing information until he gradually becomes more and more capable of sorting through sensory input and filing it in the proper places. If he "puts out" a particular emotion through sounds and facial expressions and gets back the same thing he sent out, he's receiving the message that his emotion is appropriate, that it has been registered and makes sense to this other person out there, his parent. If he's crying because he's cold, for example, and you show an appropriate expression and response, such as making soothing sounds and wrapping your baby in a blanket, he'll understand that you've received his message and your response made him feel better, so he will no longer have to worry about what will happen the next time he's cold. He knows how to tell you and he's confident that you'll do something to make it better. Eventually, as he gets older, he will be able to make inferences and extrapolate from the appropriate messages and responses he's acquired through his interactions with you to other relationships and interactions in the world. In short, this is the beginning of what is known as social cognition.

Without your responses, however, he will have no consistent way to categorize and integrate sensory information. It may be that very inability that overwhelms autistic children, who are constantly being bombarded with sensory input they can't make sense of—sights, sounds, textures, even flavors—and, therefore, rock and bang their heads as a way to block out the input and soothe themselves. Interestingly, several studies, including one conducted at the Fay J. Lindner Center for Autism, North Shore–Long Island Jewish Health System in Bethpage, New York, indicate that autism may be the result of an abnormally functioning mirror neuron system.

When Mirroring Becomes Less Instinctive

Most parents are instinctively pretty good at mirroring and connecting with their infants. We don't need to be taught how to coo at, smile at, and mimic our baby. But at around the time our child begins to acquire language, about the age of two, I believe that, just as instinctively, we often begin to react differently. When we lift our four-month-old baby out of the bath and she's screaming, what do we do? Usually we hug her and use our most soothing voice to say something like, "Oh my goodness, look at you. You're so cold. You're shivering. Come, let's get you warm . . ." By doing that we're letting the baby know with our words, tone of voice, and body language, as well as by matching his affect, that we understand he's uncomfortable and all we want is to make him feel better. That is our only agenda.

But when our two-and-a-half-year-old does the same thing, we tend to say things like, "Oh, honey, stop crying; there's nothing to cry about; you'll be fine. Here's your towel. Be a big girl now." Now our agenda is for our child to stop crying, and instead of mirroring her feelings we are, in effect, telling her that she has no reason to cry. In addition, from the child's point of view, the same behavior that used to elicit one kind of response is now eliciting another. Whereas she had previously been confident that we understood what she was experiencing and feeling, she may now begin to doubt both us and herself.

Depending on how sensitive and anxious she is to begin with, the child will react more or less dramatically to that shift. At this point it's important to acknowledge that some children simply are genetically more anxious than others. At least to some degree it's a matter of how the brain is hardwired. And the more anxious, emotional, and sensitive a child is, the more often in the course of any given day he'll be getting back messages that don't match those he's sending out—that he has no reason to be so upset, that there's nothing to be frightened about, that whatever has happened, it isn't really so bad. In other words, you'll be saying, directly or indirectly, that there isn't any reason for him to be feeling what he's feeling. We let our children know this all the time, for example when they tell us they're not tired and we tell them they must be tired, or when we tell them to put on a sweater and they say they're not cold and we tell them they must be cold (usually because we're cold).

Because all the instinctive mirroring you did with your newborn made him feel so good—both loved and understood—when you stop doing it, he's naturally going to feel a bit shaky and nervous. Why has your response to him changed? Why is it that now when he cries, instead of cooing, "Oh, I'm so sorry you feel so sad," you tell him there's nothing to be so upset about and he just needs to stop?

All those invalidating responses can be extremely emotionally disorganizing for a child, because he'll begin to think, *Well, if what I'm feeling doesn't make sense to her, maybe it really doesn't make sense at all.* And if he's feeling something that doesn't make sense, what is he supposed to do about that? For anyone, but especially for a small child, being told that your emotions are inappropriate or incomprehensible to the one person you had always believed understood you can be quite distressing.

The Terrible Twos

I believe that this shift in the way you respond to your child, and the child's reaction to it, can at least in part explain the phenomenon we call the "terrible twos." Interestingly, this is also about the time when you may be having a second child, which means not only that you'll be busier, more distracted, and have less time for your toddler, but also that he will see the new baby receiving all those good-feeling mirroring sounds and expressions that were formerly his alone. And because he has by now acquired language, you may also think it's time to stop your baby talk and start speaking to him as if he were a very small adult. As a result of all this he may, quite reasonably, become a bit anxious about his place in your life, and you may see a regression into increased clinginess and "babyish" behavior. It's my theory that when a toddler exhibits these behaviors he may be trying to recapture those soothing reactions he got from you when he really was a baby.

Connection Creates Individuation

At about the same time we as parents tend to start mirroring less instinctively and less often, our toddlers are also beginning to separate from us and push their own boundaries, which means they'll also be testing our limits. That may make you angry or frustrated, and you may become upset in return, all of which is perfectly natural. The problem, as I've said, is that your agenda no longer matches that of your child. You want one thing—basically for him to "behave himself"—and he wants another—to make sure you still love him no matter how he behaves. You assume that he knows you love him, and on some level, of course he does. But we all need to put more care into maintaining that bond than we tend to give it on a regular basis.

Building Confidence Through Connection

Psychologists and researchers, including John Bowlby, one of the originators of attachment theory, and Dr. William Sears, author of *The Attachment Parenting Book*, point out that the more a child is bonded to his parents, and the more he receives responses that accurately reflect his feelings, the more he will be able to trust himself and his intuition, and, therefore, the more he will believe that he is able to manage in the world. And with that self-confidence he'll be able to go off on his own for longer and longer periods of time. At first this might mean simply going off to another part of the room; after a while it might mean going off to play with other children in the park. He's able to do this because you've taught him, through mirroring and connecting, that whatever he's expressing makes sense to you. You may not always agree with it, and you may offer an alternative way to look at it, but you always listen first. From that he will likely come to understand that his feelings and his ways of expressing them must be appropriate and to trust that they will make sense to others as well.

Beyond that, however, you've also let him know, by forming those strong connections, that the relationship between you is good and strong, that love can easily withstand separation, that you'll be there when he comes back, and that whatever happens when he's away from you, he can count on you for support and understanding when he needs it.

When you're trying to explain something—such as what you're feeling—to another person, and that person doesn't respond the way you want or expect, you feel disappointed; you may even feel an actual "drop" in the pit of your stomach. Mirroring to your child is letting him or her know that you're not going to drop him.

I like to compare this going off to play and then coming back to check with you to the experience of rock climbing. When you rock climb, you often have a partner on the ground who is wearing a harness with a rope. The other end of the rope is looped through a carabiner on the wall and then attached to the climber's harness. The rope literally connects the climber to his or her partner on the ground, who, in effect, gives him enough slack to move upward. And because the climber trusts the partner and feels the safety of the tension on the rope, he will have the confidence to reach farther and climb higher because he knows he can't fall. The tension needs to be just right—too much and the climber can't move, too little and he can't feel the tension.

As children begin to explore their world, they're constantly testing the tension on the rope that connects them to their parents to be sure it's still there. Think of the rope as an invisible umbilical cord between you and your child. When the tension is just right, the child feels safe because he knows you are there. He can take risks, explore, and push himself. If it's too tight, he can't move, try, or learn. If it's too loose, he will be afraid you are not there and will freeze, cling, and become rigid. He may also yank aggressively on that rope to remind you he is hanging on the wall.

When a child is very anxious about separating from his parents, I believe it's because he doesn't trust the tension on the rope. If you're dropping him off at a birthday party, for example, and he's clinging to your leg, he very well might be thinking, *Can I really leave my mother and trust that she'll still love me when I get back? I've been so bad today. Will she be thinking about how bad I am when I'm gone? I'm not sure I'm lovable enough to leave her and trust that she'll still love me when I get back.* What mirroring does is to assure your child that the rope is there even when you are not.

When he's confident of that, he will feel safe, and he will take that sense of safety with him as he moves beyond toddlerhood and goes out into the world—to school, on playdates, and throughout all his interactions with others. He'll be better able to take risks, to share his toys, to show concern for other people's feelings, because he will actually be happier.

When he lacks that confidence because he doesn't feel connected to you, he'll be mainly concerned with taking care of himself because he will feel more vulnerable. He may seem angry or obstinate or oppositional. You may hear from the teacher that he doesn't share well or that he doesn't participate in activities, or he may become timid and clingy to the point where he refuses to go to school at all.

That said, however, keeping the proper tension on the rope also means correcting when his behavior is unacceptable or inappropriate. Children feel safe and loved when consistent and reasonable limits are placed on their behavior. In the chapters that follow, we'll be talking about correcting and containing, but before you can do that effectively, you need to do the mirroring that allows your child to know you will always be at the other end of the rope.

In addition to worrying unnecessarily that their bonding might make it even more difficult for their children to separate from them, parents often ask me whether their constantly empathizing with their child won't lead him or her to expect everyone else in the world to do the same thing. In fact, the exact opposite may be true. If you are doing it, he will be less likely to need others to do it. He will be better able to shrug off disappointments and difficult situations because, as I've said, you will be helping him become more resilient and self-reliant. As a result, he will be better able to deal with his feelings, he will be less anxious, and he won't *need* everyone in the world to understand him the same way you do.

If you make your connections strong enough, your child will be able to go out into the world and survive being kicked out of the sandbox because you'll have created a safe haven. He'll know there are people at home who understand him, who care about him, and who are watching his back—or holding on to the other end of the rope, regardless of how unlovable his behavior has been. Children need that sense of safety in order to separate from you, go out into the world, and test their own individuality. This may be the effect mirroring has on the brains of tiny infants, who gain the ability to grow, explore, and separate from their parents, and it has the same effect on older children as well.

Mirroring Creates Empathy

When you relate to your child by mirroring and containing, you are teaching him how to relate to other people in a way that is empathic and understanding. You are modeling what it means to be a kind and understanding person rather than one who intimidates to get what she wants.

If you are constantly getting your child to do what you want by yelling and threatening punishment, you may be creating one of two possible scenarios. He may determine that this is the *only way* to get another person to do what he wants and, therefore, become an aggressive child who kicks other kids out of the sandbox. Or—and this is equally if not even more likely—he won't have the self-confidence that comes from knowing you've got the other end of the rope, and will, therefore, become the kid whom others see as an easy target for bullying.

Mirroring provides a base for social competence and lays down the groundwork for fulfilling and satisfying relationships. Arguments, falling-outs, and disappointments will happen because that is human nature, but these issues will tend to be resolved more quickly, as your child will take responsibility for wrongdoings more readily and will take things less personally in the long run.

Mirroring to Build Your Child's Social Skills

Good social health is important. Having meaningful, reliable friendships and interpersonal relationships is incredibly important to one's overall happiness, even one's success is life. Mirroring as a part of the parent-child relationship nurtures social health.

As part of my practice, I do social skills training with children who, for one reason or another, have difficulty making friends or understanding the kinds of social interactions that most of us take for granted. Sometimes the problem is caused by an underlying condition such as a learning disability or ADHD, but there is almost always an emotional component, and sometimes it is exclusively emotional. Good social skills are a function of many factors, including good mental and emotional health, good parenting, and feeling good about oneself. Children who are anxious, for example, may be so busy protecting themselves that they may retreat inward and may not have the time or the emotional energy to consider other people. Children who feel bad about themselves often sabotage themselves by behaving in a way that they know will elicit a negative response. That way, if the other person isn't nice to them, they can tell themselves it's because they did such and such, because, if they'd tried their best and still got a negative response they wouldn't have been able to handle the rejection. Whatever the underlying issue, however, children who lack self-confidence and resilience are also those who are most likely to be more defensive and jealous, less likely to share, and more likely to "tell" on others. Needless to say, they won't be much fun for others to be around.

In order to have good social health and feel empathy, you need to feel healthy inside—and this is as true for adults as it is for children. As parents we are as responsible for our children's emotional and social health as we are for their physical health, and this means that we need to nurture them well.

Before I even see a child in my practice, I work with the parents for several sessions, teaching the techniques I've been giving you and asking them to go home and practice mirroring with their child. Very often, the parents will call after a few weeks to tell me that, even though we haven't begun to directly address the issues they originally came for, there has been significant improvement in the child's social functioning. I particularly remember one little boy whose parents were very concerned about sending him off to summer camp because he'd had so much trouble getting along with the other campers the previous summer that the camp had almost refused to take him back.

When they called me in the late spring, it was only a few weeks before camp started. I began working with the parents—coaching them on how to mirror and teaching them behavioral strategies; I had just a few sessions with the boy himself. With my help the parents began to rebuild the relationship with their son that had been frayed by years of negative behavior and power struggles, and when I later called the camp to see how he was doing, I was told that he was "a different child." In fact, he wasn't a different child. He was the same child, who now knew what was expected of him and had the confidence to use the skills he'd been taught. Mirroring and containing go hand in hand. If your child knows what's expected of him but doesn't have the confidence to do it, the knowing won't be translated into behavior.

One of the most amazing things I find about mirroring is that once you begin to do it regularly with your child (and with your partner or spouse as well as other people) you will begin to hear your child doing it with his or her friends and with you. Children tend to learn intuitively, which means that they are likely to pick up on whatever you are modeling. Modeling self-control, taking a non-defensive stance, being empathic, not overreacting to whatever life throws your way will help build your child's self-esteem, and once she has that self-esteem, she won't have to worry about herself and can begin to start thinking about other people, which will make her a lot more pleasant to be around.

Then, if a sticky situation does arise, you can also begin by mirroring and then, once she feels safe, teach her didactically by introducing the idea of thinking about the other person's feelings. If, for instance, your child is playing with a friend and the sounds you hear coming from the other room indicate that things are not going well, you can step in and guide the play. One way to do this effectively is to speak as if you were your child. "Oh, I've got my favorite game piece. I love that piece, it's a great piece. Anna must think that too, because she also wants to have that piece. This is when sharing can get tricky. Can I think of something I can do so we can both be happy?" This is a way, in the moment, for you to mirror and present the problem so that both children learn experientially while they're actually playing. What you're doing here is actually mirroring and showing your child that you empathize with her feelings while, at the same time, you also recognize the other child's feelings.

The more empathy you show your child, the more she will show empathy to others, and being empathic is the key to having good social skills. At the same time, however, you need to understand that a child's ability to grasp perspective is developmental. We can assist and help it along, but it will come when the brain is ready. Children from the ages of two to six may have a hard time with the concept, but from six on they begin to develop an increasing awareness of other people's feelings. So don't get frustrated if you're doing everything you can and your toddler just doesn't get it.

To help a young child understand that there may be "two sides" to the issue, try asking him to think about a mug with a smiley face on one side and a sad face on the other. You can only see one side of the mug at a time, and if you're sitting at a table with the smiley face on your side, you won't know what the kid across the table from you is seeing, so you need to turn the mug around and look at it from the other side to get the other child's point of view. Talking about an abstract concept like perspective in concrete terms (in this case by getting him to look at both sides of the mug) is a good way to help a small child "see" both sides of the problem.

Another way to reinforce a positive social dynamic in children of all ages is to explain and implement the friendship moves and friendship blocks discussed on page 139. And don't worry if your child doesn't seem to get it at first. As you continue to mirror and use these techniques, your child *will* become more empathic. Children with Asperger's disorder or nonverbal learning disabilities can really benefit from learning these skills. (For more on special-needs children, see Chapter Twelve.)

We Need to Feel Safe to Act Rationally

Intuitively, we seem to believe that if we yell at someone and make him feel bad enough, he will logically choose to change his behavior, or, if we explain things rationally he'll understand. But when you yell at or try to rationalize with a child who's already upset, something else happens, something that has nothing to do with logic. In fact, the more you yell at or try to reason with your child, the more anxious and upset he will become and the greater will be his need to *make* you understand what he's feeling and why, which means his behavior is likely to escalate—the very result you were trying to avoid. Moreover, while all of that is going on, he actually won't have the *ability* to think rationally and control or change his behavior.

In the simplest of terms, one of the many functions of the human nervous system is to set off an alarm whenever we feel threatened. When the alarm goes off and we become scared or angry, our attention becomes completely focused on the source of our fear or anger, and we are literally physically unable to see the "bigger picture." This is a totally involuntary reaction controlled by a part of the brain called the amygdala that you may have heard referred to as the "fight-or-flight" mechanism. Fight-or-flight is a primal response designed to keep us alive, and when it kicks in it literally shuts down access to rational thought. It doesn't matter whether we're feeling anxious and upset because we're being attacked physically by a tiger or verbally by someone who's yelling at us or negating our feelings; our nervous system reacts the same way to both.

As adults we've all been in situations where we were so upset that we said things without thinking even though we knew they were totally inappropriate. Kids, however, go into fight-or-flight all the time. As we mature, we are better able to differentiate between real and imagined threats and to develop better impulse control (although some people never get very good at it and wind up in anger-management therapy), but young children generally aren't very good at either making those distinctions or controlling their impulses.

That being the case, what we need to do if we want our child to listen and be able to change his behavior is first to make him feel safe. The more your child believes you understand what he's upset about, the safer he'll feel. And, once again, you do that by mirroring, by letting him know through your words, your tone of voice, and your body language that you've received and understood not only the message, but also the urgency of the message he's sending. When you do that, you're effectively saying not only that you "get it," but also that you've "got his back"—that's you're still there at the other end of the rope—and he can begin to relax. Until he is confident that his message has been received, however, you can argue, yell, or rationalize all you want; it won't make a bit of difference.

I experienced this in my own family not so long ago when my older daughter, Zoë, who was then eleven years old, learned that her very best friend in the world was moving to France because her father was being transferred by his company. On the day she found out, I was working, and a family friend was visiting. Zoë came home from school totally devastated and convulsing in tears. Our friend—an extremely empathic and sensitive woman who had been a teacher for many years—was overwhelmed by how upset Zoë was and knew that she needed to make her feel better. The problem, of course, was that there was really nothing anyone could say or do that would change the reality of her best friend's moving to another country.

Zoë was very upset. "This is *awful*. I'm never going to have a best friend again! This is the *worst* thing that could ever happen! She's moving to *France, France, FRANCE!*" And my friend was doing her best to sound calm and rational, and was saying things like, "I know it's hard, but you'll find another friend. It seems bad now, but you will get over it, and France, well, how many people can say they have a best friend in France? That's pretty exciting when you stop to think about it." And Zoë was crying, "*Noooo,* it's not exciting! It's *terrible and I don't want to get over it, and I will never have a friend like her again, ever!*"

Then my friend started offering suggestions like, "It's not the end of the world. You can write letters, and you can instant-message her on the computer." She even tried to empathize by saying, "I know this must be hard for you . . ." all of which just made Zoë more upset.

By this time I'd come home and was listening to their exchange, and I could tell that my friend was beginning to get a little exasperated. From her point of view, she'd been making a huge effort to cheer Zoë up, and Zoë wasn't responding very well. What Zoë was hearing, however, was that she shouldn't be so upset about this, that it was actually a *good* thing her best friend was moving to France, and that was making her angry. Why couldn't my friend understand that it wasn't a good thing, it was a *terrible* thing, the worst thing that could ever happen to her? And her escalating reaction was simply a function of her trying to get that across.

Later, I talked to Zoë. I mirrored, and the first thing I said was, "*France! Are you kidding me? France! Did you know* she was moving to France? It's so far away and so sudden!"

And the rest of the conversation went something like this:

> ZOE: No, we didn't know *anything*; it just happened *out of the blue!*
> ME: This is your best *friend*, you spent all your time with her. I bet you can't even *imagine* a day without her.

I know it sounds as if I should have been making her even more upset, but that's not what happened. Zoë went on . . .

> ZOË: Yeah, this is the *best* friend I'll ever have; I'll *never* find anyone else like her!
> ME: So you can't even *imagine* at this moment that there'll ever be a better friend for you.

This went on for maybe three or four more sentences. Zoë was saying things like, "What am I going to *do* without her? School's not going to be the *same!*" And I was saying, "I can see that. You spent *every minute* with her. You don't even know what a day without her will feel like."

By this time, however, there were far fewer tears, and it wasn't long before Zoë was sniffling and asking, "Do you think there's any way we could visit France? Can you teach me to use instant messaging? Can I call her on the phone?"

What I was thinking in the middle of all this was, *This really was a wonderful friendship. Zoe wanted a best friend so badly, and this little girl was perfect for her. They adored each other. My best friend moved to California when I was in eighth grade and I remember how much it hurt, how lonely I felt, and how I feared that I would never see her again. This is awful. I wish I could make it go away. How is she ever going to get through this? I want to take this pain away for her.* It is so painful when your child hurts emotionally; you want so much to make it better, and you wish it had happened to you instead. But I knew I had to put all that aside and be brave enough to stay in the moment with my daughter. Because I was able to do that, Zoë was thinking, *Oh, wow, my mother really gets it. She really understands how much this hurts me and how scared I am not to have my friend.*

I knew that I couldn't fix the problem and that what I needed to do was just sit there and go through my child's pain without trying to minimize or go around it. I knew that was the *only* way my child could get through this painful moment and learn that she was strong enough to deal with it. Often, it's our own agenda that gets in the way when our child is sad and hurting. We want so *badly* to make her feel better (so that we, too, can feel better) that we move in and try to fix it. The problem is that this can actually get in the way of our children's wanting to talk to us. If we can't tolerate their pain, either they find it invalidating to talk to us or they worry that they are hurting us, and so they choose not to. Being brave enough to stay in the pain with your child is what makes her feel better and encourages her to tell you what's going on in her life. I remember one mother who said, "You have to dare to be there."

At this point in our conversation, Zoë no longer needed to convince me of the urgency of her message. After only four or five statements on my part, she'd heard that I appreciated the seriousness of her problem and why she was so upset, and because of that she was able to calm down enough to finally take in what my friend had been trying to tell her and move on to problem solving. The final step was to give her a message of competence by reassuring her that I believed she had everything she needed to get through this.

I had only one or two more conversations with Zoë about the move after that, and I firmly believe that if I hadn't allowed her to feel her pain, there would have been multiple encounters like the one she had with my friend. Instead, she got through the situation well and made new friends she had not had a chance to get to know before.

When you have these conversations, you don't have to be brilliant and get caught up in what great things you're going to say. It's not so much *what* you say (although that, too, is important) but *how* you say it that matters. Your child is going to walk away remembering how the conversation *felt*, not the specific words you used. Our conversation made Zoë feel embraced, loved, understood, and emotionally held, whereas my friend, despite her most heartfelt efforts, made her feel invalidated and that the urgency of her message was not registering.

How Often Do You Listen to Your Child's Feelings?

We have to stop and consider how many times in a day we tell our children they shouldn't be feeling what they are feeling. Let's say, for example, little Sarah comes into the kitchen and whines, "Mommy, I'm hungry." You're likely to respond with, "What are you talking about? You just ate lunch. You can't possibly be hungry."

At that point, Sarah might escalate to, "I am *too* hungry. I'm *starving!* Don't tell when I'm hungry and when I'm not!" At which point you'd probably be irritated and say something like, "Don't talk to me like that. You're not going to get anything if that's how you talk . . ." And so it goes.

These kinds of exchanges happen all the time. Children are dramatic. They don't regulate their emotions well; they live in the moment; and they exaggerate. To us, many of the things they say and feel can seem pretty ridiculous. Who cares who gets to push the elevator button first? What difference does it make if they don't get the front seat on the way home? To us these issues may be silly, but to them they are very important and very real. So we disagree and correct. I am not saying that we need to agree with our children all the time, but we do need to listen and hear them, and try to understand what *they're feeling* before we introduce our own agenda.

The following three-step formula for doing that is the one I teach my clients and the one we'll be discussing and using throughout this book. No matter what the specific situation might be, whenever you need to set boundaries or correct your child's behavior, the formula you need to follow is this:

1. **Mirror** in order to show through your words, tone, facial expression, and body language that you understand and appreciate what he is feeling.
2. **Present the problem** by letting him know that even though he may be upset, anxious, or just plain angry, his behavior is not acceptable and why.
3. **Find a solution** either by letting him know what you want him to do (instead of what he's been doing) and seeing that he complies, or, if necessary, by imposing a consequence for the unacceptable behavior.

Parenting comprises two distinct roles that often don't seem compatible—hard parenting and soft parenting. Mirroring and connecting with your child, loving and nurturing, are what I call "soft parenting." Setting limits and containing bad behavior is "hard parenting." The three-step formula above is what brings hard and soft parenting together.

When the Bond Breaks

One of the problems many parents have following the above formula is that, quite logically, we feel that what we need to do is let our child know that things are not as bad as he seems to think they are—in effect, that he's wrong. But, as I've said, trying to do that will, nine times out of ten, have exactly the opposite effect. And then what happens? The child becomes even more upset, so you become more upset. He wails louder and you become frustrated, and, if you hadn't been yelling already, you probably will be now. It becomes a self-perpetuating phenomenon that ends as illogically as it began.

The more you yell, the less lovable your child will feel and the more he'll act out. Again, this may not seem logical, but for a child (or anyone for that matter) it's a protective mechanism. Because he can't tolerate the thought that he might be doing the best he can and you still don't love him, he acts more negatively just to show you how unlovable he really can be. That way, in his mind, if you don't love him at least he will know why. I'm not saying that you *don't* love him; of course you do. What I am saying is that he *feels* unlovable because he knows he has behaved badly and is stuck in a cycle of acting out, becoming anxious, and acting out some more.

The longer this continues the more frayed the bond between you becomes, until you really do begin to think of your child as unlovable—because that's the way he's acting more often than not. If he's not getting a response from you that lets him know his message has been received, he's going to keep sending it, more and more urgently, using capital letters and multiple exclamation points.

TWO

Create CALM by Mirroring and Joining

Up to this point I've been explaining *why* it's so important to mirror and bond with your child, but you may still be wondering exactly *how* to do it. What I've found, both in private practice and in the many seminars I've taught, is that when I first begin to explain mirroring, everyone nods enthusiastically, and when I ask how many of them already mirror with their children, almost every hand goes up. But then, when we begin to role-play, it becomes immediately clear that what they're doing isn't really mirroring at all. Mirroring is a therapy technique, not a parenting technique, so it isn't something you can be expected to do intuitively, and even though it sounds simple, it may not be as simple as it sounds.

When your child is upset, sad, or hurting in another way, your parental instinct is to tell him it's okay and make him feel better. You want to cheer him up because when your child feels bad, you feel bad, too. And when your child is misbehaving because he feels bad, your instinct is probably to make him stop, because that, too, will make you feel better. In both these instances, however, doing what instinctively feels right to you may not be what is best for your child.

Here's an example of how parental instinct can go wrong:

Zachery is a six-year-old boy for whom just about everything is a catastrophe. He tends to act out and overreact to every little thing, and because of his behavioral problems, he has a hard time making friends. He did, however, make one good friend in school. All went well until, one day, he sat down next to his friend, Shawn, at circle time the way he always did, but this time Shawn got up and said, "I'm not going to sit next to you at circle time today because when we sit together we always get in trouble. So I'm going to sit over there, and then I'll play with you afterward." For a little kid, this was pretty sophisticated logic; who knows, maybe his mother had suggested it. It didn't really matter, however, because all Zachery heard was that his friend didn't want to sit next to him, and to him that meant Shawn didn't want to be his friend anymore.

When Zachery's mother came to pick him up at the end of the day, he was extremely upset and began to explain tearfully that Shawn wouldn't sit with him at circle time and that he wasn't his friend anymore because a real friend would never do such a mean and terrible thing. He actually told the story pretty accurately, so his mother reacted to what he was saying rather than what he had experienced—which were two very different things.

She naturally wanted to make him feel better, and so she said things like, "Oh, honey, you know he didn't mean it. He just didn't want to get in trouble. He's still your friend." But the more she continued to try to "fix" the problem, the more hysterical Zachery became.

They happened to be on their way to an appointment with me,

and by the time they arrived, Zachery was a mess. I asked his mother to stay in the room while I talked to him so that she could hear and see the difference between what she'd been saying and what our conversation would sound like. I sat him down and leaned in close so that he could see I was really paying attention, and then I said, "So, you *really* believed Shawn was your friend, and you don't think a *real* friend would act like that. And when you tried to sit down next to him the way you always do, he just *got up and moved away.*"

ZACHERY, GULPING: "Yeah, he just *moved somewhere else!* And that's not *nice*. A *real* friend wouldn't do that."

ME: "You play with him all day and you trust him, and then he just *moves* away from you."

ZACHERY, NODDING BUT STILL CRYING: "Yeah, that's right."

ME: "This is hard because he really hurt your feelings and, in your mind, how could a friend do that?"

And the very next thing Zachery said was, "Well, he *did* say he didn't want to get in trouble."

Because I was accurately reflecting what Zachery was putting out, he was able to calm down enough to make a judgment about whether what Shawn had said actually made sense. By hearing from someone else what he'd been saying, Zachery got a new perspective on the whole situation. I didn't even have to suggest it; he came up with it all on his own. After that, we were even able to have a conversation about how other friends had hurt him, and to talk about the fact that sometimes friends do things for reasons that don't actually have anything to do with us.

It's important to point out here that Zachery's mother was able to go back to him the next day and say, "You know, I was thinking about how upset you were yesterday. It must really have hurt when you thought Shawn did that on purpose, and I'm not sure I really got that." As we are learning to mirror and practicing our technique (and yes, it is a technique, which doesn't mean that it isn't also sincere and heartfelt) we often look back on moments when we could have mirrored and didn't. In the beginning it's easier to see what we could have or should have done. Because of that, it's reassuring to know that you can always go back and fix it.

In addition, by continuing to mirror, Zach's parents helped him become more resilient, so that he would no longer be so injured by incidents like the one that had happened that day.

Learning to CALM Your Child

When your child feels sad or bad, what he really wants is for you to let him know that you understand what he's feeling and that it's okay. You need to help him become CALM, and you do that by mirroring. If you keep that acronym in mind, you will understand what it means to mirror.

Connect

Affect

Listen

Mirror

C: Connect

Connecting is showing undivided attention. It means making eye contact, using your body and your voice, leaning forward, looking involved, maybe even chewing on your pen—in short, doing everything you can to show your child that you're really trying as hard as you can to understand what he's thinking and feeling. When you really feel the connection, you'll know you are getting it right. When you do that, your child will automatically think, "Oh, finally someone is listening to me!" What you're doing is matching the urgency conveyed by the child's body language with your own.

If your child is really upset and you're sitting back calmly saying things like, "It sounds like you feel . . ." or "That must make you feel very angry," this is a different technique and may not be as effective. Also, at this point, make sure that you don't insert stories about your own experiences into the dialogue. Leave those stories for later, after the connection is established and your child has felt very heard. If you try to tell those stories too soon, your child may feel that the conversation has somehow shifted to you and that his own feelings are being invalidated. To mirror effectively it is essential that you put your own agenda aside for the moment and devote all your energy to making the connection. Your child won't be able to hear or accept your agenda until he is CALM.

A: Match the Urgency of Your Child's AFFECT

The term "affect," used as a noun, means, in psychological terms, feeling or emotion—or, more specifically, the outward display of feelings or emotions. Affect is composed of facial expression, body language, tone of voice—all the nonverbal means we have of projecting emotion. When you're mirroring, if your child is really angry about something, for example, you need to join with him in showing this emotion. If he's angry, you might do that by scrunching up your own face, bunching up your shoulders, narrowing your eyes, looking intense, matching in subtle ways the faces he is making, and sharing in his urgency. When you do this, remember that it is important to look genuine. It can't be too over-the-top, and it must appear sincere, and not exaggerated or comical. Once he sees that you understand his feelings, he will begin to defuse and de-escalate his intensity, and start to organize his feelings. Again, I know this is counterintuitive, but letting him know that the urgency of his message has been delivered and understood allows him to move on to the next step.

Of course, you also want to do this in a controlled way. You don't want to rant and rave and sound angry yourself. You don't want to make your child think this is suddenly about you. You just want to let him know you *really* understand that *he* feels this way. You're doing this in order to give your child the sense of safety that comes from knowing someone else understands the seriousness of the problem so he can stop carrying the entire burden himself. That also means he needs to know you're in charge and not just as anxious or hysterical as he is.

A prime example of how this works occurred when a mother brought her extremely anxious daughter to see me. Sharon was terrified of *everything*, and when she spotted a fruit fly in my office she immediately flew into a frenzy, climbed on the sofa, and started shrieking, "Oh my God, it's a fly, it's a fly, get it, kill it, get me out of here!" at which point her mother tried to calm her down by repeating, "Sharon, calm down, it's fine, stop it, it's okay. It's only a fruit fly. It's smaller than a mosquito. It can't possibly hurt you," which only got Sharon even more hysterical. This presented an opportunity to demonstrate mirroring in action to Sharon's mom. With affect that demonstrated I was taking her fear seriously but not afraid myself, I looked around the room and said, "Tell me where you think you saw it last. Is it over there? Fruit flies are a big problem for you. You don't care if they're small. They move all around and you can't see them, and they're bugs. A bug is a bug, and you hate bugs." And after only a very few minutes Sharon completely forgot about the fly, because she knew her message had been received and someone was dealing with the problem so she didn't have to worry about it anymore.

Later, when she was calm and no longer in fight-or-flight mode, we were able to talk about the fact that fruit flies are harmless. It is important to stress that it was her fear, not mine, that I reflected to her. I did not run around the room yelling, "A fruit fly, oh my God, that's horrible!" thereby sending the message that she was actually *right* to be terrified. I simply showed her that the urgency the situation had for *her* was registering for *me* and that I was going to listen to her concerns before rationalizing.

Parents sometimes become so anxious about their child's anxiety that they unintentionally transfer their own tension to the child. Using the birthday-party scenario again: If your child is terrified and clutching your skirt for dear life and what's going through your head is, *What on earth is wrong with him? Every other kid is in there. Are we going to go through this each time he's invited to a party? Why can't my kid just be normal?* and, in your frustration, you try to peel him off, saying, "It's only a birthday party, for goodness' sake. Just get in there! What's the big deal? You'll have fun," your child will sense (not without reason) that it really is a big deal for you, and that will make him even more anxious and hysterical.

What you need to do in these situations is respond rather than react. Reacting is generally automatic—hence a "knee-jerk reaction." Responding is generally more thoughtful and thought out.

L: LISTEN to What He's Saying—the Actual Words

Words are your child's most direct means of letting you know what's going on in his head. Too often we seem to listen to our kids with one ear while we're in the middle of doing something else. But now you're going to *really* listen. And you're going to use his words to let him know that.

What you're *not* going to be doing is commenting on what your child is saying, as in, "Oh, that must have been really hard for you!" or repeating what he or she is saying as if to be sure you got it right, as in, "Gee, it sounds as if you're really angry that your sister took your Lego." When you do either of those things you may be showing that you are trying to understand, but you are also separating yourself from the child by commenting on his feelings rather than joining in the experience. What you *are* going to do is say the things your child might be saying *as if* you were in his shoes.

See if you can hear the difference:

Kristen was in the car with her mother, who was driving her to gymnastics class. Kristen was whining and complaining that she was having a good time at home and she didn't want to go to gymnastics. Her mother *thought* she was mirroring by saying things like, "I understand that you don't want to go to gymnastics, and I know that you were happy at home, but you go to gymnastics every week and you love it." But instead of calming down, Kristen got really angry and yelled, "Stop saying what I was saying, and I don't love it or I would want to go!"

Now listen to this:

"Here you are, *dragged* into the car. I'm *making* you go to the gym when you were perfectly happy at home. You were feeling like you were in control of your own life, and here I am *dragging* you off somewhere you don't want to go!"

In the first instance the mother was actually distancing herself from Kristen even though she was indicating that she knew what Kristen was feeling. By doing that she was, without even realizing it, implying that her daughter's feelings were inappropriate. In the second example she was jumping into Kristen's shoes, joining with her in those feelings, speaking *as if she were* Kristen and articulating what her daughter might be feeling out loud like an empathic commentary.

After the mirroring statement, Kristen would probably have said something like, "Yeah, you're right. It's not fair!" To which her mother would respond, "Yep, you know what? I get it. I get why you're so mad. I get why you don't want to go." By then Kristen would be de-escalating and might say, "Okay, fine! Let's just go." She'd likely remain sullen, but would be compliant. Not every child is suddenly going to become cheerful about the situation, but, after you've made two or three mirroring statements, most of the time he or she will do what you ask.

To really "get it," you need to understand that from the child's point of view, his or her reaction is not inappropriate because it truly reflects his *perception* of the problem in that moment.

Whatever the specific situation might be, you need to listen to your child and choose your words carefully. As you mirror, you can do any of the following. You can clarify: "You mean you weren't doing anything and he just came along and pushed you?" You can paraphrase: "So there you were minding your own business and got a whack on the back?" Or summarize: "So he pushed you and you don't think you did anything, and you have told me before in other conversations that people do this to you." Using any one of these tactics will help you come up with the words you need. And if you absolutely can't think of what to say, you can just say, "Wow, you just told me so many things, I don't know what to say. Give me a minute to think about it because I really want to understand it," and ask some clarifying questions. It's okay to take your time. So long as you look like you are working hard, your child will wait eagerly for your response.

In the beginning it will feel awkward and unnatural. This is a therapy technique, not a parenting technique. We aren't born knowing how to do it; it's a skill that must be practiced and acquired. If you try it and it doesn't come out right and your child stands there looking at you as if you'd just grown a second head, or if he says, "Why are you talking like that?" you just need to continue following the CALM technique and say, "I know I sound weird. I've been thinking about you lately, and I realize that I don't always listen to you. So I'm trying to be a better listener. I guess I still need to work on it." When you do that, your child will be understanding and probably quite moved to hear that you have been thinking about him. In fact, it will most likely be a very nice moment. And the more you practice, the more natural and conversational it will feel.

Not so long ago, my son, Jacob, was feeling a bit down because summer was over and school would be starting again soon. We were sitting on his bed and I was doing a lot of mirroring and chatting and just having a very connected conversation. Jacob was already fourteen and intimately familiar with connected-parenting techniques, but when I got up to leave the room, he called out after me, "Hey, Mom, how come you weren't doing any of your connected-parenting stuff with me?" I just looked at him and said, "What do you think I've been doing? I've been doing it for the last half hour." "Oh," he said. "It felt nice. It didn't feel like a technique." That is how it should be; it shouldn't feel like a technique.

M: *Put It All Together to MIRROR*

Connecting, accurately reflecting your child's affect, and listening to what he or she is actually saying are the three tools that, used in combination, create genuine mirroring and a sincere moment of deep connection.

Practice Makes Perfect

It's important to point out here that you don't need to wait for your child to act out or be upset before you mirror. It seems to have the same impact on the child when he's happy as it does when he's upset. Mirror when he tells you a funny story, when she's recounting something that happened to a friend at school, or when he's talking about a TV show. Comment on the details in a drawing or a sand castle. Try to say out loud what you think your child would like you to notice about the work he's done. It makes no difference to the brain if what you're mirroring is positive or negative. Feeling heard and understood is something all of us need, crave, and appreciate. It brings us close to others and makes us want to share our feelings.

When I was a little girl I had an extraordinary aunt. I was very young when Auntie Maude died, but I still remember her. What I remember most is how she made me feel when she listened to my stories, leaning in, looking fascinated, and indicating through her other reactions that she had nothing more important to do in the entire world than listen to what I had to say. That attention made me feel warm and wonderful, and I adored her for it. Showing that kind of attention is a wonderful gift to give your child, and it creates a very close and special moment for both of you.

At the same time, however, you'll need to remember that more often than not you will not feel like mirroring. As I've said, this isn't something that just comes naturally. If you wait to feel like it, you'll be waiting a long time. In the beginning at least it will be something you have to be consciously working toward. And it will be particularly difficult to do when you're angry, so if you practice when your child is being good, and see how much she loves it, you'll be more likely to do it when it's hard.

In one particularly difficult situation, I was working with the mother of a five-year-old boy who was having so many meltdowns, not only at home but also at school, that his teachers finally ran out of sympathy and simply tried to ignore him. The least little thing would leave him limp and sobbing on the floor. When she came to me, his mother really didn't know what to do. If she overempathized it made matters worse, and if she didn't empathize at all, that wasn't good either.

Instead of trying to deal with the meltdowns directly, I put her on a program of mirroring whenever the child was happy. After a few weeks, he was so much better that his teachers couldn't believe it and actually asked the mother whether she had put him on meds. It's not that he never gets upset, but he doesn't get *as* upset, he gets upset less often, and when he does he recovers more quickly.

Mirror with all your children, not just the difficult one. In fact, practice on everyone—try it on your spouse, your friends, your relatives, and people at work. The more you do it the more proficient you become. And you'll also begin to see just how powerful this technique really is.

Below you'll find a couple of other scenarios to help you get the hang of mirroring and then follow it up with steps 2 and 3 of the formula that I gave you on page 25: (1) Mirror; (2) Present the problem; (3) Find a solution.

Tyler and the Train

You and your little boy are at a friend's house, when your child, Tyler, comes to you furious because his friend Matthew wouldn't let him play with his train. Your instinctive reaction might well be to say something like, "I'm so sorry Matthew is not sharing, but, you know, you have trains of your own, and you don't always like to share either. Why don't you just forget about Matthew's train and play with something else?" That would be most parents' perfectly reasonable and normal response, but it's not necessarily what's going to help Tyler in that moment. In fact, it's likely to escalate his anger to the "But I don't want to play with something else! I want to play with that train!" stage, which just might get you to the "Well, that's too bad, because you *can't* play with his train" level of response.

As you can probably see, going down that road (or track) is just going to escalate the problem to point where Tyler throws a full-blown tantrum and you wind up dragging him home, swearing that you will never take him on another playdate as long as he lives.

What you're doing here is, in effect, telling your child he shouldn't be feeling what he's feeling. He just needs to get over it and get on with it. To him, however, that's confusing; it tells him that you think what he's feeling is inappropriate, which means that he'll have to work even harder to convince you that it isn't. It is all in the message-delivery system. If a child sends a message and you send a different one back, he will keep sending the message in different ways until he feels it has been heard.

To **CALM** him instead of creating more anger here's how you might respond instead.

> TYLER: I *hate* Matthew. He's so mean. He's got this really great train and I wanted to play with it and he wouldn't let me. I *hate* him and I'm never going to play with him again!"

You **C**, **Connect**, by looking right into Tyler's eyes, leaning toward him, and trying to look as though you understand his urgency. You might be thinking, *He better not start this again*, or *He is going to embarrass me in front of the other child's mother*, or *My child does this to other kids all the time. How is he ever going to keep friends if he keeps doing this?* but you set all those thoughts aside and leave them out of this part of the conversation.

Instead you **A**, match his **Affect**. He is angry, so you make sure your body language and facial expressions reflect this.

You **L**, **Listen**, to his words and paraphrase them back to him *as if* he were saying them.

You **M**, put it all together and **Mirror** to your child.

When you do that, your conversation will sound something like this:

> YOU: I saw Matthew with that train. It looked *amazing*. And he won't share it at *all*, he won't even let you *touch* it.
>
> TYLER: No, he wouldn't *let* me; he's *mean*. I'm not going to be his friend anymore. *Tell* him he has to share it with me.
>
> YOU: So here's this *great* train. It looks so amazing, and he won't even let you near it. You can't see any other way to do this. You really need me to tell him to share it with you?
>
> TYLER, VIGOROUSLY NODDING: Yes, could you, please? I *really* want to play with it.

. . .

Now that Tyler is actually hearing what you say, you can present the problem and offer a solution.

> YOU: I can see how you are stuck here. It feels too hard to do it on your own. It just feels like he won't listen to you. You guys are really good friends, but this isn't the first time this has happened. You've had fights before. You were so excited to come to his house today, and this train is really getting in the way of the fun you wanted to have together. What about finding something else to play with that doesn't get in the way? (If the child is under five, feel free to shorten this to one or two sentences, such as, "This is hard. You were so excited about this playdate. Let's see if there's something else you can play with.")
>
> TYLER: Fine, but the next time he wants to play with something of mine, forget it.

In this scenario you are not just *telling* your child that you understand what he's feeling and why he's feeling it; you're actually allowing him to viscerally experience your joining with him in that emotion. The amazing effect of mirroring is that it allows the child to actually shift his own perspective. In fact, you will probably find that once he feels heard, he will no longer need to convince you how important the problem is, and he'll let it go and accept your solution, just as Tyler did.

Occasionally, however, kids don't respond, and when they don't, you need to move on to the problem *you* have by saying something like, "Sweetie, I have tried to understand, but you are still mad. You are telling me with your words that you would like to stay and play with Matthew, but you are showing me with your behavior that you need to leave." And then you go.

Later you can reconstruct the situation and offer your interpretation of the other boy's side, or you can remind your child of times when he did the same thing to someone else. You just can't do this at the beginning of the conversation or while he's in the middle of a meltdown. If you try to do that, all the child will feel is that you are being mean or taking the other child's side, and he'll never feel the need to look inward or rethink his behavior.

Here's another scenario that may be familiar to you.

Rebecca and the Battle of the Raincoat

You need to get to the supermarket. It's raining hard, and Rebecca won't put on her raincoat. You're running late and you really don't have time to argue with her about this. A typical interaction in this situation might go something like this:

"Becca, it's time to go. You need to put on your raincoat."

"*No*. I don't *want* to!"

"C'mon now, just put it on, please. We have to go."

"No! I said no."

"Rebecca, put it on, please, right now. Don't do this to me."

"Nooo" (as she runs away from the door).

"Enough of this. Please get this coat on, right now!"

"No!!!!"

"Get back here, I mean it! I'm going to count to three and if you don't put your coat on . . ."

And so it goes.

All the while you're probably thinking, *Why does this have to happen all the time? What's the big deal? Why is everything "no"? Why can't she just once say, "OKAY, MOMMY"? I don't have time for this!!!* But Rebecca doesn't see it that way, and her behavior continues to escalate. You now have conflicting agendas. You don't understand how much she doesn't want to put on her raincoat. It may not seem like a big deal to you, but clearly it's a really big deal to her, and you need to get out the door and accomplish the four thousand things you need to do that day.

What you need to do in this situation is first suspend your agenda and let her know that you understand hers. So, if you are going to say this in the way your child needs to hear it, it might sound something like this: "Yeah, raincoats are so stiff and bunchy. It would be so much nicer if you could just run out the door in your T-shirt and not have to wear any coat at all."

You will need to say at least three CALMing statements, and put everything you've got into the performance. Get down to her level; make icky faces; let her see that you really "get" how much she doesn't want to wear that coat, or how hard it is not to be allowed to make your own decisions. By the time you've done that, Rebecca will have stopped screaming and will probably be nodding emphatically because you'll be articulating and acting out exactly what she's feeling. If you're not fighting her, she has nothing more to scream about, so she stops.

And *then* you can move on to presenting the problem, because she'll be able to really hear what you need from her. So the next stage of your dialogue might go something like this. Staying calm and being neutral, you might say: "Here's the problem, Becca. It's really raining hard outside, and if you don't wear a raincoat you're going to get all wet, and then when we go into the air-conditioned supermarket you're going to get very cold, and you're going to hate that. So what I need you to do is put on your raincoat and get in the car."

At this point Rebecca will either put on her raincoat, even though she lets you know by her hunched-up shoulders and icky expression that she really doesn't want to, and tramp out the door—in which case your problem will be solved—or else she'll continue to refuse, which means that you'll need to come up with an alternate solution, one that involves a consequence.

I know that mirroring bad behavior may sound like the last thing you ought to be doing, and you may be thinking that the kid should just put the coat on and get out the door. The more you mirror, the fewer struggles you will have, and, in any case, it doesn't take any more energy than it does to yell and run around the house chasing her with the raincoat, or dealing with the tears and arguing that will follow. The difference is that you're putting that energy in at the beginning of the conversation rather than the end. And if you are having these types of interactions, what you have been doing was not working anyway.

Think of it this way; imagine a giant pole in the middle of the living room. If you walk into the room and whack your head on the pole, you will go around it the next time. Parenting is one of those rare times when we continue to whack our head on the same pole over and over again, doing the same things that do not work. If a behavior is still happening, it's time to walk around the pole.

I'm not saying the heavens will part every single time and Rebecca will immediately run to put on her raincoat (although that will happen surprisingly often), but the entire scene will play out better even if she has to put it on to avoid a consequence you've imposed. And the more often you mirror before you try to correct, the easier such interactions will become. There will be fewer power struggles, more compliance, and when your child does have a tantrum or a meltdown, it will be less intense and of shorter duration.

Yes/No Battles and "Yeah, but"

This is a frustrating phenomenon that many of you may recognize: getting stuck in a looping argument that starts with a simple question but has no end and no way out. Here is an example:

CHILD: Mom, where is my blue shirt? I want to wear it today . . .

A seemingly harmless question, but wait.

YOU: It's in the dirty laundry basket, honey.
CHILD: But I want to wear it!
YOU: It's in the dirty laundry so you'll have to wear something else.
CHILD: I don't want to wear anything else. I want that shirt!
YOU: Then you will have to wear it dirty.
CHILD: Gross! I'm not doing that.
YOU: Okay, then wear something else.

Here comes the loop. . . .

CHILD: But I want to wear that shirt!

The situation then spirals into a revolving argument that has no end. Some children can spin out, get incredibly stuck, and have complete meltdowns over these impossible, unsolvable situations. Stay calm and neutral and use the CALM technique. Here is an example:

> CHILD: Mom, where is my blue shirt? I want to wear it today.
>
> YOU: It's in the dirty laundry basket, honey.
>
> CHILD: But I want to wear it!
>
> YOU: You're talking about that gorgeous one with the lace on the bottom?
>
> CHILD: Yeah, that one.
>
> YOU: That's a great shirt, I know you love it . . . but it's in the wash.
>
> CHILD: But I want to wear it.
>
> YOU: That is your favorite shirt and I know it really goes with those shorts. I can see you have everything picked out around that shirt. Without that shirt your whole plan is blown.
>
> CHILD: What am I going to do? I'm not going to school if I can't wear that shirt!
>
> YOU: You put a lot of thought into your outfit and you didn't plan on its being in the wash. Is there anything else that could work with what you've picked out?

At this point your child will probably look for something else to wear—maybe in a huff, maybe not, but feeling heard. Walk away and be busy doing something else. If she escalates, follow the recommendations for how to deal with a vortex (see page 50) because that's where you are headed.

Keep Your Mind on Your Goal

Setting aside your agenda doesn't mean that you forget about your ultimate goal; it just means postponing it so that, in the end, you'll have a better chance of implementing your agenda in a more positive and meaningful way. Whether your child is sobbing because she's hurt or sad, or kicking and screaming because he's angry, your immediate goal is to de-escalate those feelings so that your child can calm down, hear you, and begin to look inward. Certainly you want (and need) to let him know that his behavior is unacceptable, but if you do that before you've CALMed him through mirroring, he won't be able to hear you.

If your child is screaming and you're screaming back even louder, de-escalation is virtually impossible. Sometimes we yell because it makes *us* feel better, but if yelling were an effective parenting tool there would be a lot more very well-behaved children in the world. We seem to want our children to be able to stop being angry or upset and start to be reasonable just because we tell them to. But if you think about how you're feeling when you are angry or upset, you'll understand how difficult that is.

Imagine that you are very upset and yelling at your kids and your spouse comes in and tells you you're overreacting and need to cut it out. How well would that go over? In fact, many parents have told me how difficult it is for them to control their own anger and not yell when they feel like yelling. Yet that's exactly what we expect our children to do all the time.

Children watch us, and if they see that we are having difficulty controlling our behavior they may feel it just can't be done. So the more *you* yell, the more hysterical you'll both become. What you really want to do when your child is throwing a tantrum is stop yourself from giving in to your instinctive need to yell. You want to drop your agenda temporarily to let him know that you understand and that he can, indeed, control his emotions. Try to imagine a switching station in your head, and ask yourself, *Am I about to say something I feel like saying or am I about to say something my child needs to hear?* You will find that often those are two very different responses.

How Do You Know When He's Ready to Listen—and What to Do When It Isn't Working

Parents ask me all the time how they will know when they can move past mirroring to presenting the problem. My answer is, just try it and, if you're doing it right, you'll know. In part it's intuitive, but your child will also be telling you with his words, his expression, and his body language. He'll be nodding his head, probably saying things like, "Uh-huh, yeah," and looking at you intently instead of scrunching up his face and shaking his head. He'll have stopped screaming or sobbing or holding his breath, or whatever he'd been doing to try to convey to you the urgency of his situation.

If you've mirrored properly, it will work 70 to 75 percent of the time, even with the most difficult child. But there will be times when your child simply unravels and nothing you do is making it better. Maybe there were three other kids in Tyler's class that day who wouldn't let him play with a toy. Maybe Rebecca had a fight with her best friend in kindergarten. You know that you react differently to the same issues depending on what kind of mood you were in to begin with, whether or not you got enough sleep, and how many other things have already gone wrong with your day. Children are the same, and you may just be running into a whole piggy bank full of real or imagined slights they've already encountered and are now choosing to empty on you. When that happens, you need to drop it and move on. If after three mirroring statements your child hasn't begun to de-escalate, it isn't going to work this time.

Kids can really whip themselves into a frenzy. This can be challenging for us as parents because we don't want to invalidate their feelings (which can be very real even though they're over-dramatizing), but we also don't want to be responding as if they're going through something really huge if it isn't. By doing that, we'd actually be feeding the frenzy by making them think that maybe the problem or incident or issue is even worse than they thought it was.

The problem is this: If we allow them to suck us into the vortex of their emotions, what's likely to happen is that we and they will unravel together and a conversation about something that didn't go well at school, for example, might last for hours and rotate in circles full of "Yeah, but" and "You don't understand." It's important that we parents don't allow that to happen.

It's up to us, then, to try to have some sense of how much is real and how much is drama. If the emotion is real, making three or four mirroring statements ought to work fairly well because your child will *want* to feel better. If it's drama, however, what he really wants is attention or to remain invested in being upset; he won't want to feel better, so you won't be able to mirror him out of the vortex. What you *don't* want to do in that situation is to start screaming, "This is drama! This isn't real!" because kids get just as upset when we don't believe their lies as they do when we don't believe their truths.

As I tell my clients, if you're mirroring and your child is still carrying on after you've mirrored well *at least three times*, you need to say, "You know, I'm really trying very hard to help you and I don't think I'm being helpful. I don't feel that my presence in this conversation is making you feel better. In fact, I feel as if I'm part of what's making you upset, and I love you so much that I'm going to leave you for a little bit to figure it out on your own. I promise I'll come back and check on how you're doing." And that statement needs to be followed up with a message of confidence, such as, "You know, this happens to you sometimes, and I know you'll get through it. You're going to be okay, just like all the other times." And then you walk away.

We sometimes work way too hard at these conversations. Disengaging in a neutral way is very important for children who work themselves up. It is important to recognize that we can become part of the problem by providing them with an audience and a target for their display of emotion. They need to learn that they can soothe themselves and that they can and will recover from whatever they're feeling. I am not saying that you should never comfort a child who is hysterical or extremely upset. What I am saying is that if you have tried to mirror, tried to hold her and soothe her, and she continues to escalate, you are in a vortex, and it is best to disengage. Don't walk away in a huff or lecture about how hurt you are; just walk away as described above, being very matter of fact, and check back in a few minutes. Often, when you check back the child will re-escalate. If so, repeat the steps by trying to mirror, and leave again after three statements if it doesn't work. Repeat until the child is calm.

This protocol works for tantrums (which I define as yelling, screaming, and throwing things) that can come from anger, tiredness, overstimulation, hunger, anxiety, or control issues. Tantrums often result from the child's not getting her way and venting her frustration by taking you down with her. It also works for meltdowns, which are less about anger and more about something like profound despair, when the child's whole body collapses, he falls to the floor, and he wails that "this is the worst day of my entire life." But whether it's a tantrum or a meltdown, if the child is so wrapped up in the moment that no matter what you do, he'll resist feeling better with all his might, you will never win. Your choices are to walk away or to get stuck for hours in a useless, draining, "Yeah, but . . ." circular conversation.

If your child is having a tantrum, and your mirroring efforts have not worked, he may be screaming, "I hate you, I hate you," but you need to keep walking. If she's in meltdown mode you don't ignore her, you just disengage and remind her that you are still there but you're waiting until she calms down. She may hang on to your leg, in which case you will need to stand there, but remain neutral and silent. Don't get down on the floor and become even more involved, and don't try to tear yourself away, because that's exactly what she wants at that moment. I call this "noise," and children will often escalate their behavior in order to pull you into the pattern the two of you have always danced before. Sometimes by staying involved, you're just enabling the behavior, and the longer you stay, the longer the child will stay stuck. Most likely, if you walk away or disengage, by the time you come back he'll have calmed himself.

You may find that you have to come back a couple of times. When your child starts to settle down, you can go in and ask how he is or if he would like to talk again. This may cause him to escalate all over again, but if that happens, you just repeat the pattern until he is calm. Eventually your child will learn that he has the skills and the ability to calm himself and that he can control his emotions rather than allowing his emotions to control him. This is the beginning of improved emotional regulation and resilience.

There will be much more about limit-setting and correcting in the second part of this book, but before we go there, we need to talk a bit more about how to reconnect if you've gotten to the point where the bond with your child is so frayed that nothing you do seems to CALM him.

THREE

Reconnect and
Repair the Bond

Not so long ago I received a phone call from a mother who was sobbing. "I have a nine-year-old son," she gasped, "and of course, I love
him, he's my child. But I just hate him. I can't stand him. I don't
even want to look at him, and I can't feel sorry for him, because he's
ruined my life. I don't like who I am. I don't like the kind of mother
I am, and I need help." Because his older sister had always been what
this woman called an extremely "easy" child, she was having a particularly hard time coping with her younger child's challenging
behavior.

As she began to tell me her story, it became clear that this woman
truly was in a very difficult situation. Her nine-year-old son, Charlie,
had exhausted her to the point where she couldn't really parent him
effectively anymore. She hated both herself and her child, and who
could blame her? Charlie was adorable, with curly blond hair and
bright green eyes. He was also very smart and very, very anxious.
Basically, he controlled his whole world. When he said jump, his

parents jumped. He wouldn't get out of his pajamas on weekends, and if his mother tried to take him anywhere he screamed, threw a tantrum, swore at her, and called her names. Just getting him out of the house to go to school was a three-hour process. When his mother first called me, her entire goal was nothing more than getting to the point where she would be able to take Charlie to the corner store and back without his throwing a tantrum.

The more Charlie misbehaved and acted out, the more frayed the bond between him and his mother became, and the more she started to rely on hard parenting. This is perfectly understandable because (1) your child doesn't appear to want the cuddling and snuggling that characterizes soft parenting, and (2) you don't really feel like doing it. But, as I explained to Charlie's mother, it's exactly when you feel like doing it the least that you need to do the most soft parenting. When your car is in a skid, your instinct is to steer in the opposite direction, but what you really need to do is steer into the skid until the car comes to a stop; then you can correct your direction. Using that analogy, when your child's behavior is skidding into a danger zone, you need to go with that, acknowledge his feelings, and *then*, when the bond between you has been strengthened and your child has calmed down enough to listen, you can begin to contain and correct.

I knew immediately that Charlie's mother couldn't afford to get into any more power struggles with her child. Because just about everything she said or did was perceived by Charlie as an injury, their relationship could not tolerate it. So the first thing I did was to get his father to commit to staying at home a bit later in the morning and taking over the hard parenting job of getting their son up, teeth brushed, dressed, and out the door to school. It wasn't going to be easy, but Charlie's father knew his family's mental health depended on healing this bond.

At the same time, I told Charlie's mother that she was going to be on a two-week soft-parenting program. Every morning before he got ready for school, she was going to take Charlie into her bed, snuggle with him, hug him and kiss him and tickle him, and tell him how much she loved him. I made it clear that I knew she'd be doing this through gritted teeth—at least at first—but that she needed to put her whole heart and soul into giving an Academy Award–winning performance.

The Power of Baby Play

What I asked Charlie's mother to do is what I call "baby play," which I have found to be a powerful way to "redo" or repair a frayed bond. It's one of the most effective soft parenting tools I can give you for making an empathic repair and reconnecting with your child so that he or she will able to "hear" what you're saying when you use the CALM technique to mirror and you will be able to follow the three steps that let him know you're holding on to the other end of the rope that's keeping him safe.

Growing into a "big kid" can be pretty scary, and I believe that these days we tend to push children out of babyhood much too soon. They're exposed to an enormous amount of "adult" information that they're really not equipped to handle. So baby play is a way to let children know they're still your babies and to redo some of the attachment bonding you may have missed or that may have unraveled along the way. In fact, the more frayed your relationship has become, the more your child has been misbehaving, the more important baby play becomes.

Like mirroring, baby play isn't so much about what you say as what you "tell" your child through your attention and body language—looking into her eyes, rubbing her nose, touching her face, tickling her, using a baby voice. It's about a feeling, creating a moment of connection and closeness between you and your child. In fact, this is really mirroring in its most basic form because it's re-creating what you did instinctively when the child really was a baby.

Get out your child's baby books, pictures, and videos and look through them with her; take out a favorite toy if you've saved it; or bring out her baby blanket. Tell her stories about what she was like as a baby and watch the delight in your child's eyes. Tickle her, rub noses, tell her that she's "still your little baby." Have fun with this, make it playful and light, not forced. Kids love this interaction, even children who are a little older. And while, as I've said, it is a powerful way to reconnect with your child when the bond between you has become frayed, it is also a way to simply feel closer to your child, no matter how connected you already may be. I believe that *all* parents and children will benefit from engaging in about twenty minutes of baby play every day. If the bond is really stressed, I suggest that parents do it twice a day. And if you have trouble getting yourself to do it because you're already so angry or frustrated, try doing it for shorter periods of time—about ten minutes—three times a day.

Many parents tell me that this is not new for them; they do it all the time, but often it is not done as much as they think. Make sure, though, that it is something you do in a mindful way. Put boundaries around it. You don't have to walk around all day talking to your child as if she were a baby. Tell her that for a few minutes she is going to be your little one, and when the game is over she'll have to be big again.

If your child doesn't want the physical cuddling, it just means that it's too frightening or overwhelming for him or that the attachment is so frayed that he doesn't want you to touch him. You can then do this exercise using props such as a stuffed animal, by looking at pictures, or through stories. Get out a stuffed animal (if you still have one) that your child used to love, hold it up, and address the toy instead of the child directly: "Oh, look at this lamb; you used to love this lamb. You were just about this size, and I used to hold you in my arms just like this . . ." Or look at a baby picture and look at the photo instead of the child, saying: "Oh, look how cute you were! I remember when you used to wear that snowsuit . . ." I have had an overwhelming number of parents tell me that this technique has been incredibly helpful, not just for the child but for the parents as well. Even if it starts out as something they don't want to do, it soon becomes an interlude to look forward to. We get into the habit of talking to our kids only when we want them to do something or stop doing something. Or we get so busy and so preoccupied with what's wrong that we forget to have these wonderful moments of closeness and joy. Instead of always telling your kids to stop being silly, join in and watch the look of sheer delight on their faces. The more often these interactions occur, the more rewarding they are. Even if you feel very close with your children, baby play is a wonderful way to nurture that connection and remind them just how lovable they are.

Remember that your initial mirroring was helping your baby develop neuropathways, and that it's something the brain actually craves. That craving doesn't go away just because your child is now older. Baby play takes the child back to the safety of when he was a baby and, therefore, brings down his anxiety level dramatically.

Parents often ask me if this won't just make their child want to be a baby all the time since he loves it so much, but the truth is that it won't. Instead, he'll be filled up, and he'll let you know when he wants to move on. The other question parents ask is whether their older children won't be mortified by such an overt display of affection. The answer to that question is no as well, although with an older child you'll probably be doing this in a more playful way than you would with a younger one. That said, if you try it, you'll find that bigger kids love it too (so long as you don't do it in front of their friends).

I will never forget a two-day workshop I did a few years ago at a small private school. One of the teachers in the room snorted and laughed out loud when I talked about baby play. I asked her why she found it so funny, and she explained that her fourteen-year-old son was a Goth and they had been fighting for years. She said he would "puke on her" if she ever treated him that way. So I challenged her to go home and try it in a playful, fun way.

When I saw her the next morning, the expression on her face said it all. She explained to the group that when she arrived home the day before to find her son in his usual position splayed out on the sofa, she'd called out playfully, "Where's my little fourteen-year-old?" and started to tickle him. She was absolutely flabbergasted when, instead of "puking" on her as she'd expected, he threw his feet in the air and they wrestled around and had a great time for about ten minutes, after which, without having to say anything, they both knew game time was over and she went into the kitchen to start dinner.

Then, later that evening, as she walked past his bedroom door, he called out in a playful baby voice, "Mommy, will you tuck me in?" So she went in, kissed him good night, and then, when she was back in the hall, she slid down the wall to the floor, crying as she thought of all the time she'd wasted tiptoeing around the house and trying to stay out of her son's way for fear that she'd say something to set him off when they could have been connecting instead.

Baby play is a way to cement a bond or re-create one that is frayed, so that your child will be better able to survive the slings and arrows coming at him in the world, because he knows beyond a doubt that you are there to be his safe haven—that you're still holding the rope. The more difficult your child is, the less you feel like doing it, the more he needs it and the more important it is that you *do* do it. It's a powerful component of the connected-parenting program, even for older children; you just need to modify the play so that they will enjoy it.

Your Child Is Not a Monster, and Neither Are You

As for Charlie, the problem began when he really was a baby. We all seem to believe that our child is going to be born the perfect, textbook "Gerber baby," who coos and smiles with delight every time we appear. Charlie's big sister was apparently that kind of child. But not all children are born the same. At one end of the personality spectrum, some really do seem to take things in stride and remain smiling and happy all (or at least most of) the time, while at the other end, some have very strong reactions to just about everything and, as a result, don't self-regulate very well. Every one of us has certain personality characteristics hardwired into our DNA. They may be developed or discouraged by nurturing and environment, but the bottom line is that every one of us is unique, and our children may be more or less like us—or the way we expect them to be and think they should be.

That's one of the reasons parents sometimes find it so difficult to understand *why* their child is behaving the way he does, and what I help them see is that *whenever* a child acts out, throws a tantrum, and tries to control her world by controlling you, at the root of her behavior there is always some kind of fear or emotion she doesn't really understand and can't articulate—and if she doesn't understand it, why should you? The point is that when you respond by yelling, becoming confrontational, or punishing, what you're doing is reinforcing your child's fear and increasing her anxiety level so that she becomes even less capable of controlling her feelings.

Charlie was, from the beginning, difficult to calm and soothe. He cried a lot, and the more he cried, the more frustrated his mother became. Then, as the crying baby grew into a crying toddler, it became more and more difficult for her to cope. Sometimes she yelled at him and sometimes, when she was just too tired to do anything else, she ignored him entirely. As a result, Charlie had been receiving constant mixed messages from her, which only made him more anxious. Although he certainly could not have articulated it, he eventually discovered that the only way he had to get his mother's attention at least some of the time was to make her angry. As a result, he began to act out more and more, and his mother became angrier and angrier.

Charlie's mother was actually embarrassed to tell me her story, because, to large degree, she blamed herself and felt an incredible amount of shame for having allowed the situation to deteriorate so badly. The first thing I had to do was reassure her that what she'd been doing was her psyche's natural reaction, and that many parents would have found themselves stuck in the same cycle. Then I explained that the first order of business for her was going to be repairing the bond that had been so badly frayed by the negative dynamic that had developed between her and her son. That's what her morning cuddle time with Charlie was to be all about.

Interestingly, because the dad had been less caught up in the dance of disconnection that had been driving Charlie's behavior with his mother, he had been doing more instinctive mirroring and connecting all along, and Charlie didn't feel the same need to act out with him, so Dad didn't have too much trouble getting Charlie up and out in the morning. As a result of this new regime, things began to improve very quickly, and because of that, Charlie's mother also began to feel better about him.

The Magic of Mending the Bond

After just a week and a half, I received another phone call, and again Charlie's mother was crying, but this time they were tears of joy and gratitude. On that morning she'd been snuggling with Charlie as she had been doing every morning, when he turned to her and said, "You know, Mommy, I really love you, and I know you love your snuggle time with me, but I've really got to get ready for school now." As she spoke those words, I could hear the wonderment in her voice, but that's just how powerful making this kind of connection can be.

What had happened to shift the dynamic between them so completely? As I explained it to her, in that very short period of time, because there was so much less tension in the house and because of the time she'd spent doing nothing but reconnecting with him, Charlie had calmed down enough—and felt safe enough—to consider his own behavior. He was joining with what his mother had showed she was feeling, letting her know he understood *her* agenda but *he* needed to take responsibility for himself and get on with his own day. That, in and of itself, seemed miraculous to her, as it does to many of my clients.

Very often when people come in after just a week of working with me and I ask how their week went, they'll tell me that "for some reason" it was a pretty good week and they "didn't have to" mirror very much at all. I then have to remind them that their child's behavior probably hadn't just coincidentally improved to such a degree for no reason and that the changes they'd noticed more than likely resulted from the mirroring they had been doing.

After the initial two weeks, I felt that Charlie's mother's bond with her son was strong enough to withstand some hard parenting. Dad went back to leaving for work at his regular time, and she started getting her son ready for school. I explained that from then on when Charlie started to act out (as he certainly would), she'd first be mirroring, then, if necessary, she'd present the problem and seek a solution. It went surprisingly well. A new morning routine had already been established by Charlie's dad, and Charlie was also feeling closer to his mom, so when he did get upset by something like not being able to get his belt through the belt loops, with a bit of mirroring from Mom and a minimum of fussing, he got himself dressed and out of the house. Within a few months, Charlie didn't just go to the store and back without throwing a tantrum (which, you may recall, was his mother's initial goal), he went on a family vacation at the seashore for a week without having a single significant meltdown.

As you mirror with your child, you help him better understand his emotions, organize his feelings, and regulate his responses. By doing that, he gains confidence, resilience, and improved self-esteem. He also, more or less by osmosis, learns to mirror and show empathy for others, which will, in the long run, help him develop better relationships not only with you but with everyone else in his world.

Charlie's case was extreme but far from unusual. If the bond between you and your child is so frayed that he or she—like Charlie—appears to have turned into a monster, repairing it is going to take both courage and commitment. But the payoff, I assure you, will be worth it. If you have less serious issues with your child, the results will come more quickly, but in either case, you will be giving a powerful gift to both yourself and your child.

Once a child feels truly loved and understood, he'll feel better about himself. He'll no longer have to throw a tantrum to get your attention, and he'll want to behave not because he fears punishment but because he knows it's the right thing to do and he wants to make you feel good because you've made *him* feel good.

FOUR

The Power of
Parenting Together

As you read in the previous chapter, Charlie's parents worked together to repair the family bond. That is, of course, the best and most effective way to parent in any situation. But when you're having a problem with your child and trying to deal with a number of negative behaviors, it's normal to be stressed and probably a bit anxious. Whatever anxiety you're experiencing can then spill over to affect your relationship with your spouse or partner—and vice versa. You may become extra prickly with each other because of the stress, and because of that, it's important to find a time when you're both calm and relaxed to coordinate your agendas. The important thing is to appear united in front of your child. Try not to argue and try not to undermine or put each other down in his or her presence.

I know that isn't always easy, and you're not always going to succeed, but it's important for everyone involved that you really do make this a priority. First of all, the more your child hears you arguing, the less confident he's going to feel about your ability to protect him. If his mom or dad is constantly telling the other parent how useless he or she is, it stands to reason that the child is eventually going to start thinking that Mom or Dad must really be incompetent. Second, if the primary way you relate to each other is by yelling and arguing, your child will also pick up on that and begin to think it's the way to communicate with her siblings and friends. And finally, but perhaps most important, listening to you fight is extremely painful for your child.

We adults seem to think our children understand that we fight and then we get over it and everything is fine, and we expect them to realize that it has nothing to do with them. But kids don't contextualize behavior the same way we do, and they almost *always* think it's about them. I sometimes ask parents if they would slap their child in the face, and, of course, they're horrified by the very thought that they would do such a thing. But it hurts a child just as much to hear you screaming and calling each other names as it would if you physically hit her. In fact, during my more than twenty years of working with children one-on-one, I've found that the pain of having to watch or listen to their parents fighting is one of the issues they most want and need to talk about.

I know it's not possible to anticipate every eventuality that might arise, but, as much as possible, it's always a good idea to agree on your agenda in advance. Then, if something does come up, take your partner aside, out of earshot of your child, to discuss it, or if possible, wait until you get home and are alone to talk about the problem. You can even devise a signal to use when you're in public to let each other know you're not happy but will discuss it later. I sometimes suggest to my clients that if they can't hold in their anger when their child is present, they might text message what they have to say to their partner. Don't laugh! Anything is better than fighting in front of your child.

I once worked with a lovely teenager who was so sad and so tired of listening to her parents fight that she cried herself to sleep every night. I remember her telling me about a trip her family took to Disneyland when she was six years old. What she remembered was not the magic and wonder that should go along with a trip to Disneyland, but the faces of other parents, smiling, laughing, and holding hands with their children while her own parents were scowling and fighting in public. She said she had felt so sad, hurt, and disappointed that she sat down and sobbed right in the middle of the park. At the time, her parents apologized and told her they would stop, and they did for about half an hour, but then they were back at it again. She cried again in my office as she remembered that trip, and she still wonders why they couldn't have stopped arguing just once in such a happy place.

When One Parent Is More Anxious

We adults may be better able than children to regulate our emotions, but that doesn't mean some of us aren't hardwired to be more anxious than others. When our children are acting up or acting out, the one who is more anxious may overreact, and very often that just causes the less anxious parent to compensate by becoming even calmer. In a way, what can happen then is very similar to what happens when you try to calm a child by telling her that she has no reason to be so upset. Rather than calming the anxious parent, his or her belief that her message has not been received will only cause her anxiety to escalate.

One father I worked with told me that his wife was driving him nuts, calling him at work and "going on and on until I want to scream." His solution was to put her on speakerphone and keep on doing his work while he periodically said, "Yeah, yeah," "Uh-huh," "Okay." I suggested something really radical—that he try to just listen to her for once. "Are you kidding?" he said. "That will just make her talk more!" "No," I assured him. "She's talking more because she knows you're not listening." So the next day he tried it. He actually gave her his full attention, and because she knew he was responding, she had nothing more to say. The dad was amazed, but their mutually changed modus operandi actually had a very positive effect on how they felt about each other.

If you know that you and your partner or spouse are at opposite ends of the emotional pole, try mirroring instead of shouting or ignoring each other. As I've been saying, we all crave that mirroring connection, and the craving doesn't go away just because we've become parents.

When One Parent Is Stricter or More Lenient

I remember one incident related to me by clients who had taken their little boy out to a restaurant with buffet-style service. The dad took him to the buffet to choose his meal and because nothing really appealed to him, they settled on a waffle with fresh fruit. When they returned to the table, the mom was very upset. To her, choosing a meal from the dessert table was totally unacceptable, while to the father it had seemed like a perfectly reasonable compromise. The upshot was that they were arguing with each other in the middle of the restaurant while their child watched. He didn't know whether to eat the waffle to please his dad or not eat it to please his mom. The entire meal was ruined, but, beyond that, I can virtually guarantee that the little boy will remember the incident long after his parents have forgotten it.

In the best of all possible worlds parents would always see things the same way, but that's not always the reality. What happens most often is that the one who spends more time with the children becomes the limit-setter, and the other parent, who, for example, gets home after a long day at work and is excited to see the kids, doesn't want to spend his/her little time with them being a disciplinarian. For that parent it's playtime, a time for reconnecting; everything is fun. Let's assume for the moment that it's the father. He comes home shouting, "Daddy's home!" and the kids go screeching down the hall as he picks them up, flips them over his head, and generally whips them into a frenzy. Generally this happens just as Mom's gotten them fed, bathed, and ready for bed. Now that agenda is more or less tossed aside. Maybe they've been little angels all day, but just as likely they've had a couple of meltdowns. Mom may be saying, "You have no idea what I've been through today. It took me forever to get them settled. Andrew did this and Emma did that," and Dad is saying, "What do you mean? They're just being kids." In other words, from the mother's point of view, he just doesn't get it, and she gets resentful. He has not, however, shared her frustration. He just wants to reconnect with his kids, and in his mind she's being too tough.

Or, it may be just the opposite. Dad may be the one who is firmer with the kids. When he gets home they've been running around all day. Mom is by now totally frazzled and can't get them to do anything. Dad is angry and lays down the law because he's had an exhausting day and cannot deal with this chaos. Mom then feels the children have been treated too harshly and extends their bedtime or spends a great deal of time comforting them.

What happens then is very much the same as what happens when one parent is more anxious than the other: the strict parent is likely to become even stricter and take on all the hard parenting chores, while the other becomes more and more lenient and does the soft parenting. In other words, each one begins to compensate for what he or she believes is a weakness in the other's parenting style. They become more and more polarized and each, possibly without even realizing it, winds up undermining the other.

Not only is this extremely confusing to a child, but it also creates a situation in which neither parent is participating in all aspects of the parenting experience.

When I see this happening, I generally suggest that the firmer parent start looking for what I like to call "connectors," moments that provide an opportunity to connect with your child in some way that isn't disciplinary. Say, for example, that little Jody comes into the kitchen whining that "there's never anything to eat around here. This house is stupid." Instead of giving in to the temptation to say, "I work very hard to buy things you like, and I don't appreciate you talking to me that way. Why don't you try doing the shopping for a change? There are lots of children in this world who have nothing to eat," and so on, you might connect by saying something like, "That's the *worst*, when you have a craving for something and you look in the fridge and there's nothing there you want to eat." When you do that, Jody will register, *Hmm, that felt a bit different from what I'm used to.* It's not a big deal, just a little moment. (In fact, if you make too big a deal of it, your child will see it as a "tactic" rather than a connection.) But it is a moment of mirroring, a moment of being understood, and the more of those you and your child experience together, the closer your child feels to you, the tighter the tension on the rope, and the more the child wants to hold on to that feeling.

Tagging Out

One great benefit of parenting together is that you can "spell" each other, and your child will know that he can't play one of you off against the other.

Tagging out is a great tactic to use when your child is having a tantrum or a meltdown (which will happen, even when you've been mirroring and connecting and things have gotten so much better) and you know that you're at the end of your rope (or your patience). So long as you know that you and your spouse or partner have agreed on your agenda, and he or she is available and a willing team player, you can simply say to your child, as calmly as possible, "You know, I love you, but I don't think we're getting anywhere here and I need a break. Daddy [or Mommy, or whoever] is going to take over now." It is so important to be an observer of yourself and recognize when it's time to step out, take the help, take a break, and gather yourself together.

Or, if the other person has been aware of what's been going on, he or she might come in voluntarily and say, "You know what, you guys have been at it for a while now and you need a break, so I'll take over." You can even agree in advance on a signal that lets the other person know you're tagging out. What you *don't* want is for that person to announce, "You know, you look like you're totally out of control here, so let me handle this." Very often, the one who's been outside the fray, so to speak, will feel that he or she needs to protect the child, and you don't want the one who's tagging in to undermine or counteract whatever you've been saying or doing. Nor do you want that person to start screaming at the child, as in, "Look at what you've done. Look how you've upset your mother [or dad, or whomever]!" And finally, you don't want your teammate to sabotage your efforts by resolving the issue and then saying, "I don't know what all the fuss was about. I took care of it in a couple of minutes."

Of course, the one who's coming in fresh is going to be able to handle to situation a lot better than the one who's already overwhelmed and completely frazzled. That's the whole point of tagging out. You just need to make sure your child knows that you're agreed on the issue and it doesn't matter who is taking over. That way he or she will understand that this isn't a golden opportunity to play one of you against the other.

When One Parent Can't or Won't Do It

I've often had clients tell me that their spouse refused to "get with the program," and wasn't interested in learning all that mirroring "stuff."

When that happens, more often than not it's because one parent is so angry with the child that the parent simply can't get himself (or herself) to do it and thinks it's the kid who ought to be getting with the program. When a parent feels this way, instinctively he thinks he just needs to get tougher. When I hear that, I remind the parent that what he has been doing hasn't worked, and I tell him that he *needs* to do it for himself because it will change the way his child responds and, ultimately, the way he feels about that child.

One of the most extreme examples of this involved an eleven-year-old boy named Dillon. In this case it was the father who called me in tears because, as he put it, their household had become a "war zone" and he was at his wit's end. Dillon was absolutely horrible to his mother, calling her names and generally making himself as unlovable as possible. I worked with both parents, and the dad seemed to "get it" very quickly. The connectors between him and his son began to fall into place, and within a few weeks Dillon's anger, aggression, and rages had noticeably decreased.

His mother, however, simply could not get herself to mirror with her son. Her general reaction to his behavior was to say, "Don't you dare talk to me that way, and if you do . . ." Sometimes their fights became so intense that the father would literally have to restrain his son or put his body between them.

No matter how hard I tried to convince her otherwise, the mother's mantra was, "Why should I be nice to him? Mirroring and being nice when he's being such a monster don't make any sense." That reaction isn't unusual and it's also perfectly understandable, but what I try to explain to people is that sometimes you need to do it for yourself. Do it because it will bring a better result and you'll feel better about what your child does back to you.

In this case, after a while the mom could see that what the father was doing was, in fact, making a difference, and that caused her to challenge her own initial rejection of the plan. One day she was sitting in the living room watching television when Dillon stormed in and angrily confronted her: "What did you do with my drawing? You always move my stuff. You're such an idiot . . . You never care about anything I do . . . Where is it? *Where is it?*" Which would normally have caused her to respond in kind with something like, "Don't you dare speak to me that way. If you cared about your drawing you would have put it someplace safe to begin with. Keep it up and you'll lose a lot more than your drawing!" Which would, of course, wind up in another screaming fight. But this time, for whatever reason, a lightbulb went off in her brain. She stopped herself, took a deep breath, and said, "You know, Dillon, I watched you working on that picture. I saw the hours and hours you spent on it and the detail you put into it. No wonder you are so upset."

What she did was perfect mirroring. And Dillon looked at her, his mouth fell open, and he mumbled, "It's okay, I'll go look for it," and walked out of the room. Even more amazing, he came back a few minutes later and muttered, "I'm sorry." She told me afterward that she sat on the couch and cried because she'd suddenly realized just how many opportunities she had missed to connect with her son and how far they apart they had drifted. It was a major turning point not only for her and her son, but also for the entire family. Her relationship with Dillon continued to be tenser than that between him and his father, but from that day on, the whole family dynamic shifted for the better.

One of the many benefits of connected parenting is that even if only one parent is following the program, the child is likely to begin behaving better, which means that, as in the case of Dillon's mother, the other will begin to see the positive results and will then become more open to doing the same, so that ultimately both parents will begin to behave more consistently.

In another situation, I was counseling a family in which both parents were extremely intellectual and had always treated their five-year-old daughter, a very bright child, as if she were a little adult. The child, however, was showing classic signs of feeling unlovable and displaying what I call attachment sensitivities. There is an actual, clinical disorder called attachment disorder, but that's not what I'm talking about here. Even when the parent-child bond is strong and healthy, a child may have attachment sensitivities—if, for example, you've been away, or you get mad, or if you're just sick for a few days. Anything that temporarily disrupts that fragile bond can create some odd or erratic behaviors.

This particular little girl was miserable, sullen, throwing tantrums, and controlling the entire family with her moods. When I suggested baby play to her mother as a way to repair the bond between them, she basically told me, "I don't do that kind of thing." In fact, she was so angry and distanced from her child that she simply couldn't tolerate the idea. I explained that the child needed it emotionally, and that she, the mother, needed to find some way to make it work for her. Ultimately, she found that she could "tolerate" looking at baby pictures with her daughter and directing the baby talk to the photos, saying, "Oooh, look how cute you were in that snowsuit," or "Oooh, I remember how much you used to love that doll." From there she was able to move on to telling her daughter stories about when she was a baby, and even though she was truly putting on an Academy Award performance, it made a tremendous difference. Initially, her daughter was a bit overwhelmed by the baby play and needed somehow to sabotage the moment by clinging or squeezing or pinching her mother too hard. But in a very short time she stopped doing that, and these became very genuine bonding moments. Within a month her behavior had improved so much that the connecting and baby play started to feel much more natural to both of them.

That's the magic of mirroring and connecting. Even more magical, however, is the fact that once the reluctant or recalcitrant parent experiences his or her "aha" moment, he or she will automatically become not only more willing, but also better able to join his or her spouse or partner in connecting with their child.

Getting the Rest of the Family on Board

Parents, of course, are the primary caregivers, but none of us lives in a vacuum, and many of us live with parents and in-laws who are close enough to have some impact on our children's lives. In these situations, there can be a significant amount of tension and friction created by the parenting generation gap. There really is a difference between the culture in which you parent and that which prevailed when your parents were raising you. You, no doubt, were raised in a parent-centric culture, whereas we are all living in a child-centric world. Therefore, your parents (or your in-laws) might observe the way you parent, and think—or more likely say—"That kid just needs a good kick in the pants." Whereas you might see your mom offering your child a hot dog and let her know in no uncertain terms that in your home everything is organic and certainly nitrite-free.

Then, of course, there's the added stress of worrying whether your child will misbehave—again—during your weekly dinner with the in-laws. You may spend the entire car ride over lecturing her about how to behave, not running around, being careful not to break anything. And she, either because she knows it's a great way to get at you or because she's absorbed your tension and is so stressed herself, will almost immediately have a meltdown or throw a tantrum. You then either underreact and try to laugh it off, or you overreact to compensate for your embarrassment and yell at your child—which, of course, just makes it all worse.

Grandparents can sometimes undermine your efforts, saying things like, "Don't be hard on him, he's fine, leave him alone," after your child has done something you have been trying to correct. Or they can be very critical and dismissive of either your parenting or your children, which can then bring up issues from your own childhood. You may feel that you have to choose between protecting your child and offending your parents. Remember that mirroring to your parents can be a great way to de-escalate conflict and open lines of communication.

That said, however, grandparents can also be incredibly supportive and wonderful, and most grandparents really have a lot of wisdom. They've raised children to adulthood, which we haven't yet done. One insight they often have is to see how much we tend to overindulge our kids (unless, of course, they are the ones who do the indulging). So we shouldn't automatically discount what they have to say. Instead, why not try to get them on board?

If you find yourself in conflict with or being undermined by the older generation, I suggest, as I do to my clients, that you try explaining what you've learned from this book or offer them a copy to read. The more united a front you present, the more consistent you all can be in how you react and the messages you send to your child, the more confident and resilient he will become, and, therefore, the better able he will be to control his emotions and behave the way you want him to.

Teamwork Makes It Easier for Everyone

When your child is acting out, you become disconnected from each other, and that disconnection may then extend to your spouse or partner and to other members of your family. When you are able to reconnect not only with your child, but also with each other, you will find that dissension begins to dissipate and battles become less frequent. You begin to work as members of a team, and that means less stress for everyone.

You won't always be perfect at this—nobody is—but the beauty of this method is that there will always be an opportunity for a "do-over."

FIVE

In the Game of Life You Always Get a Second Chance

As I said at the beginning, there are times when you will forget all about connecting and lose your temper with your child, times when you're just so busy, worn down, overloaded, and focused on getting through your own day's agenda that you won't have time to worry about anyone else's.

As parents, we sometimes get so frustrated that we rely on bribing, cajoling, or begging to deal with exhausting behaviors. We can also fall into what I call parental numbness, where we tune out and ignore behaviors because we just don't have the energy to deal with them head-on. Whatever the reason, we don't always keep proper tension on that rope connecting us and our children, which leaves our kids feeling less lovable and increasingly confused by our mixed messages, ultimately leading to more negative behavior.

Nobody's Perfect—Certainly Not Me!

I teach families, coach parents, and believe in and have personally experienced how powerful mirroring can be; and yet I, too, have times when I'm so overwhelmed that everything I know goes flying out the window and I blow it with my own kids. Not so long ago, in fact, I blew it big-time with my son and older daughter.

My son, Jacob, who was eleven at the time, needed braces. Zoë, who was ten, did not. So, of course, Zoë desperately wanted braces, and Jacob, just as desperately, did not. When the day came to take Jacob to the orthodontist to begin the process, I asked Zoë if she wanted to come along. (That, as you'll see, was my first mistake, but I was so focused on my own agenda that I really wasn't thinking about Zoë's at the time.) While Jacob was in the chair, having impressions taken, gagging, and not coping particularly well, Zoë was in the waiting room playing a video game. When the whole ordeal was finally over, I went to Zoë and asked her to let Jacob play with the game while I settled the bill. "Your brother was having a hard time in there," I said, "and it would really help him to calm down if he could play with the game for a few minutes." Zoë's reaction, which was totally out of character for her, was to say, "Why do I have to? How come I have to give it up? He always gets everything!" At that point I was already at the limit of my stress level, so, instead of mirroring, I said, "You know what, that's not very nice of you. You know what your brother's been through in there. He's really had a hard time, and you didn't have to come," and on and on I went. Everything I shouldn't have said just came pouring out.

Then, to top it all off, I'd promised to take them to one of their favorite fast-food places for dinner, but I had forgotten my wallet and didn't have enough money to cover the cost of everything they wanted. So I suggested that we get milk shakes and fries to take home, and I'd call my husband to put chicken nuggets in the oven. This seemed like a reasonable solution to me, but Zoë was already so upset that she began to wail all over again. "Now I don't even get dinner," at which point I lost it: "You're lucky to be here at all, and I don't have to get you anything. There are children in this world who are starving and would be happy to have what you have . . ." and so on all the way home, even while, at the same time, I was saying to myself, *Mirror, you idiot, what are you doing? You teach this stuff.* But I just couldn't stop myself.

When we finally pulled into the driveway, Zoë wouldn't get out of the car. I left her there and stormed into the house, and my husband informed me that we didn't have any chicken nuggets. Somehow that jarred me into realizing how poorly I'd been responding to my daughter. So I went back out to the car and said to Zoë, "Honey, this has been a terrible ride home. I didn't take the time to find out why you are so upset, and I know this isn't like you, so there must be a very good reason. I've been yelling at you for half an hour and I've missed something important."

And that's when it all came out. "I'm sorry, Mommy, it's just that Jacob gets to have braces and I don't, and I would have been happy to have them and I would have handled it much better . . ."

So I mirrored again: "You really wanted those braces, and you would have been so brave." She immediately said, "Oh, Mommy, I'm so sorry. I should have shared the game, and I knew you were tired. I know it was hard and I know Jacob was upset, and it wasn't your fault you didn't have enough money . . ." Everything I had wanted her to do and say in the first place.

There are two lessons to be learned here. The first is that if I'd mirrored starting out, I would have saved myself an hour of stress, but I didn't. The second—which is probably the most amazing thing about connected parenting—is that when you do blow it and blow up, you get a second chance.

The Power of Wondering

I should have known what was going on with Zoë; I do this for a living, and as I'm writing this I can't believe I missed it. But sometimes you may not have any idea what it is your child is upset about, or you may be so upset and overstressed in that moment that you simply don't have the mental energy to try to figure it out. Unlike adults, children don't usually come home from school, sit back in a chair, and say, "Boy, what a day I had! It all started in the sandbox when Nathan took my truck . . ." Instead, what he's probably going to do is come home irritated, agitated, and grab his little sister's toy or hit her. And you won't have any idea what's prompted his behavior. What do you do then? What I tell parents is that they can "wonder out loud." You can simply say something like, "Something must have happened today to make you feel this way. You're a great kid and you wouldn't be acting this way if something wasn't really bothering you." Doing that wondering lets your child know you're on his side and you're really *trying* to understand his feelings. What you'll find is that, unlike the interrogation method we so often tend to use (*What did you do today? Did someone bother you? Did something happen? Did you get in trouble? Who did you play with?*), which usually just causes children to shut down, wondering aloud actually gets them to open up and tell us what happened and what they're feeling, because it gets them to think about their feelings. As a result, one of the collateral benefits of mirroring out loud to your child is that she will become more likely to use words instead of behaviors to express herself.

But what if you're wrong? What if you say you think your child must be feeling something he isn't? Well, the truth is, you're a parent, not a mind reader, and it's not always easy to determine what a child is trying to communicate through his behavior. So you may have to become a bit of a detective. But the point of connecting isn't to let him know how smart you are. The point is to make it clear that you're genuinely trying to understand him. He'll let you know if you're on the wrong track.

So if he does get mad, tells you that you don't know anything, and starts to escalate his behavior, you can mirror that too. You might try, for example, "I'm not even close to understanding what you're trying to tell me." Doing that usually gets a child to start talking because he's so amazed and disarmed that you've said exactly what he was thinking. The fact is that sometimes when you bumble around, it's the bumbling that shows the child you're really trying to understand and not just outsmart him. The key is that when you're doing it, you're doing it honestly. And that you let your child know, through your facial expression, body language, and tone of voice, that you're really trying.

Sincerity Is the Key

People often ask me if mirroring isn't manipulative, and my response is that if you're being manipulative and that is your intention, then it is. If, however, you're truly being empathic and trying to figure out what your child is feeling so that you can guide him in the right direction, that's not manipulating. It's manipulative only if your intention is to manipulate. Or they ask if it doesn't sound patronizing or sarcastic, and my answer is that it will sound that way only if that's how you're feeling. If you are genuinely suspending your own agenda and trying to understand what your child is experiencing or feeling, it will come across as genuine and it will work. If you're doing it just because you want your child to sit down and be quiet, or if you really are being sarcastic, he'll know it.

We've already discussed the fact that doing it honestly can be difficult when your child is acting out and you're at your wit's end. But again, even if at first you're using every acting skill you possess, the more you mirror, the more honest and authentic it will become. And in the beginning, the honesty may come from the fact that you honestly do want to get to the bottom of the situation so that things will get better, and you're willing to do whatever it takes to understand your child's experience.

Your Child Knows Who's in Charge

When your child is continuously acting out and you're continuously yelling or giving in just to get her to be quiet or stop embarrassing you in public, you may think that you've totally lost control. But, you can manage these situations so you can keep your child safe and help her make good choices. Whenever a parent tells me her child is out of control, I immediately ask if he wears a seat belt. And, invariably, her response is, "Of course." "So, how did you get him to do that?" "Well, he just knows."

Your child already knows you're more powerful than he is, which is all the more reason for you to be mindful of how you use that power. In fact, if you think about how we talk to our children much of the time, you'll see that they spend a good portion of their young lives being ordered around: "Go to your room. Pick up your toys. Come to the table. Stop doing that." We talk to our children in ways we would never speak to other adults or tolerate being spoken to ourselves. Imagine how you'd feel if your spouse or partner came into the kitchen while you were loading the dishwasher and said, "How many times have I told you not to put the glasses in like that!" Or, what if you arrived at a friend's house for dinner and the hostess greeted you by saying, "Hang up your coat. What's the matter with you?"

Now consider that your child already knows he's totally dependent on you. He can't quit his job; he can't move out; he can't get a divorce. You're his parent, not his boss or his roommate or his spouse.

Because we, as parents, occupy that position of power, it's really incumbent upon us to be more mindful of our children's feelings than we are on a daily basis. I believe that we ought to spend more time simply conversing with our kids, finding out how they are, what they like or don't like, and what great or gross thing happened in school, instead of spending so much time talking *at* them, lecturing, and teaching. Not every interaction we have with our children has to be a teaching moment. Sometimes we need to connect just by letting them know that we're interested in them and want to be involved with what's happening in their lives.

When "Life" Gets in the Way

I started this chapter by saying that no one is perfect, and there will certainly be times when you're too stressed or too tired to see your child's behavior (or, more likely, misbehavior) for what it is, and you'll take it much too personally. When that happens is when most of us revert to all those knee-jerk Mommy and Daddy responses like, "Well, if you think Josh's parents are so great, why don't you just go and live with them," or "I don't know why you can't be more like Emma. You don't see her . . ."

Things happen in our lives that have nothing to do with our children, and we too will get cranky and short-tempered. That's when we won't be paying as much attention as we probably should to keeping the right tension on the rope. If there's too much slack on that rope, our kids will tug just to be sure we're still there, and if we overreact to that tug or start tugging back by getting annoyed, lecturing, or talking too much, all the child's negative behaviors will start flooding back.

Undoubtedly, just as you're beginning to see the results of the mirroring you've been doing and you're starting to think, "This really seems to be working," your child will have a bad day and both of you will likely revert to your old, worst behaviors. Your brain will be saying, "Oh, no, I'm not going back to *that* again," and you'll overreact. You just need to understand that this will happen, and recognize it when it does, so that you are able to go into recovery mode. It's exactly when you feel the least like mirroring that you need to do it the most. If you really pay attention to your gut feeling of not wanting to do it, and *make yourself* do it, within twenty-four to forty-eight hours you'll probably be right back on track.

Nothing Is Irreparable

Whenever you blow it, remember that you'll always have a chance to make the necessary repair. Growing up in a household where no one ever makes a mistake, no one ever gets angry, and parents mirror every minute of the day is not reality. Children do need to experience reality and learn that they can deal with it. Mirroring is like putting money in a bank. It's an investment with a great return. The more you mirror, the more you'll have in the bank and the more you'll be able to make a withdrawal now and then. You might yell at your child after mirroring for a few weeks and see that he shrugs it off in a "What's wrong with her?" way, when just weeks before he would have been hurt and upset. This is resiliency, this is what will help your child navigate through the world. She will have her feelings hurt, she may fail now and then, things won't always go her way, but you will have helped her to be resilient—loved so well that she can handle it, learn from it, and move on.

SIX

Time Well Spent, or Giving Your Child What He Needs

Yes, we're all going to blow it from time to time, which is all the more reason why we need to bank as many connecting moments as we can. One way to do that is to give our children as much of ourselves as we can whenever we have the opportunity.

Think how you feel when you're trying to explain something to someone who is scrolling up and down on his BlackBerry, or when you're talking on the phone and hear the computer keyboard clicking on the other end of the line. It's annoying, insulting, even hurtful because you know the person with whom you're trying to communicate isn't really listening, which means that you, or whatever you're saying, isn't worthy of his undivided attention.

I like to explain to my clients that there's a significant difference between what I call "standing up" and "lying down" parenting. Too often, when our children really want our attention, we give it to them "lying down." We might be literally lying down in front of the television while our child is trying to get our attention. We're pretending to listen, but, at the same time, we're also trying to follow the program we're watching. When we do that, our child knows we're not fully present, and we can't really watch our program anyway. What we need to do instead is get up and turn off the television for fifteen minutes and give our full attention to our child. If we do that, he'll get what he needs from us and he'll go away content, leaving us to watch the rest of our program in peace.

Let's say, for example, that Andrew brings you a drawing he's just finished while you're working on the computer. Lying-down parenting would be to glance at the drawing while you continue to check your e-mail, say, "Oh, yeah, that's nice," and then go back to whatever is on the screen.

What you need to do is give Andrew and his offering your full attention. The point is that you shouldn't wait for your child to be upset in order to mirror. You also need to mirror pleasant or positive things. So use your voice and follow the CALM technique, saying something like, "Oh, wow! What a great-looking truck! You put in all the chrome and the headlights, and I can even see the driver sitting behind the wheel." Point to things as you mention them; use your body movements and facial expressions to let him know that you appreciate how much work he's put into the drawing. If you do that, when you look into his eyes you'll see that they've grown bigger and he's puffed up with pride.

At that point you can explain that you would like to finish checking your e-mail (or doing whatever you're doing) and will talk to him in a few minutes. He will most likely be happy to let you get back to work because you made him feel good. If he doesn't, and he keeps trying to get your attention when you feel you've given him enough, use your CALM technique again and let him know what the consequence will be if he doesn't let you finish what you're doing. The worst that can happen is that you'll stay neutral, consequence him, and get back to your e-mail later. The key is to make sure your child is getting enough stand-up parenting.

Sit down with your little boy the next time he's playing a video game and let him know how interested you are in what he's doing as he moves to the next level. Comment on his playing by saying things like, "I had no idea you were on such a high level; you are really good at this. Who is that character?" And so on. Watch as his face lights up in absolute joy. Or sit down with your little girl as she works on a craft project and comment on the beautiful colors she has chosen or the amount of detail she put into her art. It's not as simple as saying, "Oh, that's really great. Let's stick it on the fridge." It's about really taking the time to comment on the child's creativity or noticing the effort he or she put into an activity. Pulling out special details you know he'll be proud of is a wonderful way to mirror your child. Whatever the activity, put yourself in his or her world for a little while. It doesn't have to be for very long. In fact, you can mirror and make it clear from the beginning that after whatever length of time you determine, you need to go back to your own project. But while you're doing it, give it your full attention and do it well.

When you parent your child that way, even if you have only a limited amount of time to spend with him, you'll be doing a better job than the parent who may be home all day but who is, essentially, parenting while lying down.

Sometimes "Later" Is Too Late

I know it's hard when we have so much on our plate to simply stop what we're doing even for a short time. We tend to think that we'll deal with our child later, when we finish what we're doing. We like to believe that our children will always be there, which means that, too often, when we have multiple obligations, we send them to the back of the line. Stop and think how many times a day you tell a child you'll be with her "in a minute," or say, "Tell me about that later." Now think what you want your children to remember about you when they grow up. Do you want them to remember your saying "Just a minute" and missing special moments, or do you want them to remember you rolling around on the floor with them and laughing?

When a child grows up feeling truly loved it has a profound effect on his or her development and personality. That feeling can act as a shield against whatever she encounters in the world. It doesn't mean you'll never fight; it just means that he'll know the bond is there so that you can fight without either one of you ever feeling terribly injured. Invest in the moment and your child will feel incredibly important.

Once again, I don't mean that you have to drop everything and pay attention to every little thing your child does; just make sure you're paying *enough* attention. The truth is, if we're honest with ourselves, we know in our own hearts how much that is. We can tell because we can ask our kids to "wait a minute" and not feel guilty if we know we're staying connected. When we feel guilty or unsettled about asking them to wait, it may be time for self-examination. Children need to keep themselves busy and be proud of their own work or their own pictures, but they also need you to stand up and be present. I have had so many kids tell me how bad it feels that their dad is always on his BlackBerry or fixing things in the garage or that Mom is always on the phone or the computer. Take time to stand up and be there for your children; it will be worth it, and they will pay you back in many ways.

One dad who struggled with this was a doctor who had a busy practice in town where he worked all week long and a second practice in a rural area several hours away where he worked on weekends. The result was that he was almost never home, and when he was, he was so exhausted that he couldn't deal with any amount of misbehavior from his kids. In his mind they should have been so thrilled to see him that they would be happy and perfectly behaved. In other words, his expectations were totally unrealistic.

He told me that his plan was to work really hard for five years and make enough money so that he could retire. After that, he'd have all the time in the world to spend with his children. The problem, as I explained, was that the children were eleven and thirteen, which meant that in five years they'd be sixteen and eighteen. The younger one would be a teenager and the older one would be heading off to college. By then neither one of them was likely to be spending very much time with their father, and he'd have missed out on important and precious years he'd never be able to get back.

That was a real wake-up call for him, and he actually wound up selling his weekend practice. While he still worked long hours in town, he at least had weekends to enjoy and participate in his children's formative years.

It Doesn't Take that Long

I saw the power of stand-up parenting just recently with my own daughter Zoë. She's the middle child, very sweet and patient, who often takes a backseat to her little sister, who is eight years younger and much more demanding of my time. On this day, Zoë had been trying to tell me about how she'd hurt her toe. I had been working on a presentation I had been asked to do on stand-up parenting for parents who work long hours and travel a great deal. And all the while she was talking to me, I was muttering "Uh-huh" as I was sorting through the mail, thinking about my workshop, and not really listening. At a certain point it occurred to me that I needed to check my e-mail, and I actually started to walk out of the room while she was still talking. But I caught myself, realizing how ridiculous it was that I'd been working on a presentation about not doing this very thing. At that point I got down on my knees and said, "Zoë, I'm so sorry. You've been talking to me about your toe and I've been hearing you, but I haven't really been listening. Let me see your toe." Then I sat down on the floor, took her foot in my hand, and looked at it and rubbed it, all of which took no more than two minutes. But it was two minutes of total stand-up parenting, and when it was over, Zoë went away happy. If I had practiced stand-up parenting from the very beginning, I would have experienced a great two-minute moment instead a not-so-great fifteen-minute moment. It's hard to do this when we're multitasking and constantly on the go, and you won't always catch yourself lying down. But as a parent you do have to make a special effort to catch as many of those moments as you can.

Catch Your Child Being Good

In addition to practicing stand-up parenting, we need to keep reminding ourselves to "catch our child being good" and mirror the good choices they make. We all want to know that someone has noticed when we've done something right, and, too often in our society, doing things right is expected. It's only when we do things wrong that we hear about it. So we need to remember to praise as well as to correct. When we let our children know just how lovable they are, we are, in effect, letting them know that they have no need to be anxious, to worry that we won't always be there to protect them, or to act out just to get our attention.

The truth is, you can mirror any time your child speaks—or doesn't speak, for that matter. Whenever a child communicates with us in any way, we can mirror. Mirroring accomplishments or good behavior seems to have the same positive effect as mirroring when your child is upset. Truthfully, it's easier to mirror when you and your child are both happy, and there's nothing in the world that feels better. You should be able to lay your head on the pillow each night and think, *I had at least two or three really good mirroring moments today.*

Keep Track of Their Accomplishments

If your child is struggling with negative behavior or anxiety, one way to show her that you've noticed the positive things she does every day is to keep a special notebook that I call an accomplishment book. It's a way of gathering and remembering those moments when she could have done something negative but made a different choice. For example, a typical entry in the accomplishment book might be, "I loved the way you shared your doll with your little sister this afternoon. That wasn't easy, because it's very special to you. It would have been easy to say no, but you chose to share it." Another example would be, "I noticed this morning that when your brother took that toy out of your hand you probably wanted to shove him, but you didn't. You took a big breath and you came to me." Be careful how you do this. You don't want to say, "Normally you would have snatched that doll out of your sister's hands but . . ." or, "Normally you would have hit your brother . . ." which would simply put the child on the defensive and remind him of how bad he usually is. The point here is to accentuate the positive without invoking the negative.

If you're feeling a bit disconnected from your child, you can also use the accomplishment book as a connecting strategy and write little notes like, "You looked so cute this morning when you went bouncing off to school," or "I love the way you laugh."

Or if your child is challenging himself in some way, you can make note of that. So, for example, if you have a child who is trying to control his anxiety you could write, "I loved the way you were really nervous, but I saw you take a deep breath and you went into the birthday party anyway."

What you want is for your child to read what you've written and feel proud. Use cuddling up with your child and reading through his or her accomplishments as part of your bedtime routine. This will become an important ritual for both of you. It's a lovely way for you to recognize and relive the moments when your child is really trying so that you're not always looking at the bad moments. When you're constantly criticizing your child for something he's done wrong, he'll often say, "Well, you don't care about all the times I did this [other, good thing]," and he may be right. We don't recognize the good things often enough.

Also, change may come in such small increments that we fail to notice it when it's happening. I like to compare this to marking your child's growth on the doorjamb. You may not notice how much she's growing until you actually stand her up against that wall and make a new mark, at which point, you look at where the previous mark was, and say, "Wow! Look how much you've grown!"

If you've been reconnecting frayed bonds, you'll begin to see your child not just as the tantrum-throwing, manipulative, out-of-control kid you thought you'd been living with, but as a child who does have loving moments and who is really trying to please you. And she'll be able to look at the good things she's done and begin to understand that she actually has more control over some of her behaviors than she thought. By doing that, she'll also begin to see herself as lovable, which means she'll have less and less need to act out and test the limits of your love.

Part Two

Setting Appropriate Limits

SEVEN

Letting Your Child Know What's Okay and What's Not

Up to this point I've been emphasizing the fact that before we can change behavior we have to connect and strengthen the attachment with our child. The second half of the equation, however, is to let him know what's okay and what isn't, and that there are consequences for negative behaviors. If you did nothing but mirror, your child would likely have some difficulty understanding what behaviors were expected of him; if you did nothing but set limits and impose consequences, your child would just think of you as mean and the bond between you would suffer. Ideally the two aspects of connected parenting should occur simultaneously, but if the attachment bond between you and your child is too fragile, he will interpret any effort you make at setting appropriate limits as an injury, in which case the limit-setting may not work. Once the bond has been repaired, your child will be able to tolerate consequences, and your connection will be strong enough for him to withstand and benefit from containment. When the two halves of the equation are in balance, they work together to help your child understand and organize her feelings so that she is better able to control her behaviors.

All Children Need Limits

Your child may look for all the world as if he doesn't want limits, but don't be fooled. Deep down, all children need limits. They need to know what's expected of them, and they need to know that you have the ability to guide them. When I explain this to parents, I like to tell them the following story. It may seem irrelevant at first, but bear with me. My daughter Zoë had always wanted to take horseback-riding lessons, and when we moved north of the city I thought it would be something fun that we could do together, so we signed up. I didn't realize, however, that I was going to be more or less thrown together with my horse and expected to deal with getting him tacked up and ready for our first ride. The instructor led me into the stall, and there was this *enormous* animal (his name was King, and he definitely lived up to it). We more or less looked at each other out of the corners of our eyes and I started to brush him. Then the instructor left the stall for a minute and King turned around and snapped at me. I jumped and he jumped, chains rattled, and we were both spooked. Just then the instructor came back and asked me what had happened. When I told her he'd tried to bite me, she just said, "Oh, King, cut it out," and that was that. Still extremely nervous, I went back to my brushing, she left again, and the same thing happened. Of course, as soon as she came back, the horse gave her this innocent look as if to say, "Who, me? I didn't do anything." At that point the instructor looked at me and said, "You know, you've got to show him you're in charge. He doesn't want to be in charge. He's scared and he wants you to demonstrate your authority so that he can relax."

At that point I wasn't really thinking about children. I was just thinking, *Why on earth did I ever sign up for these lessons and how can I get out of this?* But I got up on the horse, not very comfortable, my body totally stiff. Zoë, meanwhile, was having the time of her life. The instructor turned to me again and said, "Look at your horse, look at his body language. He's not comfortable. He's not going to have fun with this lesson and neither are you. He doesn't know what you want him to do. Horses are pack animals; it's stressful for them to think they're in charge." And suddenly a lightbulb went on in my head and I thought, *That's just like kids. That's exactly what they do!*

So, if you're a parent giving your child mixed messages, looking nervous and afraid that you don't know what to do or that you're not going to be able to control your child, your child will pick up on that and won't feel safe. Instead, he'll be thinking, *Maybe this person can't protect me. Maybe she can't control me, and if she can't control me how can I be safe?*

As parents, we are the ones who need to help our children learn which behaviors are acceptable and which are not. We need to do that because we have more perspective than they do, and because it's the only way they have of learning what we expect of them.

They Don't Want to Be in Charge

I believe that we very often give our children more power than they are emotionally capable of handling, certainly more than they want, and definitely more than they need. When children have too much control, they don't become happier; rather, they come to believe that adults in general, and their parents in particular, aren't well equipped to take control—which, as I've said, is what they really want. I can think of one family, for example, who told me their six-year-old daughter had direct control over the purchase of the family car. This concerns me. Why would a six-year-old have a say in something like that? What kind of burden is that to place on a child?

When we give children too much power, they become anxious, and that's when they start acting out. In terms of our rope analogy, they're not feeling the connection to you because there's too much slack on the rope. I used to rock climb with my husband, and whenever he gave me too much slack I was terrified and would find myself yelling at him or yanking on the rope to find out if he was still there. This is very much like what kids do. If you give them too much slack they will metaphorically yank on the rope as if to say, "Are you still there? Where are you?"

Conversely, when you set limits that are fair and predictable—keeping the proper tension on the rope—they can relax and focus on the business of being kids. It's like walking into a room with the lights off: you have to grope your way around the perimeter, touching the walls to avoid hitting your head and bumping into the furniture. That's what children do. They use behavior as a kind of sonar and keep feeling you out until they hit something and it gets sent back to them. At that point, they know they've gone as far as they can.

What they're trying to find out is how much power you're really willing to give them, pushing the envelope, trying to find the point at which you will no longer tolerate their behavior. And if you, in turn, keep moving the wall because you want to avoid the behavior, your child will keep escalating until he finds the place where the wall no longer moves. While he's doing this, however, he will be feeling more and more anxious, which means he will be moodier, more difficult to please, and less happy. It's stressful not to know where the walls are. Think how hard it would be for you to walk around in the dark all the time. And while this is going on, your child's brain is wiring and pruning itself to deal with stress.

One little boy I remember, who has since grown into a bright and delightful teenager, was well on the way to controlling his entire household when he was only five. Luke was a dramatic kid whose tantrums kept his parents in line and got him whatever he wanted. Although his mother loved him, she was beginning not to like him very much.

One of the first things I ask parents who come to see me is whether their child will go to time-out when they ask him to. Using time-out as a containment strategy is controversial, but I've found that it is useful as a way of measuring what your child will do when you ask him. If your child can sit down quietly and contemplate his own behavior, at least you'll know that there is one thing he will do for his own safety. And for younger children, it also acts as an interruption, sort of like shutting down and rebooting the computer. I like to consider it "thinking time." You do not have to put your child away from you; they can be nearby. It is more about an interruption of behavior than exile. Luke, however, wouldn't go to time-out; he would actually laugh at the request. If he was acting out, hitting, kicking, and screaming, the only way his mother could get him to go to his room was to pick him up and take him there, then go out and hold the door closed while he proceeded to trash the entire room. He toppled his bookcase, pulled down the curtains, tore the bedding off the bed, and literally ripped the wallpaper off the walls until she let him out. Clearly, this was an extreme situation that required extreme measures.

Luke's mother was understandably angry, exhausted, and constantly worried about the next fit or tantrum. She had been kicked, bitten, and head-butted until she was almost numb to it all. She described walking around with a knot in the pit of her stomach, constantly afraid that her son would not listen to her. As many parents end up doing, she was walking on eggshells and Luke knew it. In actuality, he was frightened, because no child wants to think that the adults around him can't control him. It makes them scared of themselves and very angry at their parents.

What I told this exhausted mom was, first of all, that she would have to do a lot of mirroring and baby play to rebuild the bond frayed by years of her child's unlovable behavior. She would have to catch him being positive, responsible, and thoughtful, and then acknowledge and encourage this behavior. But at the same time, she needed to make sure that when he did become agressive, his behavior was contained so he was safe and so that he would not continue to hurt her. She was to stand near him outside the door. If he came out and was still aggressive, she needed to walk him back, saying—in a neutral tone—"No, sweetie. You're not ready; you need to stay in your room until your body doesn't feel like hitting, kicking, or biting anymore." She did this time after time until it became almost robotic, and after a while he did stay in his room but he also continued to trash it.

The next step was to take everything out of the room that was breakable. She explained to him that his anger was getting in the way so much that it was making him destroy the things that were important to him, so she was taking them away to keep them safe. When he was able to take care of them, all of his things would be returned. After that, she continued the time-outs, saying, "You know, sweetie, you've made a choice, and you just have to understand that every time you do this, this is what's going to happen." She also told him that he'd have to earn his things back by sitting quietly in his room when she asked him to for a specified period of time.

At first Luke tested her wildly and tried his best to pull her into their old familiar pattern of backing down and giving him his way. Children do this almost as if they had a giant fishing rod. They bait the line with the right trigger and throw it out there, and we have to learn not to take the bait. Luke's mom stayed neutral and continued to mirror and use baby play. Each time he came out of his room, she was loving and normal and life went on as usual. She didn't keep warning him or reminding him that he "better be good now." Sure enough, his behavior gradually improved. Day by day, he showed he was responsible enough to have his things returned to his room, and after a while, he stopped destroying things altogether. In addition, and more important, within just two weeks he became a different child. Whereas previously, in his opinion, everything "sucked" and everything was "stupid," he was now happy and generally positive instead of negative and moody.

Ironically, it was his mom's giving in, to avoid tantrums and aggressive behavior, that was partly responsible for guaranteeing that Luke's behavior would continue. Our children's behavior often has much more to do with us than we would like to think. I say this not to place blame—since most of us take the bait at one time or another—but to empower you by helping you to understand that you *can* create change.

After a couple of months Luke's mother called me one day. She was in tears and I was afraid something had gone terribly wrong. But what she said was, "My son is singing in the back of the car. My son never sings!" Before we worked together, he would have been sullen and complaining and kicking the back of her seat. She'd never seen him so happy and buoyant, so this was truly an amazing moment for her.

What Luke had been exhibiting was almost adolescent behavior—at age five. Frankly, I believe that what we generally think of as normal adolescent behavior is actually a symptom of a child's feeling disconnected from his or her parents, and it can show up very early. As we've already noted, adolescents don't really hate their parents, no matter how much they try to pretend that they do. In fact, what they really need and want is to feel loved and connected.

Another little boy I worked with was so out of control at the age of eleven that he actually pulled a knife on his mother in the kitchen one day. Granted it was a butter knife, but a knife nevertheless.

This was a family truly in crisis. There were two sons who literally could not be in the same room without fighting. The situation was so bad that the parents were actually taking the boys on separate vacations. The eleven-year-old was responsible for most of the aggressive behavior, and his older brother, whose experience was that no one appeared to be in charge, was trying to act as the parent.

The mother was so disconnected from her younger son that she truly hated him. And the father was so stressed that he was actually having chest pains. The knife-pulling incident paradoxically turned out to be a blessing in disguise. The mother was so undone that she called me on the spot, and when I got her to put the boy on the phone with me what he said was, "Doesn't she get it? I'm only eleven. How can she let me do that?" This was a true "lightbulb moment" for the mom, who realized that her child needed her to be strong. She'd been emotionally injured by him in the past, and the more he saw he'd been hurting her, the weaker she appeared in his eyes. As she began to rebuild the bond, once the attachment was strong enough, she began to work on what I call being a strong mother. Instead of yelling or pleading, she would respond to his verbal out-pourings by saying something like, "You know, I like myself way too much to allow you to talk to me that way." The more she did that, the more he began to respect her, and gradually she began to see remarkable changes in her child. The craziness of this destructive dynamic is that your child will keep at you and at you until he finally gets you to stop him.

One day, when her son had run out into the yard and she went looking for him, he said, "Mom, can you do that thing where you come caring after me?" He wanted her to mirror; he wanted to feel held and loved even though he was scared and angry. So she sat down and held him and mirrored right there in the yard. It was a profound moment and the beginning of extraordinary change for the entire family. This was the same child who had been telling me, "I belong in juvie. I'm going to end up in juvenile hall."

But how does it get to that point? It can start with just a little bit too much slack on the rope so that the child is getting away with too much and begins to ramp up the bad behavior to find out just how much you'll let him get away with. And eventually, if you don't tighten your control, the child will misbehave because he has no sense of attachment and feels totally untethered. That negative behavior, the fact that he's acting so bad, is what makes a child feel unlovable and what makes the parents pull away, which makes the child act out even more. It took almost two years for this family to reconnect and restore the bond, but the eleven-year-old who was convinced he'd wind up in juvie is now a great kid, and the family's life has completely turned around. His father called me last year with a completely unrelated question and said about this child, who is now fifteen, "I can't thank you enough. I have the most wonderful relationship with my son now. He's close with his brother. He's such a great kid."

My caveat to parents is that if we think it's hard to control our child when she's four, imagine how much harder it will be when she's fourteen and instead of asking for a drink of water she's asking for a drink, instead of wanting an ice cream cone she'll be wanting to attend a coed sleepover party with drinking and drugs. Many parents believe that when it comes to something really "important," they'll be able to say no. But often it doesn't work that way. The older the child, the higher the stakes, and by the time a child who's been used to getting her own way reaches adolescence, she can be quite vicious and entitled. The truth is, it's never too late, but it's never going to be easier than it is right now.

How damaging it can be *not* to set limits was brought home to me not so long ago when I was shopping at Ikea. If you've ever been to an Ikea, you know that the stores are enormous, and they generally have supervised play areas where parents can leave their children to amuse themselves while they shop. In this particular instance, a child who appeared to be about five or six years old had taken a toy from the play area, and an Ikea employee politely asked her to give it back. I could see from the expression on their faces what her parents were thinking: *What, you're not going to take that away, are you? You don't know what's going to happen!* The child immediately threw a full-blown tantrum in the middle of the store and the parents went into full-scale panic mode. I could see the looks of pure horror and sheer panic on their faces, and they started to scream at each other: "Where's her teddy bear? Did you bring the teddy bear?" "I thought you were bringing it." "No, I told you to bring it. We can never go out without that teddy bear, never!" Then the father began to interrogate the employee: "Do you sell this toy here? Where can I go to buy it, what part of the store is it in?" The clerk didn't know, and the father ran off in even more of a panic. About ten minutes later he came running back, wild-eyed and dripping with sweat, and handed the toy to the child.

What was that teaching this child? First of all, certainly that if she screamed and cried enough she'd get what she wanted, but also—and this is the real key—that her not being able to keep that toy she'd taken from the play area really was a really big deal. Children gauge their responses based on our own, and in this instance her parents got extremely upset. *Look at my parents; this must be worse than I thought.* And finally, she was learning that she wouldn't be able to get over it herself, that the situation required a major intervention on the part of her parents. What happens then is that the child begins to organize her world around that information.

We Know More Than They Do

A child of five or six does not, after all, have very much experience by which to judge what's really bad and what isn't. In the grand scheme of things, for a lot of children, if they are lucky, when their ice cream falls on the floor, it really is one of the worst things that has ever happened to them. We, on the other hand, should be able to tell the difference between something that's really a major catastrophe and something that isn't. We have the ability to put things that happen to us into a larger perspective. So it's our job as parents to help our children begin to understand how to react to various situations. We do this by not overreacting like that father in Ikea. But we also need to understand that what's not a big deal to us may seem really important to a child, so we don't want to underreact, thereby dismissing his or her feelings.

Think how you would feel if you'd just bought a new car. You did all the research, saved your money, found the perfect car, and as you were driving it out of the dealership someone smashed into you and totaled the car. You'd be devastated, so how would you feel if your spouse looked at you and said, "Stop making such a big deal of it. You'll get another car." That's how our children feel when we minimize their emotions.

What we need to do instead is remain calm, stay neutral, mirror to acknowledge what they're feeling, and then present the problem and reassure them that whatever has happened, they will get through it and they'll be okay.

Additionally, it's important to help children learn how to sort events into big hurts and little hurts because that's how they acquire the skills that allow them to manage disappointment or adversity. I suggest that parents sit down with their child and get him to think about something that would be a "big hurt," something he'd really be crying about. You don't want to make it something really terrifying like the house burning down or both his parents dying in a plane crash, but use something in his experience to which he can relate, such as losing a grandparent, if this has happened already. If nothing of that scale has happened, try examples like leaving a favorite teddy bear on the bus or not being invited to a birthday party. Then ask him to think about what a "little hurt" might be—perhaps someone's taking his pencil, or his not being able to find his favorite T-shirt when he wants to wear it. You can also come up with events that might be "medium hurts."

Once you've done that, when something bad happens, mirror first, then ask your child whether she thinks it's a big hurt or a little hurt. She will *always* say it's a big hurt, but you can say, "You know, sweetie, it feels like a big hurt, but this is really an example of a little hurt, and you're going to be fine. You're going to be okay." Because you mirrored first, you're not invalidating her feelings; instead you're teaching her how to organize and regulate her emotions.

You Don't Have to Be Embarrassed

When our children act out in public or at friends' or relatives' homes, it can be very upsetting and very stressful for us. When my kids were small and came to visit me at the Children's Mental Health Center, where I worked, I always used to worry that they would act out, I would be embarrassed, and my clients would view me as incompetent. Then my very wise supervisor told me that it's not about whether or not our children will act up, it's about how we handle it when they do.

As parents, we too need to make sure we're reacting appropriately in any given situation, and sometimes not doing anything just because we're in public and embarrassed to be making a scene can be as counterproductive as overreacting.

If you ignore bad behavior, it will continue to escalate because you've failed to let your child know it's unacceptable, and eventually it will get to the point where you can no longer ignore it, so you'll explode. The problem, however, is that since your child has been exhibiting the same behavior all along and you haven't said or done anything about it, he's now going to look at you and think, *What's the matter? This was never a problem for you before.*

Many clients have told me that they're afraid to set limits in a public place because they know their child will have a tantrum and they're afraid of being embarrassed. I certainly understand the impulse, but it's counterproductive for at least two reasons.

First of all, everyone knows that kids have meltdowns, and if they see you handling the situation calmly and quietly, they'll appreciate the fact that you're being a responsible parent. The second reason is that children have very powerful radar. They know when they can get away with something because you don't want to "make a scene," and will continue to escalate their behavior just to see how far they can go.

I remember seeing a mother on a checkout line not so long ago with a little girl who appeared to be about five. The child was screaming at the top of her lungs that she wanted a Barbie lunch box, and as they got closer to the checkout counter I was wondering if she'd get it. I could also see from the expression on the cashier's face that she was silently saying, *You're not actually going to buy that, are you?* But the mother put the lunch box on the counter, glaring at the cashier as if daring her to say anything, and handed it over to her daughter. What lesson had she taught that little girl, except to validate both her behavior and her need—maybe even her right—to get what she wanted? She bought more than a Barbie lunch box that day. She bought trouble, and and a guarantee that her little girl's behavior would be repeated over and over again.

Mirroring lets the child know that it's okay to be upset about not getting to keep a toy or about losing his ice cream, but the containing lets him know that those things are not, after all, the end of the world, that it's not okay to scream and yell, and that screaming and yelling or crying aren't going to get him what he wants—and actually thinks he *needs* at that moment. In other words, the mirroring lets the child know that it's okay to have these feelings, while the containing lets him know that the behavior is not okay.

Sometimes, if your child is misbehaving in public, you simply need to take a deep breath and say to yourself, "Okay, I guess everyone here is just going to have a show."

I've had to do that myself more than once. I remember, for example, one particular time when I was in the children's section of a bookstore with my younger daughter, Olivia, who was about three at the time. A twelve-month-old came toddling in, and because Olivia loves babies, she was talking to him and holding his hand, which was fine until the toddler wanted to go back to his mommy—and Olivia wouldn't let go of his hand.

First I tried mirroring persuasion: "Olivia, it's so wonderful to play with this little guy. He's so cute and you are so big—it's like having a real live doll." Then I presented the problem: "But the baby doesn't want to play anymore, so you need to let him go back to his mommy." Olivia, however, held on, and as any three-year-old who is not aware of personal space would do, she kept grabbing and hugging the baby, who was now getting very agitated. So I introduced a consequence: "Olivia, if you keep grabbing the baby, you are going to have to sit with me outside the children's section for a little while." Of course, she kept on grabbing the baby, so I tried to pick her up. But she went into that back-arching, arms-rigid-at-the-sides kicking routine that makes kids impossible to pick up. (Other impossible postures that seem to be embedded in kids' DNA: raising their arms directly over their head, so you are forced to pick them up by the torso, with their arms free to bop you on the head; and stiffening while lying on the ground so that you can't peel them off the floor.) Off to the bench Olivia and I went, to settle down. With children this age I like to use a time-out as a way to interrupt negative behavior, but I don't believe that you should lecture or ask the child if he knows why he's in time-out. Even at the age of three, the child knows.

After we'd been sitting for three or four minutes, I told Olivia we could return to the children's section, and reminded her that if she started to touch and hug the baby again, we would be going back to the bench. She went straight for the baby and grabbed him, so back to the bench we went. After two or three of these episodes— and remember, I'd already mirrored and I'd remained neutral—she headed back in and did not go for the baby. Instead she went straight to a pile of books and knocked them down (nice). I mirrored about her wanting to make her own choices and talked to her about how her anger was now getting in the way of her fun; we would have to leave the store if she did anything like that again. Down went some more books, so off to the car we went. Olivia went completely limp and into full tantrum mode. I carried her and her boots and her coat out of the store, stayed very calm, and told her gently that I loved her enough for her to be mad at me, but because she had chosen to throw the books on the floor, her behavior was telling me it was time to go home.

By that time I was sweating, but still trying to say calm; I knew I had to follow through, and I finally did get her—kicking and screaming—into the car and buckled into her child seat.

Through gritted teeth, but once again following the CALM technique, I said, "You were having so much fun, and now here we are in the car, not in the store. You really were having fun until all this happened." She was too upset to react well to the mirroring, but it was important for me to do it.

I wish I could tell you that it all ended with that stellar display of parenting, but sadly, it did not. I was hot, exhausted, frustrated to the point of tears, and Olivia was yelling in the car seat. So I lost it. I even said that her behavior was so awful I should have stayed at work instead of taking her to the bookstore, and that if she behaved that way we would never go anywhere again (breaking my own cardinal rule that you should never set a consequence you cannot keep). I did everything I shouldn't do, and I knew it. The voice in my head said, "Stay neutral, you idiot," but I could not. Eventually Olivia cried herself to sleep. It was not a great moment for me. I felt terrible, I was extremely mad at myself, but it happened. I have lost it since and will again. We are human, and parenting is the most difficult job there is. It amazes me how angry we adults can get at these little people we love so much. But what I value about connected parenting is that you can always go back and repair your mistakes. Your children are strong, and the more you mirror and the closer you are, the stronger they will become.

I made a repair when Olivia woke up, with some good mirroring statements, hugs and kisses, and a dose of baby play. I'm not saying that we should feel free to lose it, but I am saying that it's okay to forgive ourselves as long as we are working toward being the best parents we can be. That said, there are limits even to losing it. I feel very strongly that we should try as hard as possible to avoid hitting, grabbing, or yanking at our children in anger. For one thing, that's something we almost always do for ourselves because we're angry. For another, it doesn't make sense for us to talk to our children about not hitting or hurting, and then to hurt them ourselves to teach them a lesson (as we would put it). When we hit or grab at our kids, we're in effect telling them that we're out of control and that our aggression is not controllable, which is exactly the opposite of what we've been trying to teach them. And finally—I've said this before, and I'll probably say it again—we have to remember how small children are and how frightening it must be to them to be the focus of our anger.

But this was a story about Olivia, and I am happy to report that I deliberately took her back to the bookstore a few days later and, as luck would have it, there were a few babies there. This time she gave them their space and had a fantastic time. One of the most important things to remember about consequences is that you have to be willing to wait to see the results.

Say What You Mean and Mean What You Say

When you set limits and introduce a consequence, especially in public, you have to mean it from your head to your toes. Making that commitment gives you a great sense of confidence and freedom. If you get a sinking feeling in the pit of your stomach every time you take your child to a shop or a restaurant because you're thinking, *Oh God, I hope this goes well, I hope she behaves, I hope he's not going to lose it and wreck this whole outing,* your child will sense what you're feeling—children have radar designed especially to home in on these thoughts—and he'll definitely go crazy. But once you are confident that you have the ability to control the situation, you'll be free to walk into a mall or a restaurant and know that you'll be able to deal with whatever comes up. Furthermore, that confidence will come through in your voice so that—maybe not the first or second time, but sooner rather than later—your child will believe you.

I remember the mother who told me this story about what happened when she and her husband took their two children out for ice cream one evening. They were sitting at the table with their bowls in front of them when her younger daughter, Julie, who was about five at the time, put her feet up on the table. The mother calmly told her that this was not acceptable, but she did it two or three more times until her mom said, "Honey, if you put your feet on the table one more time, we're going to leave and we're going to wait in the car while Daddy and Meredith finish their ice cream. Two minutes later, Julie stared her mother right in the eye and up went her feet. So her mother calmly picked her up and carried her out, kicking and screaming, "Nooooo, Mommy, I didn't mean it. I'll be good, I promise . . ." It's very easy to fall for that and give in, but it's a really bad idea because I can almost guarantee that the minute you put the child back in her seat her feet will fly up again. In any case, Julie's mom held her ground, put her in the car, and kept telling her in a calm, neutral voice, "I know this is really hard. You were having such a good time, and then your not listening wrecked it." Eventually

Julie stopped crying, and her mother told me that this one incident bought her remarkably good behavior for many weeks after.

This was brought home to me yet again when we were on a family vacation and Jacob, who was then eight or nine, threw a fit in the middle of the walkway at SeaWorld because he couldn't refold the map we'd been consulting in exactly the way it had been folded originally. I did all my mirroring and nothing was working, so I told him that when we got to the manta rays he would have to sit on the bench instead of petting them. There he was, crying on the bench, looking like a lost soul.

As a parent I struggle much more with setting limits than I do with the mirroring, so as he sat there, I ached for him. But I knew I needed to remain firm for his sake. He needed to know where the walls were and trust that they wouldn't move. Then, when we moved on to the next exhibit, it was over, and, a few minutes later, he turned to me and said, "You know, Mommy, I'm really kind of proud of you. I didn't think you were going to stick to that."

Sometimes parents who are struggling with behavioral problems tell me that they just "don't have time" for all that mirroring and presenting the problem. They just want to get the problem solved. My answer to that is, "You can't afford *not* to do it." In fact, it takes a lot less energy that all the arguing and fighting you're doing now. You won't be able to do it all the time, but you can try to do it as often as possible, and you will see the results.

So long as they feel securely bonded to you, children are happier and in a better mood, and enjoy life more, when their world is organized for them and they don't have too much power. When they don't know what the limits are, they are more likely to be miserable, ungrateful, testy, and, most important, unhappy.

Times Have Changed—No More Musical Chairs

As Maggie Mamen points out in *The Pampered Child Syndrome*, the predominant parenting model has become so child-centered that we're afraid ever to disappoint or frustrate our kids. When most of us were growing up, we played musical chairs or pin-the-tail-on-the-donkey at birthday parties, and someone won; other people didn't. Maybe that was hard and some people cried, but we got over it. I don't remember being traumatized by losing a game at any of the birthday parties I went to. Now, however, at school and at birthday parties, games are designed so that everyone wins, everyone gets a prize. But that simply isn't realistic, and it's not a good lesson for life. If a child knows she's going to win no matter how badly she does, why should she put any effort into being better? She begins to expect to win for not doing anything.

A little later, however, in middle school and beyond, things start to change. Kids try out for a team or a school play and aren't chosen; there are parties to which they're not invited. A lot of kids simply aren't prepared for that. They've been robbed of the experience of knowing that they're not going to be good at everything and that they can handle disappointment. If every little bump in the road has always been smoothed out for them, when a big bump comes along, they don't necessarily have the tools to know they'll actually get through it.

Not so long ago, Olivia and I were at an interactive center in an amusement park where there were tables of things to touch and play with. (And I'm happy to report that this story has nothing to do with Olivia.) There was a table of safari animals, and, as I was sitting there watching, a little boy gathered up about ten of them and handed them to his mother, saying, "I'm going to do a puzzle now. Hold on to these for me so no one gets them." To my amazement, his mother did just that. She held them in her lap for thirty minutes while her five-year-old son worked on a puzzle. Each time a child went up to her and asked to play with them, she replied, "I'm sorry, I'm holding these for my son," and they walked away disappointed. After finishing his puzzle, her son announced that he wanted to go get an ice cream. He never did play with the toys.

There is so much wrong with this scenario that I don't even know what to say. The lessons this woman taught her son are that it's okay to hoard, it's okay not to share, and his needs are more important than anyone else's. Consistent messages like that can only lead to unhappiness—the one thing the child's mother was most likely trying to avoid. Each and every one of our actions and reactions teaches our children something about themselves, about us, and about life.

It's extremely common these days for a parent to go to a store to buy a birthday gift for another child and buy one for their own child at the same time. Children are constantly receiving presents for no reason, and, in my experience, this is true even for families that may be struggling financially. Sometimes we do this just to get in and out of the store without having to deal with a meltdown or a tantrum, but sometimes I believe it's because we're reacting to our own childhoods. When we take our children to a restaurant or an amusement park or buy them toys, we may be thinking, *Wow, I would have loved that when I was a kid. This would never have happened to me*. I'm not saying that the pendulum needs to swing all the way back to the way things were when we were growing up or that we shouldn't indulge our children from time to time, but we do have to be careful not to overdo it. It is certainly nice to give them gifts and special treats, but I worry when I see some of my ten- and eleven-year-old clients with expensive designer bags, scarves, and clothing. Be aware of the pitfalls here and use the CALM technique to say no to your kids when you need to with compassion and their best interests at heart.

Setting Limits Prepares Kids for Life

Setting limits in a loving way is not mean. It's preparation for life. It's a way to let your child learn what is expected of her, not only within your family but also in the world, and that she is fully capable of handling whatever it might be. Your child wants and needs that kind of guidance. It's what allows him or her to feel both safer and more in control.

Think how you feel when you're thrust into a situation and don't know what the proper behavior is. And you have a lot more experience from which to figure it out than a child does. Your child wants to please you and feel lovable. It's your job to help her build for success and show her how. When you do, you'll find that you have a happier, more lovable, and loving child.

By overindulging and overprotecting our children we may actually be depriving them of the opportunity to develop inner strength and resilience. Kids who become used to being given everything they want will be devastated when things don't go their way.

That little girl who had a meltdown in Ikea might then grow into a fourteen-year-old who throws a tantrum when her mother refuses to buy her an outrageously expensive pair of designer sandals to wear to her prom. Even more concerning, however, is what will happen to all these entitled youngsters when they go out and discover that they're not as entitled as they thought, that the world isn't going to give them what they want just because they pout and complain— and, in fact, that exactly the opposite is true.

A friend of mine who works in human resources for a large national magazine recently told me that many of their younger employees do not seem able to handle stress, disappointment, or responsibility; they fall apart, don't complete tasks, and complain constantly. And a friend who works for a large American university says it is now common for parents to call on behalf of their kids and argue with the professors about grades or even audit classes for their children. I don't know these parents personally, but I guess they are the same ones who always rushed in to do things for their children rather than letting them try and maybe fail and ultimately learn to do things for themselves.

Kids want to do things for themselves, even if it's something as simple as making their own sandwich or pouring their own juice. It's not so different for us as adults; we want to feel competent and capable, able to do things on our own, and so do our children. Mirroring and then setting limits while letting them know that they are strong enough to deal with disappointment is the surest way I know to keep them safe while at the same time helping them develop that sense of competency and capability.

Sometimes it can be a rough ride, but if you just hang in there and stay the course you will come out the other end feeling more confident as a parent, and you will have a happier child.

EIGHT

Before You Set Limits, Get Familiar with Your Own

One of the most important things for any parent to remember is that limit-setting only works if it comes from a loving place, and if you're really angry with your child because he's out of control, throwing tantrums, or defiant, any consequence you set will be tough, but it won't be loving.

Mirroring helps your child from the inside out so that he is better able to accept the limits you set and fulfill your expectations of him. The other side of that coin, however, is that when you do set limits and impose consequences you must be very aware of your own agenda, of why you are setting the limits you do, and of whether they are actually appropriate to the situation. Sometimes parents believe that if they don't come down hard on their kids, the children won't believe they're serious. But if you scream and yell, if you keep getting tougher and tougher, your children will only become increasingly angry, will grow to fear you, and will use behavior to hurt or upset you. And the more vulnerable the child, the truer this will be. Yes, you need to be authoritative and serious, but you can't be vindictive or mean. If you're so angry that you're imposing a consequence on your child just to "get back at" and hurt him, it isn't going to work. And, in addition, if you're overreacting, screaming, and losing your temper, by modeling this kind of behavior, you'll be undermining what you're trying to teach—which is that your child can and should control his or her own behavior. If you can't control your anger, how can you expect your child to control his?

So again, and as always, you always need to ask yourself whether your child needs to hear what you're about to say (and the tone in which you're about to say it) or whether it's something *you* need to say. If it's something your child needs to hear, you'll be able to remain calm and neutral while you say it; if it's something you need to say, you'll probably be raising your voice, using a threatening tone, and generally behaving in a way that makes the problem worse instead of resolving it.

Achieving the proper balance isn't easy, but it's something you need to keep in mind when you're trying to teach your child. If you overreact, your child will just think you're mean; if you underreact he'll think you're a pushover. Beyond that, you have to believe and mean what you're saying. If you're thinking, *This is never going to work,* it isn't going to work. Kids have radar; they know when you mean it and when you don't. And they will keep pushing until they know you actually do mean it.

Know Your Triggers So You Don't Overreact

All parents have triggers, those particular behaviors that drive us crazy and make it really difficult to remain neutral. Your triggers might be two kids talking to you at once; your children chattering away when you're multitasking; kids smacking each other or play-fighting in the car; whining or tattling; always saying no to simple requests; calling Mom or Dad in a wailing, howling, or frantic tone—or any number of other behaviors. Whatever your triggers are, when your child engages in one of these behaviors, mirroring will feel like the last thing you will want to do. In fact, if you're already even a little bit stressed, it can be enough to put you right over the edge, which means that you'll probably be overreacting to whatever is going on with your child and thereby compound the problem.

As human beings, we have a difficult time understanding how our behavior impacts other people. We know that no matter how angry we are, we would never hurt our children, and we know that we'll be fine later, so we don't really hear the effect our words have on our kids. They always sound harsher to the one who's hearing them than they do to the one who's saying them. When people tell me that they're considering buying a nanny cam, I want to tell them that if they turned the nanny cam on themselves, some days they'd probably fire themselves.

One thing I often ask parents is, "How many times have you been yelled at and responded by saying, 'Huh, come to think of it, you're absolutely right. Thank you so much for setting me straight. I don't know what got into me'?" The answer is, probably never. So why, when you yell at your child for not being nice to his brother, for example, do you expect him to respond by saying, "Oh yeah, you're right. I really am lucky to have a little brother." Why do we expect so much more of our children than we're capable of ourselves?

Sometimes we seem to believe that children, because they're children, don't feel things the same way we do, but they do. In addition to that, they're not allowed to yell back, they're not allowed to hit, and they don't necessarily have the skills to stop.

Triggers, as I've said, are different for different parents. For you it might be your child's pulling on your shirt when she can plainly see that you're busy or talking on the phone. Being interrupted while talking on the phone is a powerful trigger for most of us, and what we usually do is try to pretend that everything is fine and carry on the conversation while we're gritting our teeth and muttering "Stop!" under our breath or making annoyed "I'm on the phone!" faces to our kid. This doesn't work. We don't sound normal, and the person we're talking to knows it. My remedy for coping with a kid who's badgering you when you're on the phone is to deal with it up front instead of trying to ignore it. The phone rings, you answer it, and then you say, "Could you please hold on for a minute." Put the phone down and talk to your child. Then you say, "Look, sweetie, sometimes it's hard for you when I'm on the phone and you need my attention. Is there anything you need right now?" (Normally the child will say no.) "Okay, then, I'm about to take a phone call, and here's what I expect from you. You won't bug me or grab me unless it's something really important or you're in some kind of danger. Then, of course, you can come and get me. Otherwise you need to let me talk. If you don't, here's what the consequence will be . . ." If she lets you talk, that's great. You can reward her with praise or by spending some extra time with her. If she doesn't, she knows what the consequence will be.

If your child is particularly needy and persistent, he will probably continue to bother you, but you can still deal with it even if it starts while you're in the middle of a conversation. Whether it's a business or a personal call, just say to the person on the other end, "You know, I'm having a bit of a problem with my child, so if you don't mind I'm going to hang up and deal with it, and I'll call you right back." Then you hang up and say to the child, "You know, I had to get off the phone. I told you what the consequence would be if you bothered me while I was on the phone." And you give him the consequence. Believe me, you will sound more professional and in control to the person on the other end of the phone and you will be far less stressed. We may think we hide these things well, but we don't.

If whining or nose talking (an equally annoying style of speech) is the trigger behavior, first listen to what the child is saying, make three mirroring statements, then ask him to repeat what he said without whining. The desired result is twofold: you don't let the behavior continue until you can't stand it anymore and lose your cool, and the child doesn't get what she wants until she asks appropriately. Be neutral and matter-of-fact but consistent, and the behavior should improve.

Monitor Your Stress Level

To avoid overreacting, whenever possible you need to determine the level of your stress. On a scale of 1 to 10, if you're at a 1 it means you're calm and relaxed enough to tackle anything. A 10 means that you're already so overloaded (probably with issues that have absolutely nothing to do with your child) that almost anything will cause you to lose your patience and say things you'll later regret. The problem is that our own changes in mood mean that we can be very inconsistent in the way we react to our children. If your child screams "MAAAAHM!!!!!" when you're calm and relaxed, your response may be, "Yes, what is it, honey?" whereas if you're already at a 10, you'll probably scream back, "What? Whaddya want? WHAAAT?" If she's bouncing up and down on the sofa when you're in a good mood, the behavior might roll off your back; then, on another occasion, if it was a bad day at the office or you just received an enormous heating bill, the same behavior will set you off and start you screaming. Behaviors that were no problem at all the day before will suddenly seem monstrous. One way to avoid inconsistency as much as possible is to ask yourself why you're about to start screaming. Is it really about your child's behavior or is it about you? Of course, you're not going to succeed all the time. Parenting is stressful and often intensely frustrating, and I always tell my clients that they shouldn't even try to be perfect. Nevertheless, our aim should always be to try to stay as consistent as we can as much of the time as we can.

Children don't have the same ability we do to think, *Whoa, she's really in a bad mood; she must have had a tough day at the office.* For children, everything is so personalized that they often think it's about them. (And that holds true for some adults as well.) So we really should try to be as consistent as possible in the way we respond to them. Inconsistency is unsettling, and leaves them wondering whether they should ever listen to us at all.

Children are also literally very small. They look up at the entire world, and they depend on adults for everything. That's an extremely frightening position to be in, and if their dad is shut up in his room for a day with a migraine, and is edgy or impatient because of it, or if their mom is in a bad mood because she's been working overtime, children don't understand why their parent is suddenly out of sorts. They just think, *Oh, they must hate me*, or *Is it going to stay this way?*

So whatever your own triggers may be, it's important to be an observer of yourself, because the better you know yourself, and know when you're on the brink of exploding, the better able you'll be to calm yourself down before you get to that point. Very often, when we're in the moment, we think that everything we perceive is objective reality, and that's not always so. We need to be brave and mature enough to step into the other person's reality and look around a bit from his or her point of view. That's what we're doing when we mirror with our children.

But what can we do when we know our frustration and stress level is at a 9 or a 10 and little Sophie is screaming from the next room that her brother is hitting her? The problem is that when we're at that level of stress, our brain perceives everything as noise and pounding irritation. (Which, incidentally, is exactly what your child is experiencing when he or she is upset and you're yelling at him.) Basically, we're in fight-or-flight mode, and what we need to do is get out of it before we go off. There are a few simple tactics we can use to achieve this.

One thing I tell my clients is to close their eyes or look away and take a deep breath. Looking at the stimulus is only going to exacerbate your stress level. And while you're doing that, try to slow down your breathing. You can even tell your child that you're trying to control your anger. If you do that, you'll actually be accomplishing two things at once: you'll be getting yourself to calm down and you'll also be doing some fantastic modeling for your child by showing her that it is possible to control your emotions rather than letting them control you. Every time you lose your temper and scream and yell, you are showing your kid that anger is not controllable, and if an adult can't manage it, how could a child? Yet this is what we demand and expect from them. We must be able to do it ourselves in order for our children to know it is possible.

The result, if you don't calm down, is often something you regret—an action or reaction on your part that is out of balance with your child's behavior. Imagine again that little Sophie is screaming because her brother hit her and you scream back, "Oh, just stop it!

Cut it out! Cut it out! I can't take you two anymore—you're making me crazy!!!!" Now think about what would happen if *you* were that mad and your spouse or partner yelled the same thing at you. How would you react? How well would that work for you?

My best suggestion is that you try to monitor your stress level throughout the day so that you can use these tactics to prevent yourself from reaching that point where your fuse is so short that the least little thing is going to set you off like a firecracker on the Fourth of July. In Chapter Twelve we're going to be talking about how you can teach your child how to control his own anxiety, but for now, I want you to appreciate how hard it really can be.

Because it is so difficult, no one can parent without losing it from time to time. So, if you feel yourself losing it, if you really can't stop yourself from releasing your anger, here's a fallback measure: try to change your words. We say terrible things when we're angry, things we don't really mean, such as, "If you don't stop I'm going to get on a plane and go away and I'm never coming back!" We know we're not going to do any such thing, but our child really doesn't. He'll remember those words, and they hurt him. So, scream if you must, but say something like, "You know, I could say some terrible things right now that really aren't nice. But I'm not going to do that because I'm really trying to. . ." That way you'll have the satisfaction of releasing your pent-up anger without saying words you'll regret.

Red Light, Green Light, Yellow Light— Avoiding Conflict Before It Occurs

Not all the issues we have with our children are equally important, but it's sometimes hard to remember that when either we or our child is already overstressed, even though the cause of the stress may have nothing to do with the immediate situation. If we don't determine in advance which battles are worth fighting and which aren't, we can find ourselves getting sucked into all kinds of secondary skirmishes we never needed to be involved with in the first place. Ross Greene does an excellent job of discussing this in his book *The Explosive Child* when he talks about having a Plan A, Plan B, and Plan C. I do something similar when I encourage my clients to set priorities by thinking of different behaviors in terms of red, green, and yellow traffic lights.

Red-light behaviors are those that can actually endanger your child's physical or emotional safety, such as running with scissors, not wearing a seat belt, refusing to hold your hand when you're crossing the street, or hurting another child's feelings. These are nonnegotiable, hard-parenting power struggles you *must* enter and *must* win.

Green-light issues are those about which we tend to get into unnecessary arguments with our children. Does it really matter if he wants to wear plaid pants with a striped shirt? Do you really care if she doesn't want her hair braided this morning? So what if he jumps in a puddle once in a while? Does it matter if she brings two toys or five toys to the restaurant? If you haven't already figured this out, when you're in a bad mood to begin with you may find yourself starting World War III over something equally frivolous—and possibly something you don't really care about, or wouldn't if you hadn't been annoyed with your spouse or your boss that day. Green-light behaviors won't be the same for everyone, but we all have them, so figure out what yours are. It will save you a lot of wasted energy in the long run.

Yellow-light behaviors are those that must occur with some regularity and that you need to reinforce with some consistency but might just let go from time to time. These might include taking a bath,

brushing teeth before bed, or eating your vegetables. They're important, but if either you or your child has been having a really bad day,
you need to think about whether or not you really want to get into
another power struggle that's focused on taking a bath. In other
words, yellow-light issues say, "Proceed with caution," but be a little
flexible, use your judgment, and be aware of your own agenda.

Yellow lights allow you to let something go while still remaining
the parent. If, for example, you have a rule that says no cookies
before dinner, you can decide to say, "You know, this is a yellow light.
I think this one time let's turn it to green and we can break the
no-cookie rule so long as you don't ask me every day." By doing that,
you've retained the right to make that decision without having to
fight another battle that day.

Now, once you've decided on your red, green, and yellow lights,
sit down with your child when both of you are calm and relaxed. As
always, you start by mirroring before going on to discuss what is or is
not acceptable behavior. So the conversation might go something
like this: "You know, it's sometimes really hard to do the things people tell you to do. You think you should be able to make up your own
mind. But what happens is that we wind up getting really mad and
fighting with each other, and in the end you have to do it anyway.
You're not happy and I'm not happy. So I've come up with this idea."
Then explain to him that there are certain behaviors that are *never*
going to be okay and that those will always be red lights. Other
things—the yellow lights—can turn red or green; it's up to you. He
will also learn that the behavioral choices he makes can turn the light
to red or green. This allows him to directly experience the cause and
effect of his actions. And green lights are choices you're not going
to struggle with except under special circumstances. (You might, for
example, insist that a little boy dress up for an important event.)

Once you've done that, all you'll have to say in the future is, "That's a red light," and if your child has already tested your red lights and knows he's never going to win a particular power struggle, he'll realize there's no point fighting about it or getting into a power struggle when you're already at the outer limits of your ability to cope.

One caveat, however, is that you can never turn a red or yellow light green in the middle of a battle. And if you've gotten sucked into fighting over something that should have been a green light, the minute your child starts to become negative and stubborn, the issue in question *always* becomes a red light. You can't change your mind in the middle, even if you realize you've done a really stupid thing by picking the wrong fight. That's why you need to prioritize and determine your own agenda *before* you start the conversation.

What you should never do is fight about it for ten minutes and then get so frustrated that you say, "Oh, okay, go ahead, have your cookie. Why don't you eat the whole box! See if I care!" When you do that your child will learn that even if it's only one time out of twenty, there's a chance that if he digs in his heels he'll win.

The problem is that every time you allow yourself to be worn down you're guaranteeing that the behavior will be repeated, and you'll have taught your child that you don't mean what you say. Avoiding just this kind of situation is the point of determining red, green, and yellow lights in the first place. Otherwise, you'll be creating what I call movable walls, and kids don't like that. They like to know what is expected; it helps them predict their world and function well within it. Using the red-light, green-light tactic allows you to be more flexible and less rigid while still helping your child to feel that his world can be predicted.

Predictability Starts with You

We've already talked about how you might feel if you had to stumble about in a dark, unfamiliar room looking for walls you couldn't see. If you keep that image in mind, you'll find it much easier to understand why it's so important for you to be as consistent as possible in the way you react and relate to your child. Ensuring that kind of consistency always starts and ends with you, which is why it's so important that you continually monitor yourself, be aware of your stress level, and make sure that your agenda is in the best interests of your child.

In the following chapter I'll be providing you with two powerful strategies for teaching your child what will be expected of him and, therefore, making the world more predictable and peaceful for both of you.

NINE

Frontloading and Intervention— Key Strategies for Containment

Aside from mirroring and remembering to stay neutral, frontloading is the most important tool for changing behavior. It's a contract with your child that predicts what might go wrong and lays out exactly what will happen if he misbehaves. Once the contract is clear, if the child then does misbehave he has, in effect, chosen to accept the consequence. That doesn't mean, of course, that he'll accept it with good grace; in fact, he'll probably get very upset. But once he's had his tantrum, you can then mirror and remind him of your contract. By doing that, you will be keeping his world predictable at the same time you're letting him know that he is responsible for the consequence he's received.

Let Your Child Know What to Expect

It is a function of our busy, crazy lives that we're constantly dragging our children from one activity to another. Sometimes it's to do something "fun," like going to the park, and sometimes it's to do something we want or need them to do, like getting a haircut or going to the supermarket.

Children don't have agendas in the same way we do. They don't have "to do" lists. Basically, they live in the moment, and we're constantly yanking them out of the moment to follow *our* program. We do need to get things done, but if what we need to get done is going to involve or impact our children, we need to give them some information in advance. Too often we simply assume they know our agenda, but they don't. Or we assume they can read our minds, or we just forget to tell them things. (How would you feel if someone suddenly announced that you had to drop everything and get in the car *right now,* without telling you where you were going, what to wear, or what was expected of you?)

Children in general have more trouble transitioning from one activity to another than we do as adults. (We'll be talking more about that in Chapter Eleven.) And when we pull them out of the playground and toss them in the car because we need to get somewhere fast, their behavior is likely to deteriorate. Think what's going on in their heads: "What are you doing? I was having a good time here. I don't want to get in the car!" Again, it's a matter of letting them know what we expect of them. This is what I call "frontloading."

If you let your child know in advance that you understand how much he loves the playground and he can play there for a few minutes, but when you come to get him he's going to have to be ready to get in the car with you because he needs to get a haircut, and he needs to sit still in the barber chair, and if he doesn't there will be a consequence, at least he'll know what's coming. You'll also need to make it clear exactly what that consequence will be. Then, if he isn't quiet and/or doesn't sit still, he'll know why you're going straight home instead of to his favorite fast-food restaurant or why he can't watch his favorite TV show that afternoon.

Many parents ask me if frontloading doesn't just put ideas in the child's head, so that he or she will be even more likely to act out. But the truth is that you know your child, and you know when he's most likely to act out—or else you wouldn't have needed to front-load in the first place. The key is to do it in a loving way—a way that lets him know you *want* things to go well and you are willing to help him achieve that.

When You Know It's Going to Be Hard, Plan in Advance

Keeping that in mind, you will also know what situations are going to be particularly stressful or difficult for your child—those occasions when acting out or melting down is most likely to occur. These are the situations when frontloading is all the more important. Here's an example many parents can relate to, along with a strategy for anticipating and containing unacceptable behavior.

You're going to a toy store to buy a birthday present for another child. You can be fairly certain that your child, who's supposed to be "helping" you choose the gift, is going to find some toy he just has to have for himself. So, before you even leave the house, you begin to prepare him for what's going to happen and what kind of behavior you expect. You're making a contract with your child. As with every strategy in this book, you start by mirroring.

Your initial dialogue might be something like, "You know, we're going to the store to buy a toy for Jackie's birthday. There are so many great things to buy, and they always have the best stuff right up front where you can see it. There will be things you want for yourself, but we're just buying a present for your friend, so if you think that's going to be too hard for you, maybe Mommy should just go by herself."

At that point your child will most likely say something like, "No, no, it's okay. I can do it. I can come." That's when you let him know what behavior you're going to expect. "Okay, then, but you have to understand that if you come, you're not going to go home with anything for yourself. I don't want any whining or begging. That's an absolute red light. Okay?"

Undoubtedly your child will be nodding vigorously and assuring you that he understands. So you need to explain that if he doesn't live up to his part of the bargain, there will be a consequence. Sticking to your guns can be a challenge because some children have enormous endurance and can keep at you long after they may have forgotten what they actually wanted in the first place. If you're struggling, keep in mind that giving in to your child will not make him happier; it will actually make him more restless and less satisfied. And make sure that when you decide on a consequence, it is appropriate and one that you'll be willing and able to carry out. If your destination is a toy store, just having to leave may be all the consequence you need.

If the consequence is too severe, you might not follow through or your child will just perceive it as mean. It needs to be something that will have meaning for your child (and that's going to depend on what's important to your particular child) but also something that fits the crime, so to speak, and that you're willing and emotionally capable of enforcing. If you announce a consequence and then don't impose it, all your frontloading will have meant nothing—in fact, it will have taught your child that he doesn't really have anything to worry about because you never do what you say. And if you follow through some times and not others, you'll be letting him know that there's still a chance he's going to get away with it this time—which, in his mind, means it's usually worth taking a shot.

Another common dilemma parents often get caught up in is the idea that the consequence has to be "big" or severe enough to get an immediate reaction. They keep waiting for the look on the child's face that lets them know the consequence "worked." And to get what they're looking for they continue to up the ante until the consequence is so absurd that they feel bad and take it back. At the risk of sounding like a nag, I want to remind you that it's really not a good idea to take it back—your child needs fair and reasonable consequences but also needs to know that you mean what you say. Taking back a consequence after you've discussed it with your child undermines all the value of trying to keep your child's world as consistent and predictable as possible. It undoes all the good work you may have been doing up to that point.

However, if you feel you have overreacted and come up with a consequence that is totally unreasonable, it is okay to talk to your child and explain that you made a decision in anger, frustration, or exhaustion, and that you no longer feel the consequence is fair or just. This shows your child that you consider her feelings, can reflect on your own behavior, and are not afraid to acknowledge that you made a mistake.

One way to avoid all this is to ask your child what he thinks the consequence should be. Quite often the child will choose a consequence that is more severe than what you would have chosen. And surprisingly, he will often remind you of what his consequence is, indicating once again that children really do need structure.

What you need to understand is that you won't necessarily see the results of your consequence right away. Many kids want to save face and will tell you to "go ahead and do it, I don't care." So it won't be until the next time you go to the toy store or the mall that you'll see their behavior is different, which will also let you know that your consequence had an effect, after all.

Once you get to the store, things may go perfectly smoothly, but just as likely they won't. The first time your little angel's eyes light on something particularly appealing and he says, "Oh, Mommy, I want that," you remind him of what you said. You mirror first with at least three statements like, "Of course you want that. It looks like a really cool toy." Your child may then say, "Yeah, it's the one in that series that I really need." To which you can reply, "Wow, so it goes with that set you've been talking about . . ." And the child says, "Yeah, so can I have it, please, please, please, Mommy?" You again: "This is so tough because here is this toy you really want and you say you really need, but remember, this is exactly what we knew was going to happen. We knew this was going to be hard, but I told you in advance that we wouldn't be buying anything for you today." At that point he'll either be very upset and disappointed but pull himself together with mild to moderate protest and move on, or he'll fling himself on the floor and have a full-blown meltdown in the middle of the store.

This is when parents panic because they imagine, rightly or wrongly, that everyone in the store is staring at them. So they either buy the toy to stop the behavior and then yell at the child later, or they start talking through their teeth with their mouth closed, hissing, "Stop that! Get up this minute. You're embarrassing me. Stop it." And then they start telling the child what he's doing to *them*: "Can't you see you're embarrassing me?"

Let me assure you that when you yell at your child to let him know what he's doing to *you*, he's not going to feel remorse in the moment. Nor is he going to turn off the faucet of his emotions even if he's capable of doing that—which he probably isn't just then. At this point he knows he's blown his chances of ever getting that toy. He's upset, so he's going to take you down with him. It's as if he were saying, "Fine, you didn't get it for me so I'm just going to show you what not getting something for me looks like."

That said, there will always be some children who would never throw a tantrum in public because they're too concerned about what people might think. Most, however, will be much more likely to act out in a store or a restaurant or anyplace where they know you'll be embarrassed. When it happens, talking through gritted teeth or grabbing at your flailing child is not going to solve the problem or make potential onlookers think better of you as a mother. What you need to do is take a deep breath and first try to CALM your child by mirroring, then present the problem and the solution. After you have CALMed your child, say in a neutral voice something like (and I know this is hard), "You know, screaming and yelling are not going to get you that toy. You've chosen to do this in front of everyone in this store, and all you're really doing is embarrassing yourself." And then you disengage by walking a few steps away.

Once your child realizes that he's lost his audience, he may very well stop. If he doesn't, you again have choices. If the child is small enough you can simply pick him up and walk out. If he's bigger, you may just have to wait it out. If you stop reacting, you'll be depriving him of the fuel he needs to keep going and he'll calm down sooner rather than later. When he does, you walk out and he'll realize that he got nothing for his behavior but the consequence you had told him in advance would occur if he chose to behave that way. If you continue to follow this formula consistently, your child will change his behavior—not because he was yelled at or humiliated, not because he was punished, but because the behavior got him nothing and you were both empathic and neutral.

The opposite side of that coin, of course, is that if your child handles himself well in a potentially difficult situation he has chosen to receive a positive consequence to reward the behavior you front-loaded. (For more on rewarding positive behaviors, see page 141.)

Friendship Moves and Friendship Blocks

Teaching children about friendship moves and friendship blocks is a specific kind of frontloading strategy that you can use in much the same way as red lights, green lights, and yellow lights (see page 127). If you have more than one child, there are certain situations you can almost predict are going to bring out the worst in them. Any situation where they're confined and need to sit still for an extended period of time—such as in the car—is sure to be one of these.

Establishing friendship moves and friendship blocks in advance is a particularly effective tactic for defusing these potentially volatile situations. A friendship move is, in effect, a statement that makes the other person feel validated and understood. So, for example, if one child holds up a new toy and says to another child, "Hey, look what I just got," a friendship move would be to respond, "Wow, that's really cool. Can I see it?" A block would be to reply, "Oh, that's stupid. Who cares about that? Mine's way better!" A friendship move feels wonderful and kind; a friendship block makes the other person feel let down and deflated, as if he's been dropped. It is an invitation to start a skirmish, if not a full-blown battle. All kids do this to one another, but older siblings seem to do it to their younger brothers and sisters all the time. Parents find it very upsetting because they quite naturally want their children to treat one another with kindness and they want them to get along with their friends.

Like red lights, green lights, and yellow lights, you'll need to sit down with your child (or children) in advance, when everyone is calm and relaxed, and explain what a friendship move is and what a block is. One way to do this, if the child is old enough, is to use the example of a chess game. There are moves that help and make people want to be your friend, and there are moves that make things worse so that people want to stay away from you.

Then, once they've understood, when you're about to get into a situation that you know might lead to trouble—such as that car ride—you mirror and frontload. First you mirror: "Okay, kids, we're going to Grandma's and sitting in the car for such a long time can be really boring. It's hot and you're all cramped in, and you just want to get there fast." Then present the problem: "But here's the problem. I really need you to not fight with one another. No teasing, no kicking, no arguing. I want to hear friendship moves, not friendship blocks." Finally, offer the solution: "I'm going to be keeping track of how many friendship moves I hear. I want you all to work together to keep things peaceful, and if you do, you will earn a collective reward, something you are both" (or all, depending on how many kids you have) excited about." This eliminates the chance that they will start competing with one another to chalk up the greatest number of friendship moves and encourages them to collaborate and support one another instead.

Like red lights, green lights, and yellow lights, this strategy also provides you with a nice, simple way of reminding your kids what's expected of them without doing a lot of lecturing. Instead of snapping, "Don't say that to your brother. That hurts his feelings. You don't like it when he does that to you," you can say, "I'm hearing too many blocks. Let's hear more moves."

It is also, incidentally, a good tool to use with children who, for whatever reason, have difficulty interacting socially with their peers. Kids have social problems for many different reasons. Sometimes they have low self-esteem and need to put other kids down so that they can feel better about themselves. Some kids, such as those with Asperger's disorder, find it difficult to pick up on nonverbal facial cues or body language. And some gifted kids may understand perfectly well what's expected of them but simply don't think it's important and just can't be bothered. Particularly for the latter two groups, explaining moves and blocks as if they were parts of a game of chess or checkers works very well because it seems more like a strategy, which appeals to the analytical side of their brain and, therefore, is more relevant for them than it would be if you tried to talk about hurting people's feelings or making them angry. (For more on connecting with very anxious or special-needs children see Chapter Twelve.)

Acknowledgment and Encouragement versus Threats and Bribes

Many parents have asked me whether offering a reward for good behavior isn't either bribing the child or giving him something for what he should have been doing in the first place.

My answer would be that positive rewards, as well as negative consequences, are part of the fabric of life. For good or ill there are consequences all around us and our children need to develop the neurological hardware to deal with the fact that all of their actions have consequences—sometimes pleasant and sometimes not.

Barbara Coloroso points out in her book *Kids Are Worth It* that constantly rewarding or bribing children with treats or privileges can encourage a child to behave for external reasons as opposed to internal reasons. And they are likely to grow up to be adults who lack self-esteem, and may have a heavy dependence on others for approval.

It is most helpful to offer encouragement, acknowledgment, and feedback to children as they develop responsible behaviors and have successes, commenting on effort rather than achievement.

Carol Dweck, a professor of psychology at Stanford University, writes in her book *Mindset: The New Psychology of Success* about a study she and her colleagues did with two groups of fifth-grade students over a period of ten years. One group was consistently praised for their hard work, while the second group was praised for their intelligence. In an interview published in the Toronto *Star* (July 22, 2008), Dweck reported that the second group tended to give up when the assignment was too challenging because they didn't want to look dumb, while those praised for hard work "remained confident and engaged, and their performance increased fairly dramatically. This was on an IQ test . . . those praised for effort became smarter."

Overrewarding or giving empty praise can go one of two ways: on the one hand, it can actually diminish your child's self-esteem by letting her know that you don't have very high expectations, and, on the opposite end of the spectrum, it can give her an inflated sense of her accomplishments. Under special circumstances, incentives and motivators can be helpful to mark achievements for children who have set their own behavioral goals and want to record their progress. (See "Help Them Complete the Puzzle" on page 151.) Any incentives need to be meaningful enough for the child to feel invested without being inflated out of all proportion to the behavior that's being targeted. It also needs to be challenging enough to get (that is, the child will really have to try to accomplish something that's been difficult for him) so that getting it feels good, but not so difficult that the child considers it unattainable and, therefore, gives up without really trying.

I believe it's our job as parents to help our children develop realistic expectations. We do that not only by letting them know there are consequences for doing less than they're capable of doing, but also that you are willing to acknowledge their effort in a meaningful way. Beyond that, there are some children for whom consequences stop being effective, particularly when the bond between you is frayed. For them, it's better to simply ignore negative behavior (except in situations when ignoring it would put them in actual danger) and focus on the positive—ramp up the baby play, mirror about positive things, and generally do more soft parenting—which, you may remember, is what I told Charlie's mother when I had her cuddling with him in the morning while his father took over the hard-parenting chores.

There are many different ways to acknowledge good choices that certainly don't involve buying your child an expensive gift. If you're working on a particular behavior, keeping track of these accomplishments help her see that you are watching and noticing positive behavioral change. Acknowledging and noting these changes, if it's sincere and meaningful, can be enough. Mirroring good behavior, in and of itself, creates a warm moment between you and your child and allows her to feel good about herself—to think, in effect, *I made a good choice that had a positive impact on another person.* But that means you really need to put your heart and soul into your comment. Instead of saying, "You were really good in the store today," try saying, "I know it wasn't easy for you when we went to the store today and you didn't get anything for yourself. You really wanted that toy. I could see how much you wanted it, but you managed to pull yourself together and get through it, and that was really amazing and made our trip to the store so much more fun." If you do that, you'll be helping your child to understand that she doesn't always have to receive something tangible to feel good and that sometimes just knowing she did a good job and someone else noticed is all the reward she really needs.

Intervention or Planning for the Worst

Intervention is a containment strategy that goes hand in hand with frontloading—and no, I don't mean cornering your child in the playroom and letting him know that you think he's addicted to Cocoa Puffs and needs to go to kiddie rehab.

When I suggest that you do an intervention with your child, I mean that you should pick a place the child likes to go, where good behavior is expected, and where he or she typically has a hard time behaving (such as a restaurant or a mall), and go there with the expectation that your child will misbehave and you will have to leave.

You then frontload by explaining very clearly what behavior you expect and let the child know that if he or she doesn't make good choices you're going to leave. Remember that you need to mirror first. Here's how that part might go: "I know it's hard to sit still in a restaurant. It's noisy and it's boring and it's hard to sit there and not move." Then you need to present the problem: "But here's the problem. If you run around in a restaurant you could get hot food spilled on you, and you bother the other people who are trying to enjoy their dinner."

The next step would be to bring in your agenda. Let your child know exactly what you expect of him and what the consequence will be if he doesn't behave the way you need him to. You have to be very specific about this. You don't just say, "I expect you to be good." That's much too vague. You say, "So here's what I need you to do. I need you to sit in your chair and use your indoor voice. You can't get down and play with your car on the floor. You can't walk around and bother other people. I can help you. I can remind you, but if you run around and you're loud, we're going to leave the restaurant."

When you do this, you're helping your child to make the right choices because you're telling him exactly what you expect of him—what being "good" means. But you can't have any expectation that you'll get to eat your meal. Your child probably won't believe you the first time, because you've never meant it before, but you *must* be prepared to leave.

Maybe he'll do what you expect, and that's great; everybody wins. Don't forget to mirror and praise him when he does. But you must follow through no matter what. Your child will survive. In fact, many parents have told me that when they followed through they discovered that their child was not as hysterical as they had expected. Not only that, but he will, in the long run, be happier and more settled, not only because he knows what's expected of him, but also because he knows that he has the ability to comply.

Once you follow through, you'll almost certainly see the results the next time you go out. (Although if you have a gladiator child you may have to go through it a couple of times.) In fact, you can often ride on one intervention for quite some time, although you may become a bit lax after a while (that's perfectly normal and understandable), which means the bad behavior may make a comeback. But then you'll just have to tighten up, mirror again, frontload a bit more, and perhaps do another intervention to get things back on track.

When I tell parents this, they often ask me, "But what about my other child? What do I tell her if we have to go home?" One thing you can do, if you have two cars, is decide in advance that either you or your partner will take the child who is misbehaving home while the other stays with the sibling. You can frontload the other child as well. Let this child know in advance that you might have to leave and why, and that, if you do, this child will get some other treat or you'll take him or her out another day. What you need to keep in mind, and make clear to the child who isn't misbehaving, is that having to leave won't be the end of the world and that the child will also survive.

Not so long ago a family with four young sons, ages four, six, nine, and eleven, came in to see me just a day or two before they were leaving for a family vacation in Florida. The little boys were adorable but wild, and the parents were dreading how they might behave on the trip. Since I didn't have much time, I thought about what tools would be most useful to them, and I told the parents that they had to take all four boys out to dinner *that night*, before they hit the road. I explained how they would mirror and frontload, that they needed to let the kids know what behavior was expected of them, how the parents would help them achieve it, what the reward would be for success, and what the consequence of failure would be—specifically, leaving the restaurant whether they'd eaten or not. I reminded them that they needed to be calm but firm, that they absolutely had to believe what they were saying, and that it was equally imperative for the boys to believe they would follow through.

When I called the next morning to see how it had gone, the mother got on the phone and the conversation went something like this: "It didn't work." "What do you mean, it didn't work?" "Well, they behaved perfectly, so we didn't have to do anything." I had to laugh because I'd heard that so many times before, but I explained to the mother that she and her husband had obviously done a very good job of frontloading because the boys had believed that they really meant what they were saying, and they'd behaved accordingly.

We spoke again when the family got back from vacation, and it turned out that the residual benefits of that one planned (if ultimately unnecessary) intervention lasted for most of the trip. They used the same techniques before the boys went into the pool or when they went sightseeing, and they only had to take one of them home from a restaurant on one occasion.

What happens when you frontload and your children really do behave is that both you and they begin to understand and actually believe that they can do it, which in turn begins to shift the entire dynamic among you for the better. The key, once again, is to be convincing and authoritative, not too angry and not pleading. You don't want to go overboard, yelling with your finger pointed and saying things like, "I promise that if you act up, that's it, you're in the car, mister. I won't stand for any nonsense, so you'd just better behave yourself." And you don't want to beg: "Please behave. Please do this for Mommy. We really want to have fun and we don't want to have to leave. Please be good, okay?" This is not a request; this is something you expect, and it is a good and reasonable thing to ask. If you believe yourself, your children will believe you.

The only caveat here is that you be realistic in your expectations. You can't ask a four-year-old to sit quietly in a restaurant with a linen napkin on his lap and his hair neatly combed to the side for a three-course formal dinner, but you can expect him to sit there for the length of time it takes you all to order and eat a hamburger or a pizza. In other words, don't take small children to places they don't belong and set them up for failure. If you do that, neither one of you is going to have a good time.

The Lessons to Be Learned

The strategies in this chapter are designed to make your child's world more predictable, helping him or her to understand the relationship between cause and effect, the fact that actions have consequences. For the lessons to be learned, however, it's important that you remain calm and neutral when you're laying out your expectations and when you're imposing the consequences of not living up to them. The more upset you become, the more you yell, the less likely it is that your child will associate his behavior with the negative outcome. Instead, he'll just think that you're mean and not think about his own behavior.

It's equally important, as I've said, to be consistent and follow through when you do set a limit or impose a consequence. When it comes to parenting, consistency is the key to having a calm, secure, happy child. Without that consistency your child will never know what the consequences of his actions might be from one day to the next, which can be confusing even for an adult.

Let's say, for example, that ever since you started your job you'd been taking an hour and fifteen minutes for lunch and no one had said anything about it. And then one day, out of the blue, your boss told you you'd been staying out too long and you're fired. You'd be really mad and really confused, even though you knew you shouldn't have been doing that in the first place. So why would you expect a child—who has no way of knowing the rules unless you clarify and enforce them—to react any differently to your "changing the rules" on him without any explanation?

TEN

A Toolbox of Strategies for Containing and Correcting Behavior

Using the CALM technique to mirror, then presenting the problem and coming up with the solution is the basic three-step process that underlies connected parenting. This is the formula you *must* remember to use whatever else you are doing. Within that context, front-loading and intervention are the major strategies you will always be using to make your child's world as consistent and predictable as possible so that he will always know what is expected of him and what to expect if he can't or won't comply.

But connected parenting also means using every loving, caring, and appropriate strategy at your disposal to cope with a virtually infinite variety of situations and to correct an equally infinite variety of potential behaviors.

The strategies I'll be providing in this chapter are a cross between a box full of tools and a bag full of tricks. Some tools work better than others in particular situations; you wouldn't, for example, use a screwdriver to hammer a nail. In addition, changing your strategies will keep them fresh and interesting for your child so that he or she doesn't wind up thinking, *Oh no, she doesn't think I'm going to fall for that one again!* If you see the same magic trick over and over, it loses some of its magic, and the same holds true for the teaching and containment strategies you use with your child.

Read through all the techniques, see which ones feel most comfortable for you, and try them out when the appropriate occasion arises. Mix them up; if one thing doesn't work, try another. Paradoxically, connected parenting is as much about being flexible as it is about being consistent.

First of All, Determine Your Target Behavior

This is really about knowing your triggers. You need to determine which of your child's behaviors trouble you the most and deal with them one at a time. For most people the big issue is probably hitting, but for some people it might be rudeness. Whatever it is for you, focus on that and make sure that whenever your child exhibits the target behavior you remain calm and neutral, and impose the same consequence every time. Behaviors persist only if they are at least intermittently rewarded. So, when you target a specific behavior and make sure that it is *never* rewarded, you will find that your child drops it from his or her repertoire. The goal when you do this is to stay absolutely neutral. No yelling, no anger, but absolute consistency, because if you yell or become hysterical you'll just be signaling your child that, *Hey, this is a good button for me to push.* If you're consistent, you will see and feel the success you are having as the behavior decreases or is eliminated, and, once that happens, you can choose a new target behavior, keeping yourself and your child hopeful that change can and does happen and that, in the end, it is better for everyone.

Here's an example using my own experience with my youngest child, Olivia. One day, when Olivia was about three years old we were at our cottage in the country, and for some reason she decided to eat the crab apples dropping off the tree in our yard. Since they were about the size of cherries, the apples presented a serious choking hazard and I couldn't let her eat one, so I decided that this would be my target behavior for the day. I gently removed it from her mouth and said, "Those look yummy and red and I bet you think they will taste good, but they're not for eating and they're dangerous because they could get stuck in your throat. So you can't have that. Let's find something else to look at or check out."

After that spectacular mirroring statement, Olivia immediately ran over and popped another one into her mouth. This went on for a while until, instead of yelling, I took her to the deck and told her she had to sit there with me for two minutes. After that, I told her she could go play. She popped another crab apple and we returned to the deck. After doing this about thirty times, we went into the house. There was no yelling and I imposed no consequence. We just did something else. Later on, we went back out and she did it again. After another twenty time-outs on the porch we went back inside. By the next morning she didn't even look at the crab apples, so we moved on to another target behavior, throwing sand.

Help Them Complete the Puzzle

Sometimes when you're targeting a behavior, it helps to give your child an incentive to change. Here's one tactic that I've found works really well with most kids. Buy a jigsaw puzzle with twenty to twenty-four pieces. Assemble it some place where the child doesn't see it so that you know which pieces fit together. Then, let's say the behavior you're targeting is hitting. Divide the day into four segments: before school, after school, after dinner, and bedtime. Each time the child gets through one of these time periods without hitting, you give him a piece of the puzzle. Kids love this, and they're so anxious to finish the puzzle that it really helps to motivate them to behave.

It also helps with anxious children who are challenging themselves. One little girl I work with had been doing very well, practicing going to a store with her mother and letting the mom walk away from her in the store for two or three minutes. She loved doing the puzzle so much that at one point she asked her mom, "What can I do? What if I go down into the basement with the lights off—is that worth two puzzle pieces?"

For some kids just completing the puzzle will be reward enough; others might need an additional reward when they complete it. Either way, puzzle-solving is a way to help resolve target behavioral issues.

Cure Bad Behavior with Kindness

Many times when children act out and engage in those trigger behaviors that drive us nuts, it's because they feel anxious or unlovable. When children feel unlovable, they behave one of two ways. Some children will respond by becoming the best little kids they can be, but most will do exactly the opposite—they'll try to show you just how unlovable they can really be. It's almost as if they are thinking to themselves, *Well, if Mommy doesn't love me at least I'll know why.*

They'll push every button you've got and do something to let you know, *Hey, I'm here. Pay attention to me*. They might, for example, do what I call bugging, which is just annoying behaviors like getting right up in your face or waving things in front of your eyes, or they may become incredibly clingy. One particular form of this is what I call "uppy-uppy," when your child is whining and cajoling you to pick her up—most often when you're already carrying a younger sibling or struggling with grocery bags.

Usually, you'll let her bug you or cling for a while or you'll pick her up for a minute and then put her down, until finally you'll say, "Honey, please, I'm trying to pay these bills. Why don't you go play?" Or, "I can't pick you up right now; you can walk yourself." What happens then is that she'll just do it even more. You start to get angry. She feels a little bit hurt or humiliated, so if it's clinging she'll squeeze harder, and if it's bugging she'll do something really obnoxious like getting right in your face or pinching you. The more you try to push her away, the more she'll come right back at you. At that point you'll have had enough and you'll say something like, "Okay, that's it. Just get off me." She'll either continue to do what she was doing or walk away upset. Now you feel guilty, so you go over and apologize, at which point she'll probably go, "Humph!" and refuse to accept your apology or just do the same thing again. I call this the attachment dance or the elastic-band response.

What I tell parents to do in these situations is absolutely counterintuitive. You need to get into the moment and, in a playful way, initiate the contact so that you are the one tickling or clinging to them, or, in the case of "uppy-uppy," giving them uppy time, particularly when they're not asking for it. Do not do this in a sarcastic *I'll show you what it feels like* way. That isn't the point. The point is to use a paradoxical approach and, within limits, get into the behavior a bit yourself. Think of it as a particular kind of mirroring. *You* do the clinging. Say things like, "I love you so much, I don't feel like letting you go yet." Or, "You're so cuddly. You're so yummy. No, no, don't go yet." If you do that, I guarantee your child will pull away from you, but will feel great and full.

When I suggest this to people, they think that it sounds crazy and that the clingy or obnoxious behavior will increase, but it works, and it works fairly quickly. In fact, the behavior usually disappears within two weeks. It works because you're giving your child something he or she needs and hasn't been getting—or hasn't been getting enough of.

In one of the most extreme and ultimately rewarding situations I've encountered, I advised the parents of an eleven-year-old boy to go all the way back and redo their relationship from babyhood. What had happened was that Michael was a child of divorce. His father was the stable influence in his young life, but his mother had taken him and effectively disappeared from the time he was four or five until his father finally got him back and got custody when he was already eleven. By that time the father had remarried, and both he and his new wife were determined to do whatever they could to repair the damage that had been done while Michael was with his mother.

He was, understandably, incredibly anxious, throwing tantrums over the least little thing and, in general, exhibiting behavior one would expect to see in a much younger child. His father and stepmother were at their wits' end but refused to give up. That's when I got the idea that they would have to go back and redo all the years when he was away from them. At that point they were ready to do anything, no matter how crazy it seemed. They started to play peekaboo, read children's books, and effectively go through all the developmental stages at an incredibly accelerated rate. One of Michael's most annoying and negative behaviors had been to constantly sabotage the attachment any time it seemed to be going well. He would constantly get in their faces, wave things at them, and bug them, trying to show them how completely unlovable he was. The key was for them never to get angry and to initiate the behavior, so that when he was busy doing something they would say, "Oh, Mikey, come here, I want to give you a hug."

It took no more than two or three weeks until the bugging disappeared completely, and within a year he had done an almost total turnaround. I truly believe that in this case his brain was actually going back and making new neurological connections, but the point is that making those connections by giving your child what his or her brain craves will have a remarkable effect on behavior.

Another option if a child is really pinching or hurting you is to say as sweetly as possible, "You know, honey, I love you so much, and this is so much fun, but sometimes it's hard to tell the difference between hugging and hurting, and right now you're actually hurting me." If you say that instead of screeching, "STOP, you're hurting me!" (to which the child often responds by doing it more or doing it harder) and then reiterate what the consequence will be if he doesn't stop, the child will usually let go and soon enough the hurting behavior will disappear altogether.

Cure It with Cuddling

Whereas baby play is a technique for repairing frayed bonds, this is a strategy to use at the moment your child is upset or having a meltdown. Sometimes it seems as if kids just lose their way, spin out of control, and need you to help them get back on the right track. You can do that by hugging and holding your child. It may not feel like what you want to do, but sometimes she will just melt into your arms, cry, and then settle down. Hold her close to your chest in a warm embrace and say, "I think I know what the problem is. Your love tank is getting low. I'm going to fill it up, and when it's full, you won't feel like doing that anymore." This can work really well and have a lasting effect, but if she pulls away and wants no part of it, don't be upset and don't look hurt. Just tell her you'll try it later, and move on to a different technique.

Let Them Be Bad

Sometimes telling your child it's okay to be bad—within limits—is the best way to defuse a potentially explosive situation. Let's say your kids are in the middle of an argument and run to tell you about it. Try saying, "Okay, you guys, why don't you go for it and have a big argument, without hitting, and get it all out of your system. You've got fifteen minutes." Most of the time, they will just stand there and look at each other. Or, if your young child is heading for a tantrum because you told her she couldn't have ice cream, even though you've used the CALM technique, try saying, "You know what, sweetie? I've done all I can. Let's move some stuff so you don't get hurt and you just go ahead and have a big tantrum." Most often it won't happen. The child's audience will be gone and she will have been given permission to misbehave. If she is being oppositional, she will, therefore, most likely choose to do the opposite.

I remember one amusing incident when a mother called me, totally distraught because her little boy had rolled himself up in the hallway rug. "What can I do?" she wailed. "He's rolled up in the rug and he won't come out!" "Just leave him," I told her. "What could possibly happen if you're rolled up in a rug? It's not the end of the world." And of course, once she stopped reacting and providing an audience, he came out almost immediately.

Using this paradoxical technique can feel incredibly freeing because it takes away our fear of tantrums so that we are no longer walking on eggshells with our child. And the child experiences what it feels like to choose an entirely different behavior.

Empty the Adrenaline Tank

Adrenaline play is one of my favorite techniques. It is especially helpful for highly active children and children with ADHD. All of us have an internal battery that's always charged and ready to give us a boost in case we need to escape from a life-threatening emergency. If that energy isn't used up, for some kids it can spill over into everyday behavior.

Not every tantrum is about wanting something. Sometimes children use misbehavior as a way to regulate their emotions by releasing or discharging their excess energy. They have a huge fit and then walk away feeling relaxed and much better, while their parents are exhausted and bewildered.

When you see signs that a tantrum is building, you can use adrenaline play as a way to help your child release excess energy in a more positive way. It will take energy on your part, but it's a great way to connect and, in many cases, ward off a pending tantrum. Try wrestling, chasing, playing hide-and-seek, or having a sock-throwing war. Go outside and have a race. Or, if you don't participate directly, let the child set up an obstacle course in a safe place, and time him running the course.

Whatever activity you choose must have an element of excitement and a tiny bit of fear, which is why chasing or hide-and-seek is great. That thrill will give your child's brain what it needs and help him self-regulate. Tantrums won't disappear altogether, but you may find that they occur less frequently.

At this point, if you have a high-energy kid you are probably thinking, *That sounds great, but as soon as we start my child will get out of control and won't know how to stop.* To avoid this, frontload the rules and tell your child that if he is hurting anyone, won't listen, or won't stop when the game is over, there will be a consequence. A natural consequence—such as not being allowed to play again until later or the next day, or getting ejected from the game after three penalties and having to sit in the penalty box—is best. He may test you a few times, but that should work. If you have a high-energy kid, I recommend that you do this at least once a day, maybe twice, but definitely not too close to bedtime. Remember to stay neutral if your child blows it, and follow through with the penalties.

Use Distraction

Especially with younger children, distraction can be a very effective technique for changing behavior in the moment. Changing the subject, pointing out something interesting, or reminding them of something they like to talk about can take their mind off what they were doing. You just don't want to use this every time because, if you do, your child may experience it as invalidating what he is feeling.

Get Him with Laughter

Making a joke or making light of the situation can often be an effective way to shift a child's mood. Just be careful that your child doesn't think you're laughing at or making fun of him. Clearly, that would be more harmful than helpful, so if the child doesn't see the humor, know when to drop it, repair, and try another strategy.

Use Imaginary Play

Imaginary play is another wonderful strategy to use with young children. Let's say, for example, you have to brush your daughter's hair in the morning before she goes to school, and she will have nothing to do with it. Little girls with long hair can make hair-brushing seem like torture, crying and screaming, "You're hurting meeee! Stop it!" These daily fits can be so exhausting it may sometimes seem better just to leave their hair looking like a bird's nest. Most often, we resort to angry threats that we're going to take them to the hairdresser and have it cut short—which most of us don't really mean. What we need to do is stay neutral and use a good detangler along with imaginary play. You might, for example, ask your child to pretend she's a princess and you are a friendly ogre or a nice witch who has to brush her hair to undo a spell.

For bathing or tooth-brushing use Pokémon or superhero images to get your little boy to comply. Be sure to choose a theme that's fun and appealing for your child, and make it a game. Doing this will help change the behavior and create new habits so that, over time, you will no longer need to do it. In fact, you will be amazed how well this strategy can work, and it is also a nice way to connect.

If you can make a game of something you want your child to do, he or she will see it as fun rather than a task. So, for example, you might "bet" him that he can't get dressed before you do. Just be sure to emphasize the fun rather than the competition.

Say It and Walk Away

The "say it and walk away" strategy is a great one for children of all ages. This involves making an observation, pointing something out or making a request, telling your child you are going to give him time to think about it, and then, without appearing angry, walking away. It can work very well for young oppositional kids whose answer to everything is "No." For example, if you have asked your child to get dressed and she refuses, once you have used the CALM technique, try saying, "You know what? I'm going to get out of your way and let you think about this. I'm going to give you some time." Then walk away, not with a huffy attitude but remaining calm and matter-of-fact. Quite often, once you have removed yourself, and your child no longer feels cornered, she will comply.

Try Counting Down

Don't underestimate the power of counting. This is a wonderful technique that works very well. Tell your child she has to comply by the count of five, but, as always, mean what you say. Be prepared to follow through—and no counting to four and a half!

If One Thing Doesn't Work, Try Another

None of these strategies is going to work every time, and not every one will work for every parent or every child. That's why the more tools you have in your bag, the more likely you'll be to find the right ones for the job when you need them.

As you continue to mirror, contain, and dip into your tool bag, your child's behavior will begin to improve, but as you're caught up in the moment, you may not notice the changes. What you can expect to happen first is that the tantrums and meltdowns will occur less frequently. Next, the child will begin to recover from these episodes more quickly. And finally, the intensity of the meltdowns and tantrums will begin to decrease. The intensity is generally the last thing to change. Once you're aware of this continuum, it will be easier for you to see behavioral changes as they occur.

In the following chapters I'll be providing you with specific strategies to use on specific occasions and with children who are particularly challenging or challenged in various ways.

Part Three

Connecting and Containing in Special Situations

ELEVEN

Homework, Eating, Sleeping, Bathroom Issues, and More— Mirroring and Containing to Make Transitions Easier

Very often, when parents come to me for help it's because of a particular behavioral problem—usually having to do with eating issues, toilet training, sleeping, or transitional times like turning off the television or the computer, doing homework, or getting ready for bathtime. These problems can seem overwhelming, and parents want them resolved as quickly as possible. Nevertheless, it is always my recommendation that before addressing the issue that brought them to me, they first master and practice mirroring techniques with their child for several weeks.

Sometimes this is difficult for parents to hear; they think that this would be ignoring the problem. But it isn't; you are actually working toward fixing the problem by helping your child organize and build resilience. Mirroring is actually the foundation of everything that follows. And without a strong foundation, everything you do afterward is less likely to last.

Mirroring, as we've already discussed, organizes the brain, lowers anxiety, and helps children to regulate their emotions. And because many of the special problems children most often exhibit are related to anxiety or self-regulation, the mirroring work almost always makes the "big issue" easier to correct in the long run. But even more miraculously, many parents find that after they've been mirroring for a period of time, their child will come to them and say, "I think I'm ready now," to do whatever it is they and their child have been struggling with for so long.

Moving from one activity to the next is particularly difficult for children because they don't have the same sense of time we do. We spend most of our time thinking about time—how much we have or don't have to do everything we need to get done. But most children don't think ahead, so a young child is not going to say to herself, *I really need to get in the shower now because the TV show I want to watch comes on at seven and I need to get my homework done before then or Mom's not going to let me watch it*. Rather, she's going to think, *I'll just watch this show now and I'll do my homework later*. She believes that some perfect, magical homework moment will present itself; except that, of course, it never does. Her present self needs to have a little fun, and she tends not to think about the fact that her "fun" is just going to make trouble for her future self.

Ordering oneself in time and space is a higher level of thinking than most kids are capable of, so we have to help them get through those transitions.

Cure Homework Headaches

Doing (or not doing) homework is one issue related to time management that constantly causes problems for parents and their children. The homework meltdown is a common event in many homes, complete with tears, power struggles, and yelling that can last well into the evening, just when family members should be reconnecting and enjoying one another, and can carry over in the form of hurt feelings, shame, and frustration. As an unintended result, your child may then begin to associate learning with stress.

The most common scenario goes something like this:

MOM: Joey, it's time to do your homework.

JOEY: Just a minute. I'll do it in a minute. I just need to finish this.

MOM: Honey, you say the same thing every night. You always say just a minute and it's never just a minute. I'm telling you that you need to do your homework *right now*.

JOEY, ESCALATING TO: I *hate* homework. I don't *want* to do it. It's too hard; it's *dumb*. My teacher's *mean*.

And how does Mom respond? Usually by saying something like: "Your teacher's very nice, and I had to do homework when I was in school. Homework is a good thing. It helps you practice what you learned in school during the day. And anyway, you have to do it. Everyone has to do it. Putting it off is not going to solve anything," and so on.

At this point Joey, who believes his message has not been properly received, will escalate his behavior in an attempt to make the urgency of his situation understood: "You don't care about me! I *said it's too hard! I'm not doing it.*"

And Mom will think: *Oh my God, he's not going to do well in school. How is he going to get ahead in life if he can't stick to anything?*

That contretemps is most likely to end with an escalation or a homework meltdown and Mom's taking away some privilege or else sitting next to Joey and holding his hand as he does the assignment

that probably could have been completed in fifteen or twenty minutes but has now taken at least an hour or two of aggravation for
both of them.

How could Joey's mom have avoided that? At the point where
Joey first said, "I hate homework," she might have mirrored by
responding, "I know, there are at least a million things you'd rather
be doing than homework. You want to play your video games and
text your friends and watch television. You do work all day at school
and you don't feel like doing it at night too." At which point Joey
would probably be nodding and saying, "Yeah, that's right." She may
have had to make three or four statements like that before saying,
"I can definitely see why you wouldn't want to do your homework,
but here's the problem . . . and *then* bring in guidance and teaching
by explaining why she is insisting that he do his homework. Joey
most likely still won't be thrilled to memorize spelling words or
whatever he's supposed to do, but chances are, he will comply. And
after going through the same routine a few times, he will probably
realize that he still winds up having to do his homework, and that
it really isn't so bad. He might even gain enough insight to figure
out that the sooner he gets it done, the more time he'll have to do
what *he* wants.

For anxious children, as well as those who have learning disabilities or ADHD, homework is just another time of the day where
they may feel incompetent. But homework does not have to end in
tears and fighting. It is possible to find balance and manage negative
homework behavior. It is possible to work toward establishing homework time as a positive learning experience.

Homework Tips for Parents
  • Stick to the school's guidelines on how long children
    should spend on homework; do no more than that

(unless your child is happy and motivated to continue).

- If very little gets done, write a note to the teacher stating that homework time did not go well and that this was all that was accomplished.
- Never get in a fight with your child about homework; no one wins.
- Organize a homework buddy—an older child in the neighborhood who can help your child at homework time.
- Empathize with your child about how he is feeling before lecturing him on why homework is important.
- Stay neutral; sometimes kids argue with you as a way to avoid doing the work. If you are eager to oblige with an argument you become part of the avoidance pattern.
- Be careful about imposing negative consequences for not doing homework. If you do impose them, keep them immediate and stick to what you say, for instance, no TV that same evening.
- Try to use positive rewards for good choices and good work habits. A fun activity you can do together can help create good habits and change negative patterns.
- Support the teacher—try not to voice your opinions about there being too much homework. It is important that your child see you supporting the school.
- If homework battles are damaging the attachment bond, arrange for the other parent to be in charge of homework. If that is not possible, arrange with the teacher to temporarily stop homework until the bond is strengthened and can withstand the tension homework puts on it.

Create a Window of Time
to Help Your Child Manage Transitions

Because, as I've said, children often have a hard time moving from one activity to the next, it's helpful to them (and will create more peace for you) if you can give them a series of time frames or windows of time in which to complete what they're doing and move on to what you need or want them to do.

One situation that gives many parents—and kids—a hard time is getting the child to turn off the computer and come to dinner. Here's a typical scenario:

> DAD, WALKING INTO THE CHILD'S ROOM: Noah, dinner
> is ready. You need to stop playing that video game.
> NOAH: Yeah, okay, just a minute. I have to beat this level.
> DAD: You always say that. You always say you need to beat this
> level. That's going to take at least another ten minutes and
> you need to get off now and come to dinner.

By now Dad is starting to get annoyed, thinking, *Every single time I ask you to do something it's just a minute. Why can't you ever just come when I ask you to? I've had a tough day and I don't need this struggle to top it all off.*

> NOAH, SOUNDING RUDER: I said just a sec! *Jeez!*
> DAD: Don't you speak to me that way. Just get off the computer
> or you'll lose it for a week!

The outcome of this encounter is likely to be either that Noah will lose his computer privileges and throw a full-fledged tantrum or that his dad will walk away in disgust, thus demonstrating that he really didn't mean what he said in the first place.

To Noah that video game is incredibly important. In the context of his life, it's one of the most important things he needs to do, and he's right in the middle of accomplishing something he's spent a long time trying to achieve. To help you understand his sense of urgency, imagine that you're right on the brink of a discovery that you know is going to change your life forever. It's going to get you to a whole new level in your job. You know the answer is just within reach when someone walks into your office and says, "Come on, it's time to go to lunch." You'd probably respond exactly the way Noah did: "Wait just a minute. I'm in the middle of something. I'll be right there." And if he continued to badger you, saying things like, "Come on, you're always working," you might just say, *"I said I can't!"* You don't actually mean to be rude; you just want the intruder to go away and leave you alone so that you can finish what you're doing. What you need to realize is that, for Noah, beating the level on his video game is as important as the problem you're just on the brink of solving. It may not seem that way to you, but for him it's a really big deal.

Once you understand how Noah thinks, you can accommodate for it and save everyone a case of indigestion. Before I go any further, however, I want to acknowledge that I know what many of you are thinking: *You've got to be joking. I'm going to go through all this just to get him to come to dinner? Forget it.* But remember, if this is a problem for you, whatever you have been doing has not been working, and the repeated battle night after night is actually a lot more work than what I am about to suggest. Also, remember that this strategy does not create the same wear and tear on your relationship and that over time the mirroring you are doing will have a positive and protective impact on your child. Can you say the same for the way you've been dealing with the behavior up to now?

So what you want to do is this: first of all, don't wait until dinner is ready. Many computer games are designed so that if you don't complete a particular level of difficulty before turning it off, you'll have to go back to the previous level when you return to the game. It's a design element that keeps kids hooked and is certain to drive parents crazy. That said, you need to help your child manage the transition by opening a window of opportunity for him to finish what he's doing. Begin the process fifteen minutes before dinner will be served and start by mirroring. When you enter the room, sit beside your child and comment on what a high level he's at or make a statement about how hard it looks. Remember that you need to make two or three mirroring statements without bringing up your own agenda. Then you can present the problem by saying something like, "Noah, I know how important that game is to you and how long you've been trying to get to the next level, but here's the problem. Dinner's going to be ready in fifteen minutes. The window is opening. You have fifteen minutes from now to get yourself to a place in the game where you can turn the computer off. If you can't turn it off in time, that tells me you can't be on the computer so close to dinner, and from now on you can only be on it for [whatever amount of time you decide] after dinner." By doing that, you're frontloading. You're making a contract with your child, and you're also letting him know that if he doesn't turn the computer off by the time the window closes, there will be a consequence. He'll have to "pay back" that fifteen-minute window by losing fifteen minutes at the computer (or some other activity) later. Still, don't count on his compliance. Go back into the room, and if he is still not off five minutes before the window closes, you can say, "So, Noah, how are you doing? Are you getting closer?" Almost invariably, Noah will say, "Oh, yeah, yeah, I just have to do this one thing." Now you can sit down next to him (if there's room) or look over his shoulder and say something like,

"Huh, I didn't know you were at that level. I can see why it's so hard for you to complete it." Your child will love the attention. And then you need to say, "But Noah, here's the problem. The window is really closing, and if you can't find a way to complete what you're doing, you'll just have to turn it off and lose some of your work." At this point he'll probably comply, but if he doesn't, you'll just need to turn it off yourself and deal with the tantrum, if there is one. (For tantrum protocol, see page 50.)

As an aside here, parents often ask me how much time they should allow their children on the computer, and my answer to that—as with most things—is, it depends. Every child is different, and some children are still only when they're watching television or on the computer, so this might be a good way to get them to slow down and for you to get a much-needed break. Also, for kids who struggle socially, the computer is a way for them to have some sense of a social life, particularly when they're playing a game live online and talking to other children. It's a way for them to feel less lonely and to understand that there are other kids out there who actually enjoy their company. I mean all this in moderation, of course. You don't want them to escape into the virtual world and avoid real friendships, but these experiences can have a positive impact when managed appropriately.

This is probably also a good place to mention that if children are on the periphery socially, watching limited amounts of television can also play a positive role in their lives. Like it or not, television is a part of our popular culture, and I believe kids should have some knowledge of what their peers are talking about when they discuss what happened on the last episode of a favorite program. To deprive them of that entirely can set them apart from their peers. For some children this is no big deal, but for others, particularly if they already have difficulty making friends or interacting with other kids at school, this would just be putting another obstacle in their path. Television can give them a context to join in conversations or on which to base schoolyard games of "pretend."

Finally, some children are better at self-monitoring than others, so you don't really need to interfere. But if they're using the computer or television to avoid other activities or interactions with the family, you might need to limit their time. Look for markers and use your gut to determine how important that computer or TV time is for your child. Then, you can even use it as a negotiating tool if necessary.

When you do have to impose a consequence, such as taking the computer away or not allowing television, doing it in the heat of the moment will only provoke escalation. Instead, if your child won't get off the computer or turn off the TV when you ask, tell him he's making a choice to have a bigger consequence and then walk away. You can also password-protect your computer and newer television sets to help you enforce screen time. If you threaten with yet another consequence, your child will perceive it as unfair, and it will very likely backfire. Your child will think you're mean, and in addition, if you've already taken everything away, you'll have lost your leverage and he may decide there's no point in trying, because he has nothing to gain and nothing more to lose. Later, when your child is doing something else and you've had a chance to calm down, take away the mouse or unhook the cable. Just remember to stay neutral and calm, mirror, and remind him it was a choice that he made.

If, for example, your child loses his computer privileges for the evening because he did not get off when you asked him to, you can first use the CALM technique and then say, "It's awful to lose the computer. I know how much it means to you, but you knew what the consequence would be if you chose not to listen." When your child responds with something like, "You're so mean, this isn't fair!" you can mirror again: "No one likes to be told they can't do something, but why are you so mad at me? If you had gotten off when you needed to, you would have your computer time tonight." Using this technique helps you stay neutral and it helps your child see the link between cause and effect.

Create Windows to Make Mornings Easier

You can use the "window" tactic for virtually any situation that requires a child to be ready to do something at a particular time. Another typical situation would be getting up and getting ready to go to school. If you've been waking your children at 7:30 when they need to be out of the house by 8:30, you're just setting yourself up for some crazy mornings. Kids need at least an hour and a half to get themselves up and out in the morning. So, if you're giving yourself that extra half hour of sleep, you're no doubt paying for it in spades.

If you are routinely getting up and yelling at your children to get out of bed, then nagging them to hurry up and screaming at them to get in the car, both you and the kids are already stressed before the day begins. Particularly for angry or anxious kids, this means that by the time they get to school they'll be ready to chop off the head of the first person who bumps into them or else run for the hills.

My suggestion is that you try this instead. Tell your kids the night before that things will be a little different in the morning but that this new routine should help everyone get out of the house feeling better and in a happier mood. Then, explain the morning window plan, which should look something like this:

An hour and a half before you need to leave the house, wake the kids and tell them that they have a twenty-minute window to do whatever they want—go back to sleep, play with a toy, watch TV, get on the computer, or whatever you allow in the morning. It's their personal time and you won't be bugging them about it. That also gives you time to sit down, have your coffee, and pull yourself together. Then, five minutes before the window is closing, give them fair warning that the personal-time window will be closing in five minutes and then it will be time to move on. In the next fifteen-minute window they need to wash up, brush their teeth, and get dressed. The third fifteen-minute window is for eating breakfast, and the final fifteen minutes are for gathering themselves and their stuff and getting out the door. One of the greatest myths is that you can say, "C'mon, kids, get in the car," and they'll just grab their lunch box and follow you out the door. It doesn't happen, as you've probably already realized. But if you've left a window of time for them to find their homework, realize that they've forgotten their band instrument, or need to change their socks, you'll be calm instead of stressed, and you won't be freaking out—and neither will they. Instead, you will all be relaxed and calm, knowing that you have built in time for them to dawdle, run upstairs to look for things they have forgotten, or have a fit because their socks don't feel right in their shoes. Creating these windows is a way for you to pull back and allow your kids to make more choices about how they use their time. Kids love that. And if they don't get done what they need to get done before a window closes, there is a consequence to pay: they owe you that time back however you choose to collect it. Again, you don't yell, you stay neutral, but you let them know that they'll have fifteen minutes less TV time that evening or they'll have to do a fifteen-minute chore, or—my favorite because it's really effective—they'll have to go to bed fifteen minutes earlier that night. If you don't stay neutral, if you scream, your child will learn how to push your buttons and will figure that if he's going to lose fifteen minutes he might as well take you down with him. And don't think that just because you don't seem really angry and your child doesn't appear to be upset, he's not learning anything. Some kids will do anything to save face; they'll never let you see that they're upset, but you'll notice a change in their behavior the next time the situation arises.

When it comes to transitions (and just about everything else), each child is different. Some are organized, self-directed, and transition very well, while others live in their own world and will walk around with one pant leg dragging behind until you put their other leg in. Some transitions, however, are developmental milestones that you and your children will face with more or less difficulty, get through, and hopefully put behind you forever. Among the most common—and potentially most contentious—of these are issues surrounding eating, bedtime, and the bathroom.

Eating, Sleeping, and Bathroom Issues

Issues around eating and sleeping, and bathroom "accidents," while common, can be frustrating and worrisome to parents. All three of these issues are very delicate and have a strong emotional component that must be handled carefully to avoid making the problem worse or having your child associate it with anger, stress, conflict, or shame. With all three of these problems, paying attention to the tension on the rope, nurturing the connection, and mirroring all the time about unrelated issues is critical. Once your child feels stronger and more resilient, and when some of the emotional noise has been cleared away, the problem very often resolves itself. I'll discuss each issue in detail in the pages that follow.

Take the Fight out of Food

As with toilet training, parents bring their own agendas and fears about eating to the table. For some people, food simply doesn't figure prominently in the family dynamic. For others, finishing what's on your plate may be equated with love or showing appreciation. There may be strong ties to food and eating that relate to your family's ethnic background or your own family traditions. The way you were raised to think about food will certainly figure in to the way you relate to your child around issues of eating.

When it comes to food, parents generally seem to have two kinds of concerns: those that relate to what, how much, and when the child eats, and those that have to do with "table manners."

Nutritional issues and caloric intake can be highly charged if you, as a parent, have strong likes and dislikes with relation to certain foods or if you are weight conscious and extremely rigid about what you will and will not allow yourself to eat. Whether you tend to tell your child she isn't hungry (or "can't be" hungry) when she says she is or, conversely, keep urging her to eat because you're afraid she isn't getting the proper nutrients, you may inadvertently be teaching her that she can't determine for herself what her body is telling her. Beyond that, however, making some foods "good" and others "bad," or some foods allowed and others off-limits, is almost guaranteed to create a desire for what the child can't have. Ever since the Garden of Eden it's been human nature to value and desire the forbidden fruit.

I appreciate, of course, the growing problem of childhood obesity, and I fully understand the role parents play in educating their children about making healthy choices. There are, however, better or worse ways to do that—ways that are more or less likely to work. Again, mirroring about things that have nothing to do with food will address any emotional issues layered on top of eating and food choices, which can help make your child more confident about all his choices, including his ability to know when he's hungry and when he's full, and will address whatever emotional issues he might have relating to food.

While I do not in any way mean to suggest that mirroring alone will lead to healthy eating patterns, I do want to reiterate that a strong, loving, and reliable bond is the best foundation any parent can give any child. Any parent who has specific concerns should, of course, discuss them with his or her pediatrician and/or a nutritionist. That said, however, you can also use mirroring and containment to help children accept reasonable behaviors and choices with relation to food. So a dialogue might go something like, "That cupcake looks really delicious and you want to eat it right now. The icing is so chocolaty and the sprinkles are really yummy. It would be great if it were as healthy for you as a salad, but here's the problem. If all you ate were cupcakes you wouldn't be getting enough healthy food, and you need to be strong enough to play on the swings the way you want to. You need a lot of energy to do all the fun things you like. So you need to eat your sandwich [or chicken or whatever it is] first, and then you can have dessert."

What you really don't want to do is to make the table a battleground, which is a sure way to create unpleasant, negative emotions and interactions relating to food. Sometimes the battle is about getting your child to eat more—as in the classic, "just three more bites and then you can leave the table." And sometimes it has nothing to do with the food itself but everything to do with how the child behaves at the table. The struggles can begin as early as when your child is learning to feed himself and you think he should be using his spoon instead of his fingers. Maybe your friend's toddler is an incredibly neat eater who manages to spoon up her macaroni and get it to her mouth without spilling a drop, while your child finishes mealtime with more food on her face than in her mouth. Again, we're dealing with developmental differences and the fact that some children are more coordinated than others. Don't worry—she won't be picking up her peas with her fingers when she's on her first date. Children do learn to use utensils. Staying neutral, not overreacting, is especially important in the case of eating. Otherwise, children may try to control you through their behavior regarding food. Whether their eating pleases or displeases you, you must remain calm and neutral.

Whether it's about eating more or less, using a napkin, not staying seated at the table, or simply how long he has to sit there, getting into a power struggle with your child about food is going to be counterproductive. Mealtimes should be warm, comfortable, and positive times for families to talk and bond; you should work toward making sure the meal table is not associated with negativity. That doesn't mean, of course, that an argument at the table from time to time is going to leave your child permanently damaged. What we're talking about throughout this book are goals to strive for, but you need to remember that everything in life is about balance.

Finally, people often ask me how I feel about using treats or desserts as rewards. There is no simple answer to this question. Most of us at some point will use food as a reward, and if we don't someone else will. Teachers, babysitters, and other parents will offer a Popsicle for good behavior or a job well done and will bring in treats for a class party. It really can't be avoided. All I can say is, if you do use food as a reward, you need to be aware of the potential pitfalls. But the more comfortable and joyful childhood is, the less need there will be for any child to "fill an emotional hole" with food.

On an entirely different note, some children react behaviorally to hunger, becoming weepy, aggressive, or impatient. I have noticed in my practice that this tends to be especially true for highly sensitive children, children with ADHD or sensory-integration issues, and gifted kids who often do not recognize their own hunger and may have a meltdown or tantrum themselves into a vortex. If your child is like this, make sure you are one of those parents who always has snacks in your purse, car, or backpack. These kids should eat every hour and a half to two hours. They will tell you they are not hungry, and, in fact, they may not feel hungry at all. But you need to stick to what I call the "three-bite rule." They need to have three bites; then they are done. In most cases, the child's mood will lift after just this little bit of food and he will be a new person. Help your child to make the connection so that he becomes better able to recognize when he is hungry.

Take the Battle out of Bedtime

As we've discussed, dealing with any kind of transition has to do with awareness and self-regulation, and getting to sleep is all about being able to calm and settle oneself. There's a fairly substantial body of scientific data that indicates that a large percentage of adults have a problem with that, but we seem to believe that children shouldn't have the same problems we do. As parents, part of our difficulty dealing with children and sleep may be that—as with toilet training—there are so many conflicting theories on the subject. Never let your child sleep in your bed; never put your child to bed in a room by himself; let your child fall asleep on your chest and eventually she'll learn to sleep on her own. Let them cry it out; never let them cry it out. I have no doubt that many of these theories work well for some children and not for others. People are unique, and children are people, so, as with other issues you may be struggling with, you need to keep in mind that this one too will resolve itself. What works with one child may backfire completely with another.

For parents who just want to get a good night's sleep, however, bedtime can become a very challenging and upsetting time when it should be just the opposite. So, again, we need to check our own agenda and determine whether our anxiety is being telegraphed to our kids. If we get angry and turn bedtime into a fight, that emotional stress can complicate other sleep issues. Following the CALM technique and staying neutral will have a positive and lasting effect.

It's important that children get enough sleep. Little children need at least eleven hours; kids who are ten, eleven, and twelve need at least ten hours, which is why I believe that having a designated "bedtime" is important. Children grow when they sleep, the brain does a lot of connecting during sleep, and children who have enough sleep are better able to regulate their emotions. In fact, many behavioral issues, including increased anxiety and irritability, can be related to lack of sleep.

Some clients have told me that their child just "isn't tired" when it's his bedtime, that he's jumping around and completely "wired." But waiting for your child to appear tired can be a mistake. Kids who are bouncing off the walls and jumping up and down on the sofa are, more often than not, very tired, although their tiredness manifests as wild behavior and tremendous energy. Because their tiredness generally doesn't look like what we think it should, it's all the more important that they have a specific bedtime. If your child is acting out or refusing to go to bed, you need to apply all the mirroring and limit-setting techniques you have at your disposal. In many cases, people notice an improvement—sometimes a significant improvement—in behavior after just a few days of a child's having longer and better sleeps.

Parents often claim that, what with homework and after-school programs, it's impossible for them to get their children to bed as early as they would like. Or, they say, the bedtime routine takes so long that it always winds up being later than they thought. I know that we're all overscheduled (and that includes our kids), but if your child can't get to bed on time because he has so many activities, you probably need to cut back somewhere—and I don't mean on the number of hours he sleeps. Or, if getting ready for bed *always* takes longer than you thought, you might want to revise your schedule and start a bit earlier.

If bedtime in your household is always bedlam, it may be caused by anxiety or it may be a way for your child to exert her control because she knows how much you want her to comply. Many times, it's a combination of many things. In all cases, however, having a routine is important, and it should be more or less the same every night, especially in the beginning. Therefore, you need to find one that you know you can stick to and that feels right for you. If necessary, you can make adjustments along the way. Generally speaking, your routine will probably involve bathing, brushing teeth, some snuggle time, and a bedtime story, but, of course, there will also be exceptions. (Remember the yellow-light issues we discussed in Chapter Eight.) Sometimes you just need to be flexible—which is not a bad way to teach your children that they, too, can be flexible—or else you'll find that your entire life revolves around your children's bedtime.

Some children are more adaptable than others; some don't require as much of a routine. You know your child, which makes you the best judge of what will or won't work for him. And if you have more than one child, you may find, as I did with mine, that what works for one absolutely won't work for another. Some children can stay up later on weekends because they'll sleep later in the morning; others get up at the same time no matter when they went to bed and are, therefore, better off going to bed at the same time every night.

If bedtime in your house is a battle or your child has trouble getting to sleep, it's probably because children's anxiety levels tend to rise at this time, just as our own levels of patience and flexibility go down. Going to bed means being alone and being in the dark (and by the way, there is nothing wrong with using a night-light or leaving a hall light on if that makes the child more comfortable); it may bring up fears of "monsters under the bed," which are very normal, or, depending on what the child's been exposed to by the media, fear of burglars or kidnapping. Children have fears that are very real to them and we, as adults, need to appreciate that. So again—and I can't say this often enough—mirroring in the daytime about things that have nothing to do with sleep is one of the best things you can do to make your child less anxious and more resilient in general. But do remember that it will take a while for this to take effect. Just because you mirrored well one day doesn't mean your child will go to bed without making a fuss.

When it's getting close to "that time," you can also help get your child's brain ready for sleep by simply turning down the volume. Start way before bedtime. Try turning off or lowering the volume on the television. Dim the lights, and speak more softly. Get in your pajamas yourself. Give your child all kinds of messages that it is time to prepare for sleep. *Don't* decide to start tickling or roughhousing with your kid on the sofa—you'll be the one getting beaten up when you try to calm him down again. This is a time for doing quiet, cuddly things, the more loving and peaceful the better.

"Thumbs-up" and "Three Wishes" Sleep Techniques

For children who are really anxious about going to sleep, there are a couple of techniques that really do seem to work. One is what I call Thumbs-up. Start by telling your child that you'll be checking on him frequently. He won't have to worry because you'll be watching out for him and giving him a thumbs-up, and he can give you one back. Then you have to prove it by keeping your word. The key is to do it *very often,* by which I mean *every few seconds,* at least in the beginning, so that just as your child is beginning to worry that you won't come back, there you are. You need to get there in time to preempt his anxiety. Show him you are on duty. At least for the first night you won't be having much fun, because you'll be doing nothing but checking for a while, so be prepared. You won't be doing any talking, just giving him a thumbs-up, but you need to make sure you're at the door before he can ask for you. On the second night, you'll be doing the same thing but you'll probably find that after the first five or ten minutes your child will have fallen asleep. Then, by the third or fourth night, you'll be checking less frequently and for a shorter period of time. After a while, you may not need to do it at all except, perhaps, if your child has had a particularly difficult day, in which case you may need to ramp the checking back up for a while.

What you're really doing here is a kind of mirroring. You're letting your child know that you got his message and you take it seriously. So long as you remain calm, he'll know that you're in charge. You've got his back, you're watching out for him, and because you're on the case, his brain can relax and get on with the business of falling asleep. And because he will be more relaxed, he will often have a deeper, more restful sleep with fewer wake-ups.

Another version of this would be to call out frequently and ask your child if she is okay before she has a chance to call out to you. But I want to emphasize here that this technique is only for anxious children who are having difficulty staying in bed; it is not for all kids, especially not those who are fine once you've kissed them on the head.

Many children who are anxious about going to bed simply try to put off the inevitable. These are the kids who are always thirsty, or itchy, or too hot, or too cold, or who need to go to the bathroom—again. My "cure" for these problems is to give the child Three Wishes, which is a form of frontloading. First of all, you, the parent, need to think of as many possibilities as you can and build them into the bedtime routine; that way your child will have fewer things to call you back for "forgetting" once you've left the room. Then tell him that once he's in bed, he'll have three (realistic) wishes, but no more. So he'll have a chance to complain that the closet door isn't shut all the way or that he's not tucked in tightly enough—you'll be giving him a bit of leeway but only so much. The process of getting him to bed may take longer, but there will be less struggle and you'll be putting your energies into creating some peace for yourself instead of fighting with your child.

If she continues asking for things and coming out of bed, use the CALM technique, then take her by the hand and walk her back to bed, saying, "I love you. You've had your wishes. Now it's bedtime." Stay neutral, decide you will most likely spend a while doing this, and commit to it.

Stick with this and, after the first couple of times, don't speak at all, just walk the child back to bed, and keep doing it until she stays there. This will take enormous patience—and if you have a gladiator child she will probably try everything from throwing a tantrum to hanging on to the wall—but if you stick with it and stay neutral, it will pay off. By dropping your own agenda (to get your child to bed as quickly and painlessly as possible) for the moment, you'll be doing something that will, in the end, get you what you want, and sooner rather than later.

For extremely anxious children, who are often older children who have developed a real fear of bedtime, you can start by saying good night and just sitting quietly on the end of their bed. Then, after a night or two, move to a chair. A couple of nights later, move to the doorway, then to the hall. Next, stay upstairs, and finally go downstairs. It takes patience, but, again, it can help frightened kids learn that sleep is something they can master. Once they've learned to do it on their own, they will feel very good about themselves after achieving this. Just remember to mirror a great deal during the day about unrelated issues, and don't go over the top with your praise, because this may cause them to panic and actually regress.

It is always challenging for parents to sort out how much of a child's behavior has to do with being defiant or controlling and how much has to do with real panic. This is true not only for sleep issues, but also for any circumstance in which a child uses avoidance as a coping strategy. The truth is that sometimes you just can't tell, but by staying neutral, sending the child messages of competence, and sticking to what you have said, you are letting him know that you believe in him and that his fear does not define him. In the end, whatever the cause, he will learn to control his behavior and will feel proud of himself.

In the following chapter we'll be talking more about specific techniques for dealing with generalized and extreme anxiety.

Take the Anxiety out of Bathroom Accidents

Many parents agonize when their children continue to have "accidents" well past the time when the parents believe that they should be done with that sort of thing. In some cases there may be an underlying physical condition that is contributing to the problem, and I always tell worried parents that the first thing they should do is have their child examined by a pediatrician. Encopresis, for example, or involuntary fecal soiling, occurs when children are constipated or voluntarily or involuntarily hold on to their stool; they may become not only miserably uncomfortable but also chronically constipated, and may no longer even feel the urge to go to the bathroom or be aware when they are soiling themselves. In addition, virtually any personality trait a child has—such as anxiety or holding on to emotions—can be expressed in terms of bathroom issues. Having bathroom "accidents" can be a way for a child to exert some kind of negative control by communicating through his behavior (even though he may not be aware of it), "I'm not going to do this, and you can't make me," or to hold on to the perceived safety of being a baby.

One of the most effective ways you as a parent have for dealing with this problem is to mirror about things—both positive and negative—that have nothing to do with bathroom issues and stay as neutral as you possibly can about "accidents." Your mirroring will help your child to organize himself (which you need to do in order to recognize the signals your body is sending so that you get to the bathroom in time), and will help him to feel safer and more comfortable about doing or learning something new. Most often children—and particularly boys—may just be so busy doing other things (like playing) that they ignore the messages their body is sending to their brain until it's too late.

The problem is that most parents become so frustrated and frantic that they begin to say things like, "No one's going to want to play with you," or "You will smell terrible and no one will want to be around you," or "If you keep on having accidents they're going to kick you out of school." (That last one, incidentally, may be just the excuse the child is looking for if she doesn't *want* to go to school in the first place.) They begin to talk too much and to use shame as a motivation. The latter can lead to emotional problems that confuse the messages the child's body is sending. What you really need to do when you realize your child has soiled himself is just to say in a very neutral way, "Come on, let's get you changed."

Neutrality isn't the same as indifference. You don't want to make the child think that you don't care if she continues pooping in her pants, but neither do you want her to feel ashamed and mortified. What you want to do is to keep both your tone of voice and your facial expression as neutral as you can and to stop yourself from talking too much.

The story of one family I worked with is fairly typical. Their five-and-a-half-year-old son, Willie, was still having accidents, wetting his pants and occasionally pooping. He was just so involved in his play, in what he was doing, so off in his own head, that he completely tuned out the signals his body was sending, as well as the feeling and the smell. Some children are more attuned to sensory input like feeling and smell, while others, like Willie, just dissociate and ignore it. For them the bottom line is, If it isn't bothering me, why should it bother you? In any case, before they came to see me, Willie's family had tried just about everything from rewarding him with a sticker when he went on the toilet to taking something away when he had an accident. They tried lecturing and they tried pleading. Altogether they were working much too hard on this problem, making it such an intense emotional issue that Willie had figured out it was a great way to upset them, to get their attention, and to wield some control. In fact, it had gotten to the point where their anxiety had actually become part of the problem.

I told them that for the present they were to put bathroom issues on the back burner and just ignore his accidents. When he had an accident, they were to remain totally neutral and clean him up without talking to him about it. At the same time, they were to go on a program of intensive soft parenting, baby play, and mirroring about everything *but* the bathroom. They were also to set reasonable limits on his behavior in general because that's all part of feeling safe, but again, they were to ignore anything that had to do with bathroom accidents. That's all there was to it, and within a few weeks the problem was resolved. It was over.

Not so typical and especially traumatic for parents is when a much older child continues to have "accidents." One such child, whose parents came to me, was already eleven and still soiling his pants. Mark was an extremely bright and sensitive child, who was also rigid and inflexible and who tended to have a tantrum anytime something unexpected was thrown his way. His parents were both accountants and basically left-brain thinkers. They were very open and admitted that the concept of mirroring didn't come easily to them, but they were desperate and willing to learn. They approached the problem in a very systematic, almost mathematical way, but in the end they did an absolutely wonderful job. After about four or five months of mirroring about everything *but* the bathroom issue and, whenever he had an accident, remaining absolutely neutral and simply saying, "Okay, now you need to go and change," he went from having an accident several times a week to once a month, then every couple of months, and, within six months the problem was gone completely. Mark is probably the oldest child I've treated with this problem, but I've seen it resolved in the same way with many others who are beyond what we generally consider the toilet-training years.

Increasing Self-Regulation Is Always the Key

Whether you're dealing with everyday transitions or developmental milestones, the key to helping your child get through these charged moments as peacefully and pleasantly as possible is to make the mirroring connections in conjunction with necessary corrections. The two always go hand in hand. If you did nothing but mirror and connect, your child would never acquire the behavioral or social skills she needs to succeed in life. If all you did was correct, you'd be compromising those all-important connections that allow the brain to self-regulate and create emotional stability.

TWELVE

Strategies for Mirroring and Connecting with the Anxious or Special-Needs Child

I've worked with the parents of many children who have been diagnosed with various disorders or problems, and I want to acknowledge that I am always impressed by how incredibly well educated and proactive they are. I've learned a lot from them, and I hope that if you are a parent of a special-needs child the techniques in this book add to and enhance the knowledge you have already acquired.

For parents whose child has just been diagnosed, sifting through all the information out there and trying to make sense of it can be overwhelming. At the same time, realizing your child will have extra struggles in life can be frightening and deeply upsetting. We all want our kids to enjoy life and be successful, and it is hard to watch someone we love so much have to work extra hard at that. It is also very difficult, and can be embarrassing, when your child has behavioral problems, to be looked upon as the parent of "that kid," the one other parents talk about and don't want their children to play with.

Compounding all these difficulties, when a child has a disability or a problem that affects behavior, the bond between parent and child may be stressed because the parent becomes frustrated, and what happens then is that the child, in turn, becomes more anxious. The issues may be the same as those that parents experience with so-called "normal" children, but they are likely to be intensified, ramped up to a higher level.

What many if not all children who have ADHD (attention-deficit/hyperactive disorder), ODD (oppositional defiant disorder), OCD (obsessive-compulsive disorder), Asperger's disorder, nonverbal learning disabilities, or anxiety disorders, as well as those who are gifted, have in common is that they are generally more anxious than most. Just think about it. If you're a child with ADHD you're paying attention to everything. If you have ODD or OCD your brain is giving you signals that just don't make sense to anyone else. Gifted children see the world from a different perspective from others. All these kids are constantly receiving invalidating messages from the world and the people around them. For kids with Asperger's disorder or nonverbal learning disabilities, the problem is somewhat different because they don't always understand the messages they're receiving. In all cases, however, whether it's their not understanding or not being understood, the result is increased levels of anxiety that can manifest in many different ways, including heightened sensitivity to sensory input like tastes and textures. (You'll often find these children gagging or itching or being annoyed by the label in the neck of their shirt and, consequently, having meltdowns.)

Many anxious children also tend to give up quickly and to have poor self-help skills. They may not know they are hungry, let alone how to make a sandwich. And, as adults, we may aid and abet this tendency by doing too much and expecting too little. At times it really is easier to make the sandwich than to watch them struggle and then deal with the plates, cutlery, and mess all over the kitchen. But if we continue to do this, how will they learn? They will rely more and more on us, and as they get older they will expect more service. They will become ungrateful and we will become resentful.

Children have to make mistakes, and we have to be prepared to let them. If things like spatial awareness, sequencing, and planning are challenging for your child, their struggles will be painful to watch at times. Let them do things; give them some chores. Let them make mistakes and let them learn. Help and guide them, but don't criticize or hover. By letting them do things for themselves you are also giving them skills for life, confidence, and a strong message of competence.

Although what I'm offering in this chapter and throughout this book is certainly not a panacea, connected-parenting techniques will help any child, whatever his or her problems, function better and more comfortably in the world. Some of you will already have heard at least some of these principles; for others they may all be totally new. Whichever group you fall into, I believe you'll find information here that will help.

As I've said, I believe that anxiety is becoming more prevalent among children in general. In part that's because we as a society tend to give them too much freedom and too much power. Children with too much power are often negative and moody; they're not happy with anything, and whatever they get isn't good enough. They think freedom and power are what they want, but they're not. In fact, the human reaction to having too much freedom and power and too few rules and boundaries is simply to feel untethered.

Beyond that, kids today also have access to more information than they're able to handle comfortably. The media may be one of the biggest culprits in this. Think of all the scary information coming at you every day—not only wars and murders but also constant and conflicting warnings about your health and well-being. "What you eat today may be killing you!" "Your medicine cabinet may be poisoning you!" "Check your smoke alarm! Check your carbon monoxide detector!" It's enough to make even the most grounded adult nervous, and, whether you're aware of it or not, your children are getting and processing all that information on a daily basis.

Even programming designed specifically for children is more complex, sophisticated, and on some level disquieting than the programs we watched growing up. People make fun of those 1950s sitcoms like *Leave It to Beaver* and *Father Knows Best*, but the message they conveyed was that whatever mischief the kids were getting into, whatever problems or worries they had, the adults in charge were really in charge, and they were able to sort it all out by the end of the half hour. Today's programs are much more likely to show children acting bratty and outsmarting their bumbling parents. The message these shows deliver is that adults really don't know very much, which only makes children doubt our ability to guide them and keep them safe. This, in turn, may cause them to become more anxious. I'm not saying that your children shouldn't be watching television. In fact, as I've already said, I believe that television has some benefits. What I am saying is that you, as a parent, should be aware of and monitor what your child is watching, and be prepared to discuss what your child sees.

The more anxious kids are, the more they need to see that we can, in fact, protect them from whatever it is they're afraid of. We do that, in large part, by letting them know that we understand and appreciate their anxiety but that we'll keep them safe and we also know that they are strong enough to get through it. Admittedly, this can be a challenge, particularly with those kids who mask their anxiety with bossiness, anger, and inflexibility.

One of the most anxious kids I've ever met was about five years old and terrified of just about everything, but especially thunder and lightning. On one particular day his older sister was playing in a soccer game, and Matthew was sitting on a blanket on the grass with his mother watching her. It was a perfect spring day with one or two tiny, fluffy white clouds in the distance. Matthew spotted a cloud and immediately became hysterical. In his mind, that one cloud meant there were going to be more clouds, and then there was going to be rain, and thunder, and lightning, and it was imperative that they get in the car immediately. As he was crying and screaming and hyperventilating about the imminent, life-threatening lightning, his mother was doing what most moms would do, saying, "Stop it. You're fine. Don't be ridiculous. The sky is perfectly blue, there isn't going to be any lightning." She even went so far as to find one of the other parents, who she knew worked for the Weather Channel, to come over and explain that the kind of cloud Matthew saw wasn't the kind that brought lightning. But it didn't matter; there was no way any rational argument was going to make any difference. He had a full-on panic attack; he was hyperventilating and quite hysterical.

Finally she just picked Matthew and the blanket up, asked a neighbor to give her daughter a ride home, and left. When I saw her she was beside herself. She didn't know what to do. Clearly her son couldn't spend the rest of his life indoors just in case there might be some lightning. I explained that the next time this happened, she needed to mirror and match his urgency so that he would know she understood and "got" his message, because the more she tried to tell him it was nothing, the harder he'd try to convince her it was "something"—and something really bad! In addition to the generalized mirroring we have talked about, I taught her how to mirror this specific incident.

The day of the next soccer game was just as beautiful as the previous one, but Matthew was already beginning to get anxious in the car. Of course the same thing happened: Matthew saw the cloud, Matthew knew it was going to cause lightning, Matthew started to get hysterical. Only this time his mother responded differently. Instead of trying to talk him out of his fear, she said, "Oh, Matthew, what happens when you see more than one cloud in the sky? Tell me what you think it means. Oh, you think those clouds are going to catch all the other clouds in the sky, they're going to find one another and you're pretty sure they're going to group together and there will be a big storm." She said all this without sounding the least bit worried herself, matching perfectly the urgency Matthew felt about the situation. Because of that, he perceived that his message was being received and he immediately began to calm down. Once he was calmer, she was able to say, "But you know, sweetie, remember what the man from the Weather Channel told you last time?" And she was able to explain the science of weather, which she'd been trying to do the last time, but without mirroring first.

Matthew still wasn't able to sit on the grass, but he agreed to sit in the car and let her sit on the grass until the game was over. It was a major step forward for him, and by the end of the soccer season, he was able to join his mother on the blanket, although he still wasn't thrilled about it.

What I'm advocating isn't a miracle cure, it's just human nature. I tend to be a lot more anxious than my husband, and the more I remind him to be careful about this or that, the more he responds, "Yeah, yeah, okay, I get it." On one occasion, however, he was making a long car trip alone with our three children and two of their cousins. Again, I kept reminding him to be careful: "You know, you've got five kids in the car. You need to be like a school bus driver. It's really important . . ." and on and on. To which he was replying, "I know how to drive. Why do you keep telling me how to drive?" which only made me feel I had to continue to impress upon him the seriousness of the situation, until a lightbulb went on and he got it. At that point he said, "You know, you're right. I've got five kids in the car. I'll make sure Jacob watches Olivia so that she doesn't distract me, and I'll be sure I'm focused on the road." And I immediately relaxed. I'm sure he was annoyed by my nagging; I would have been, too. But then he realized what I needed was some mirroring, so he did it, and it worked. Again—and I can't say this often enough—it's a matter of knowing that you've been understood, that your point has been taken, and that someone besides you is going to take charge.

Recognizing Anxiety in Children

Most of us think we are able to recognize anxiety when we see it, but in children it can be difficult to recognize even for professionals because it doesn't necessarily manifest itself in the ways we assume it should—such as nail-biting, shyness, or timidity. It can look like that, but it can also look like purposeful naughtiness or bad behavior. Children who are anxious often throw tantrums, are more inflexible and irritable than others, and have poor control over their moods in general. Anxiety may also look like bossiness or anger, and, in fact, I believe that anxiety and anger are simply flip sides of the same coin.

It's easier for children, who don't really understand what's driving their behavior, to be angry than to be scared. Being angry makes them feel more powerful, more in control. And, in fact, children who are scared are also very often rigid because they're trying to control everything in their environment. That's really why they become so angry when, for example, you drive a different route than they're accustomed to or something happens that they didn't know about in advance. Any little change or surprise is more than they can handle.

When parents come to me because their child has a behavioral problem, the first thing I always do is to rule out anxiety as the source of the behavior, whatever it might be. To do that, I ask them to practice the techniques I've designed to reduce anxiety. Then, if the behavior improves, it's a pretty sure bet that anxiety was the underlying cause.

I should say starting out that some of us are simply born to be more anxious than others because it's hardwired in our brain. I've found that when children are especially anxious, it's likely that there is another anxious family member whom they "take after." That said, however, you can help your child become the least (rather than the most) anxious he can be. To some degree we all need a little anxiety to inhibit us from blurting out whatever comes into our mind or from throwing things or running pell-mell into the street when a car is coming. What we don't need is the degree of anxiety that prevents us from functioning successfully in the world.

The Worry Monster and Other Strategies for Reducing Anxiety or Anger

More often than not, children don't know when they're anxious. They may experience the physical symptoms of anxiety, such as butterflies in the stomach, but they probably won't connect those physical feelings to anxiety. And if they do, they don't always know what's causing it. Even as adults we may wake up in the middle of the night knowing that something is making us anxious, but it may take us a while to figure out what that something is. Sometimes we can't pin it down at all and just chalk it up to "free-floating anxiety." So why would children, who don't yet have the cognitive abilities of an adult, be any better at identifying their anxiety than we are?

One thing I often ask parents to do to help their kids recognize when they're anxious is to talk to them about the Worry Monster (or the Worry Bug if your child is afraid of monsters). If you think that your child's behavior is driven by anxiety, you might make this suggestion: "You know, I think the Worry Monster [or Worry Bug] is getting in the way of your doing things. Part of you really wants to go to that birthday party [or whatever the situation is], but the Worry Monster is making you think you can't go." Then the two of you can work together on how to defeat the Worry Monster, using the tactics I'll be explaining.

Or, if anxiety manifests as anger, give the anger a name—one little boy I know named his angry self Thunderstorm Guy. By doing that, as with calling anxiety the Worry Monster, you're making the feeling something separate from the child. You're letting him know that his anger isn't his identity, but something that he can isolate and then find ways to control. This is a particular technique called narrative therapy, which involves personalizing or naming feelings and emotions, and it works particularly well for helping children to identify their anger or anxiety. If it's an older child, you can talk about "your worries" or "your fears" instead of saying "You are afraid," or "Why are you so afraid?" You still need to separate the feeling from the person so that you can then work together on controlling the feeling. (For a more in-depth, therapeutic approach to helping anxious children, you might want to read any of the books by Philip C. Kendall listed as suggested reading on pages 279–280.)

Once a child understands that he is not his feelings and that he can control his feelings, you can go on to tell him about the Thinking Gate. The Thinking Gate is my way of explaining the fight-or-flight reaction in simple terms that even small children seem able to understand. For younger children, you can talk about it in more magical terms, and for older kids, you can be more scientific. First explain that our brain has two sides. The left side is very logical and mathematical; it's the side that likes puzzles and figuring things out. The right side is in charge of feelings and emotions; it's the side that loves art and singing and dancing; it's the part of the brain that laughs, gets upset, and has temper tantrums. Both sides of our brain need to work together, but what happens when we get scared or angry is that the right side takes over and locks the left side out. It closes the Thinking Gate. In scientific terms, this means that the brain receives some piece of information that activates the sympathetic division of the autonomic nervous system, putting us into a fight-or-flight response.

The reason for this is that back when we were living in caves we might have been sitting on a rock eating a chicken leg when we heard a rustling in the bushes. It could have been a tiger or it could have been our mother, but we didn't have time to wait around and think about that, because if it really was a tiger, by the time we figured it out, it would have eaten us. So the right side of our brain was really saving our life by closing the gate and not letting us waste time thinking about what the sound really meant. All we had time to do was either run away and hide or grab our spear so that we could stab it. But now there aren't many tigers around for us to stab or hide from, so the Thinking Gate sometimes gets us into trouble more than it helps us. Now, when we get angry or scared and the Thinking Gate closes we can't stop to think, *Hmm, maybe I shouldn't do this, because if I do this I'm probably going to get into trouble*. The only part of our brain that is working for us is the right side, the emotional side, which keeps us stuck in the loop of angry or scared feelings. When the gate closes, our right brain doesn't know the difference between our homework that is too hard and being attacked by a dinosaur. Imagine standing on a three-hundred-foot-high bridge and someone saying, "It's okay, jump, you'll be fine." You wouldn't do it; you know it's not true. When someone is in panic mode or fight-or-flight, they might as well be standing on that bridge. Rational arguments are completely ineffective. Only when we start to calm down can we hear reason. As long as we are breathing quickly and our heart is beating fast, the gate slams shut and we are in a right-brain takeover. So what we really need to do is learn to keep our Thinking Gate open so that we can control our emotions instead of having our emotions controlling us.

The first step toward doing that is learning to recognize when we're getting angry or anxious. Many children, boys in particular, feel the physical symptoms of anxiety or anger but don't connect them with the emotion until it's too late. So parents may tell me that "the least little thing" sets their child off when, in fact, the explosion or meltdown has been brewing for some time but neither they nor their child saw it coming. What you need to do, then, is help your child learn to listen to her body so that she can anticipate and judge when her feelings are escalating to the point where the gate is going to close.

Talk to your child and get her to list the ways her body talks to her when she is anxious or angry: her heart is pounding, she's breathing fast, her fists and her jaw are clenched, she may be red in the face, and she feels very strong because a hormone called adrenaline is rushing through her body. Discuss what it feels like to be anxious: again, her heart is pounding, she's breathing quickly, her stomach may hurt, she may feel a tightness in her chest, or she may be dizzy or feel as if she needs to go to the bathroom. She may feel that she needs to run and hide.

This again is something you need to do when neither you nor your child is anxious or angry. To help, you can create a visual tool, like a mountain, a ladder, or a thermometer. Just remember that the image you choose has to be interesting and relevant to your child or he isn't going to pay attention to it. Now you're going to create a scale from 1 to 10. How does your body feel when you're at zero? *I'm completely relaxed and calm. I feel happy.* How do you feel when you get angry (or anxious)? *My fists clench, or my jaw gets tight, or my shoulders hunch up, or my tummy feels funny, or I get a headache, or my heart starts to pound, and I feel like hitting someone or running away.* What you want to do is help your child tune in to the physical feelings that will give him a sense of where he is on the emotional scale. Either you or your child (depending on age or what he prefers) can write the feelings at different points that correspond to his emotional levels on your ladder or thermometer or whatever image you've chosen. It's important not to argue about this; if your child doesn't want to write them down, it's not a big deal.

The purpose of the scale is to allow your child to begin monitoring his own anxiety or anger level so that he can check in with himself at various points in the day and notice that his tummy is feeling funny or his neck is stiff or his head is beginning to hurt—or whatever physical symptoms he has that let him know his anxiety or anger is rising (just as you did in Chapter Seven).

Once he's learned to do that, you can give him the tools or weapons that will help him lower it so that the next time something makes him scared or angry he'll be starting out at a Level 3 instead of a 7, which will give him more time to get control of himself before the Thinking Gate clanks shut.

The first thing I do with the kids I work with is to name the tools or weapons the same way we named the problem. Boys love to name them things like the Happy Thought Bomb or the Deep Breathing Ray Gun. They love to connect these images to Pokémon figures and give their anger or fear cool names like Volcanox if that is what they are interested in. For *Star Wars* or sci-fi fans there are lots of wonderful images that can work with this program. The more relevant and interesting it is for your child, the better it will work. For kids who adore science, keep it technical; they will love it. Girls tend toward magic wands, wizards, and good fairies. It doesn't matter what the names are, so long as they're relevant and interesting to your child—which is the main reason you should let him or her pick the names.

Learning to breathe slowly is a cornerstone strategy for calming down that will work for your child just as it does for you. When we're scared or startled, the first thing we do is to instinctively suck in a big gulp of air in order to send more oxygen to the brain, and sometimes just doing that is enough to throw us into fight-or-flight and close that gate. For those kids who are very anxious or quite angry, the gate closes more often over smaller things, the trigger or switch is set lighter, and the brain is used to having to perceive frightening situations. When we breathe slowly and deeply our heart rate also slows down, we are better able to focus, and our brain will be less likely to think there's a threat we need to respond to immediately.

The second strategy that's also important for both of you is to turn away from whatever it is that's making you angry or anxious. That means that if the focus of your child's emotional outburst is you, you need to get yourself out of the way. The more they look at you and the more you stay engaged, the angrier or more stuck in the situation they will become.

A third tool is using imagery or thinking happy thoughts. When you have some quiet time, sit down with your child and ask her to make a list of all the things that make her happy—her favorite places, favorite foods, whatever it is. Some girls like to decorate their list with stickers. Little boys sometimes like to put it in a treasure box. Then, when they get angry or anxious, they can pull out the list and read through it to "think happy thoughts."

A variation on this theme is asking your child to write a letter from her left brain to her right brain. One little girl, who was afraid to go to school but actually did very well once she got there, wrote: *Dear Right Brain, I know you feel scared and your tummy's doing flip-flops and you feel like you can't breathe and you think maybe you're going to throw up, but you have to remember that I'm writing this at the end of the day when I got home from school and I had fun today. I had a really good time, and that feeling in your tummy goes away the minute you walk into the classroom.* If they can't or don't want to write it themselves, write it for them. This works particularly well for anxious children because they can keep the letter in their pocket and pull it out to read whenever they're about to do something like go to a birthday party or go to school, and they know that once they get there they'll be okay. And since they wrote it, they really can't argue with what it says.

To help kids figure out what makes them angry or anxious, I sometimes suggest drawing a volcano (which works well for anger) or some other picture and writing in the middle all the things that make the child angry. For example, I get angry when people say no to me. I get angry when people are mean to me. I get mad when my brother takes my stuff. Then you can draw vents that release pressure along the sides of the volcano and write in those spaces all the things that help the child calm down: talking to my mom, playing with my best friend, playing my video games, reading a book. This is totally analogous to an adult's becoming aware of his or her trigger points and learning how to avoid an unnecessary confrontation. You can then take the image one step further by talking about what happens when the volcano gets completely filled up with angry thoughts and just explodes.

Another way to visualize this "spillover" point is by filling a glass to the very brim with water and showing your child what happens when you add just one more drop.

Once your child is aware of the scale of escalating emotions, she will gradually learn to monitor them for herself. You can also help her do that simply by saying, "Hey, you know, you sort of look as if you're at about a Level 7. Try to work on your breathing or use one of your other strategies to get yourself calmed down before the Thinking Gate closes." You just need to catch her before she escalates to the point where the gate has already closed and she won't be able to hear what you're saying—for most kids that's about a Level 7 on the scale. If a child is already angry or scared, he or she will almost always say, "Stop it. I hate that stuff! There is no volcano man." This means the child is in fight-or-flight and is, therefore, unable to access logical thought. The best you can do in such a situation is to mirror (three statements) and then remind her to think about some of the things she has learned to do. Don't say anything more, and give her space. Follow the "Mirror, present the problem, and find the solution" formula. On those occasions when she does catch herself and manage to de-escalate, be sure to recognize and celebrate her progress in her accomplishment book.

All these techniques are my own variations on what is called cognitive behavioral therapy (CBT). While it is not meant to replace other forms of therapy for children who are extremely anxious, it is a very helpful, empowering, and often fun way for children to learn to control their emotions so their emotions don't control them. If you're interested in learning more about CBT, you can consult your pediatrician to find a therapist in your area who is trained in this model.

Finding the Right Time and Place

Make sure to take your time with delivering all of this. Don't try to cram it into one conversation. It may take several. If your child seems uninterested or overwhelmed, stop and bring it up again later. As I keep repeating, you have to make all of these strategies and teaching tools relevant and interesting to your particular child. And you also have to introduce them appropriately. That means certainly when both you and your child are relaxed and calm, but it might also mean (depending on the child's age and disposition) in short sessions over a period of days. For some kids, while you're driving in the car is a good, quiet time; for others, it might be at bedtime. Or you might want to take him out for a special lunch. Just remember that when your child loses interest, it's time to put the volcano or the happy list away and come back to it at another time.

Some people have suggested to me that it seems silly to talk about being angry or scared when their child is perfectly calm and happy, but the reality is that you can't do it when she's upset because she won't have access to the part of her brain that can process this information, and it will only make her more upset. She has to be calm and open to listening. And as long as you've been doing lots of mirroring and listening to her agenda first, you'll be letting her know that what you really want is to help her figure out how to have a happier life.

Most kids will be very open to this because they really do want to feel better, but there are a few who won't want to discuss it with you or who will be offended, and if that's the case, it may be helpful to have someone else, like a favorite aunt or uncle, do this for your child. In more serious cases, you may find it very helpful to seek out a professional therapist who does cognitive behavioral therapy.

Predictability Reduces Anxiety

For children who are especially anxious, surprises are never fun. They need to know in advance and be able to predict exactly what's going to happen. One of the most loving things you can do for an anxious child is to help make her world as predictable as possible, which will also make your life a lot more predictable because you won't be so anxious all the time about when she's going to have her next tantrum or meltdown.

One of my favorite tools for this is using a whiteboard or chalkboard to lay out exactly what's going to be happening each day for the next week. It needs to be big (for some reason doing this on a computer screen or a regular piece of paper doesn't seem to have the same impact) and it needs to be in a prominent place where the child can see it every day. For each day, write down all the constants, such as mealtimes, soccer practice, homework, and bath, in one color (these can be permanent so that you don't have to rewrite the entire schedule every week). In a second color, write down the things that are out of the ordinary, such as a haircut, school events, an evening meeting, a dental appointment, or a birthday party. Go over it with your child and get her in the habit of going to the board every morning so that she'll know exactly what she's going to be doing that day. If she forgets, you can remind her; if she has questions, you can answer them. That way you'll be helping her to predict, plan, and organize her feelings about what's going on in her world. Then, if she's anxious about any one of these events, she can practice her special techniques as she thinks about it.

You may not be a whiteboard kind of person. You may be someone who loves spontaneity and surprises, but if your child is exactly the opposite, you'll just have to bite the bullet and do it for her because she needs it. Our children aren't always just like us, and we sometimes simply need to put aside our own agenda and try to put ourselves in their shoes. Doing that is a form of empathy, which is a form of love.

Reduce the Anxiety of Separation

There are children whose difficulty separating from their parents (particularly their mother) has more to do with the way the child is hardwired than it does with the strength of the parental bond. The way many parents handle this type of anxiety—because, indeed, it seems logical—is to not tell the child she is going to be leaving until the moment arrives. As parents have explained it to me, they assume that the sooner they tell the child they're going to be leaving, the longer the child will have to worry about it. To a certain extent that's true. But the fact is that the longer she has to get used to the idea, the better she'll be able to handle the situation. Yes, she will no doubt worry about it, but you can mirror to help get her over that hump so that by the time you are actually ready to leave she'll have worked through the anxiety of your telling her and will be better able to deal with the leaving itself.

Another method many parents seem to have for dealing with separation anxiety is to simply sneak out when the child isn't looking. That may actually be the worst thing you could do, because it means that he'll never know when you're going to sneak out again, and he'll be worried virtually all the time, even when you have no intention of going anywhere. After a while, he won't even want you to leave the room, because if you can leave the room you can also leave the house.

So again, make your comings and goings as predictable as possible for your child, give her fair warning so that she has time to get used to the idea, and when you do leave, don't make a big deal of it. Tell her you're going, make two or three mirroring statements to let her know that you understand this is difficult for her but that you also know she can cope with it, and then go. By telling her in advance that you are leaving, you are giving her that message of confidence, letting her know that you believe she is capable of handling the information. And when you get back, don't make a big deal of that either. Remember that the key in almost every situation that you know may be problematic is to remain as neutral as possible.

The same, it should be said, is true if you're taking your child to school or to day care. If your child is upset or crying, the worst thing you can do is to hold on to her, stay there, and try to soothe her. The truth is, at that point you're no longer capable of soothing her, because you're the reason she's crying. The longer you stay, the worse it will get, because you're just prolonging the time and escalating the degree of her upset. What you need to do instead is make a few mirroring statements of confidence, such as, "Sweetie, you're going to be fine. I wouldn't leave you anywhere I wasn't sure you'd be fine." Then give her a hug and a kiss and walk away—and don't go back, no matter how tempted you may be.

As a final word here, I believe that parents—and especially parents whose children have particular struggles—need time to themselves. Parenting is more than a full-time job. It's challenging, particularly in the beginning, and everyone needs time to relax and unwind. Therefore, it's important for you to be able to leave your child with a babysitter. Call upon a family member or develop a roster of babysitters with whom your child is familiar. When you're bringing in someone new, you can first have him or her over for a short period of time when you leave the room but don't leave the house. After that you can leave for a short period of time—perhaps a half hour—until your child both knows the sitter and has gotten used to the idea that when you leave you do come back. And again, never sneak out when you're leaving your child with a sitter.

If you have two children, one of whom is difficult while the other is not, you might also call in a mother's helper to play with one while you devote time to the other. Or arrange to have one child spend some time with a grandparent or other family member who lives close by while you spend some one-on-one time with the other. Switch it up—don't always spend your own time with either the one who is difficult or the one who is easy. If you always stay with the easy one, the difficult one will think you're trying to get rid of her, and if you stay with the difficult one, the easy child will think that to get more time with you he needs to become more difficult.

Throw Them a Life Preserver

For children with milder forms of anxiety the strategies I've just given you will work very quickly. If your child's anxiety is more generalized or more severe, I urge you to speak with your pediatrician and consider seeing a good therapist. Parents worry that sending their child to a therapist will send the message to the child that something is wrong with him. But in my experience, the children I work with love their sessions, save up what they want to talk about, and see it as a safe place to discuss their feelings.

In addition, if your child is severely anxious or extremely angry, or aggressive to the point where it is really affecting her quality of life, you may want to consider, in conjunction with your pediatrician or therapist, putting her on medication. Putting a child on psychotropic medication is one of the most serious and difficult decisions any parent can make. My feeling is that the time to consider this course is when the potential side effects of the medication are outweighed by the side effects of *not* putting the child on medication. If the child is at the point of saying things like *I hate myself. I should be thrown in the garbage. I can't do anything right, everybody hates me, I'm stupid,* when he is suffering emotionally and academically, when he is few friends or positive relationships, those are major side effects of not being on medication that can last a lifetime.

I do not advocate medication lightly; it is a serious decision and I always support parents who choose not to go that route. As you struggle with the issue, however, consider this: If you have tried everything, if you have thrown your heart and soul into helping your child and your child is still struggling, it may be time to think about a medication trial. To me, it's comparable to trying to teach someone to swim while the person is drowning. You can yell, "Move your arms! Kick your feet! Roll onto your back!" but though these are good strategies, the person who is drowning won't be able to use them because she can't hear you. You need to throw her something she can hold on to so that she can then learn to swim. In some circumstances, that's what medication can do. It can get the whole family out of the crisis zone so that you as a parent can begin to use these strategies and your child will be able to hear you and respond. In some instances the medication will be a temporary measure. Once your child learns to swim he will no longer need the life preserver. In other cases, however, he may need that life preserver to keep him afloat on a permanent basis. The bottom line is that there's no right way or wrong way to help your child; whatever way works is the right way for that particular individual.

I remember the little boy who said to me, "I want to do the right thing, but my body just won't listen. I'm broken." No child should feel that way. The guilt and fear parents feel can be overwhelming, but at the end of the day all you can ask yourself is, *Have I done everything I can? Have I turned over every stone? Have I loved my child well?* That's all you can do.

ADHD, ODD, OCD, Asperger's Disorder, and Nonverbal Learning Disabilities

You may wonder what these disparate problems could possibly have to do with one another, and how one technique could be useful in helping them all. My answer is twofold. First, they are all, to some degree and in some way, related to anxiety. When you walk around in life and people don't understand you or they get mad at you and you don't know why, or when you behave in ways you don't understand, or if you don't find the same things funny as others, you get anxious. And second, mirroring—just like water—is something that we all need. It's nurturing, and no matter what the problem, it will help alleviate that part of it that's emotional or behavioral.

That said, sometimes it can be particularly difficult for the parents of a child with special needs or specific challenges to use these techniques. Because of the stress involved in parenting difficult children, the bond may be particularly frayed, and, as parents, we need to be mentally strong and genuinely able to put our own agenda aside to help our child.

Beating yourself up about your parenting is not going to be helpful. As I tell my clients, this is the dynamic you're tangled up in. Your child behaves a certain way and you react a certain way because you're human. Your child then reacts to you and you to him, and before you know it you're caught in a vicious cycle that starts to spin in its own direction. This is when you are likely to look at yourself and think, *How did I get here? How can I be this angry? This is not the mother I wanted to be; this is not the father I saw myself being.* Parenting a special-needs child can leave you feeling desperate and despairing. Parents have told me what it's like to walk around with a sense of dread in the pit of their stomach, knowing that they are constantly being looked upon and talked about, even judged and shunned by other parents and even teachers. Their hearts skip a beat when the phone rings; they're terrified it's the school calling to report yet another problem. It's a heavy, sad, isolating feeling. These special kids are like all kids, but with their own magic and their own slant on life. They can give you such joy and help you see things in a whole new way. But when others don't see this in your child, you hurt, and you are constantly in situations where you worry that others can't keep your child emotionally safe or don't see his or her strengths and abilities.

I want to say right here that parenting is not the cause of ADHD, and it's not the cause of Asperger's. Moreover, you as a parent can help, no matter how difficult your child's situation may be.

Many people mistakenly believe that the child with ADHD simply isn't paying attention. In fact, however, exactly the opposite is true. She's paying attention to *everything*. I once asked a child with ADHD what it felt like, and this was his answer: "It's like someone is vacuuming and flicking the lights on and off, and someone is talking in one ear and someone else is singing in the other ear, and the radio and television are on and I just won a million dollars." To put yourself in that situation, imagine yourself standing in the middle of an amusement park: barkers are shouting at you while bells and whistles are going off and there is competing music, and smells from the food, and people are bumping into you, and someone is trying to teach you something. Or imagine that every time you walk into a party or some other social situation you know that you're going to tick someone off, but you don't know why and you don't know how to avoid it. All that is incredibly tiring; it wears you out. And that's how kids with ADHD or learning disabilities (LDs) feel much of the time. They are intelligent and inquisitive, and are told many times in a day, "Stop it. Sit down. Stop touching that," and "We're not talking about that right now," and "I don't want to play with you." Over and over, time after time, day after day. No wonder they can be frustrated and short-tempered when they get home after school.

A baby with ADHD will notice her mother's face, but she will also notice the shadow on the wall, she will notice sounds, and she will notice her mother's hair blowing in the wind. So even though you, as a mother, may be mirroring to your baby, she won't be taking in as much of the mirroring as most babies because she'll also be busy noticing all these other things to the same degree. In consequence, she won't be receiving a full dose of the information you're giving her.

And because she's noticing so many different things at once, she may not respond to your mirroring by making faces back in the same way other babies do. You, then, receive less gratification and, without ever realizing it, you probably begin to mirror less and less.

To continue the vicious cycle, kids with ADHD are told over and over, "Cut it out. Stop it. Sit down." And because they have such difficulty controlling their impulses, they become more and more anxious. Not even consciously, they may walk into situations fearing that they're going to do something wrong, and figure, subconsciously, that they might as well just blow it and get it over with instead of prolonging what they perceive to be the inevitable. The more they're corrected, the more unlovable they feel, and the more they act out.

Children with Asperger's disorder and those with nonverbal learning disabilities can also miss out on some of the benefits of mirroring, but for different reasons. Children with Asperger's may not have as many mirror neurons, so it may be harder for them to pick up and sort through all the sensory information they're receiving, which means that their mother's voice and social input may simply be diluted by the flood of data coming at them.

Kids with nonverbal LDs may function well in the verbal world, but they often have a difficult time picking up nonverbal cues. They don't always understand or interpret facial expressions as easily as others, and may have difficulty knowing how they're supposed to respond. Clearly, this makes it difficult for them to understand what our expressions mean when we mirror to them as babies, and if they're not responding—as for babies with ADHD—we may become frustrated and mirror that much less. As a result, fewer neuropathways may develop, the children may not be as resilient as they could be, and their anxiety increases. Their anxiety is reflected in their behavior, which affects how their parents relate to them, and eventually it becomes a vicious cycle of less mirroring and less connecting.

Children with nonverbal LDs can, however, learn to pick up on nonverbal cues that will, in turn, allow them to become more socially confident and, therefore, more socially skilled. I'm sure you know people who seem to sail through even the most trying social situation while others struggle to make new friends or even to make small talk. Children, however, can be helped to develop the skills they need to participate more comfortably in the social world. You can explain and practice with them the importance of making eye contact, conversational turn-taking, timing, and all the other basics of conversation. Explain, too, that when people talk to one another they speak with their bodies and their faces as well as with words, and that it's important, when you're having a conversation, to be sure that your facial expressions and your body movements match what you're saying. When you're out in a public place, play a game that involves watching other people's facial expressions and body language and see if your child can figure out if they're happy or sad, angry or frustrated, bored or having a good time. Then ask him or her to explain to you why he or she thinks these people are feeling that way.

You can also talk out loud to help your child make the connection between what you are saying and what you are doing. Do not rely too much on your nonverbal communication. Comment out loud to help your child see the connections. For example, let's say you're in a hurry and you can't find your keys. As you are looking for them, you can narrate out loud: "I can't find those keys. I always stomp around and push things out of the way because I am frustrated with myself." It will probably feel strange, but you will be helping your child make connections between cause and effect.

Most of us learn intuitively. We are able to pick up nonverbal cues, understand what they mean, and use them ourselves. Most of us don't need to be taught to do this, but kids with nonverbal LDs or those on the autistic spectrum may need more help. Kids with ADHD may be too distracted and preoccupied to make the connections and also need a little help from you.

Not everything comes naturally to everyone, but kids who are frustrated, sad, or angry because they're missing out on social situations can be helped to acquire and hone those skills with which they may not be genetically blessed. That said, however, children with Asperger's disorder often have many of the same social difficulties as those with nonverbal LDs but may be less aware of their problems and less interested in making friends. Kids with nonverbal LDs may want those friendships and not understand why they aren't making friends, while many kids with Asperger's (although this is certainly not universally true) tend to be more detached and happier when they're alone. The point here is that if you see that your child is not making friends you need to check your own agenda and determine whether his making friends is something that he wants or something that would make *you* feel better. If he's withdrawing because he's afraid, you need to intervene, but if he honestly doesn't enjoy being around people, don't keep putting him in the middle of social situations.

One diagnosis that seems to be given more and more often these days and that is particularly frightening for parents is oppositional defiant disorder. ODD is described in the *Diagnostic and Statistical Manual of Mental Disorders* (*DSM IV*) as "a recurring pattern of negative, hostile, disobedient, and defiant behavior in a child or adolescent lasting at least six months . . ." Although, on the one hand, these behaviors can be viewed by some simply as bratty kid disorder, the diagnosis is particularly worrisome to parents because it is generally believed that ODD can evolve into a more serious conduct or mood disorder. In my personal experience, however, using connected-parenting techniques with these children, in addition to working with a therapist, can reduce the symptoms, and sometimes, after a year or so, you and your psychiatrist will find that the diagnosis was situational and that your child is no longer exhibiting ODD symptoms.

. . .

Another, relatively rare diagnosis that some children receive is obsessive-compulsive disorder (OCD), which is not to be confused with obsessive personality disorder. When you have OCD you're not happy about your obsessive behaviors; you're wondering all the time why you *have* to do these things, and you are, in effect, a slave to your obsessions. When you have an obsessive personality, you like being obsessive; you do not feel bothered as much by the obsessions because you like things that way and it does not seem as if the obsessions come from outside yourself or your own personality. In both cases, however, the obsessive traits appear somewhere on a continuum from mild to the point where they truly get in the way of daily living.

Mirroring, in combination with whatever other treatments your doctor recommends, can have a significant impact on these rituals. With time, children use them less often and sometimes drop many of them completely. Conversely, the more frustrated and angry you become with your child, the more obsessed he will become because your yelling just makes him more anxious. Once again the mirroring and connecting techniques seem to clear away much of what is emotional so that what you are left with is the disorder itself.

One of my clients, a boy of about thirteen, had not only severe OCD, but several other problems as well. There were rooms in the house he wouldn't enter, parts of the staircase he wouldn't walk on, places where he wouldn't put down his belongings. He was also verbally noncommunicative and had selective mutism. And, like many anxious kids, he also had terrible rages. By the time his mother came to me, she was worn out and sick of the rages, and had no idea what to do next. She'd been alternately nagging and ignoring certain behaviors because she no longer had the strength to deal with the rages that would follow whenever she tried to correct a behavior. She was walking on eggshells with her own child, which was a tough dynamic because it gave him more power and made him more anxious. In his mind, if his mother couldn't control him, he must really be a monster, and, moreover, if no one was in control (since he couldn't control his own behavior) the world was that much more frightening.

I explained the concept of mirroring to his mother and told her that she needed to start doing whatever version of baby play her son would be able to tolerate. She started by showing him a baby picture of himself and mirroring to the picture—"Oh, look how cute you are," or "Oh, I just found this picture today, and there you are with your favorite blanket." I suggested that she make just one statement and then walk away, leave him wanting more.

I also felt that she needed to take more control, just square her shoulders, and say, "You know, I'm not going to take that from you. I like myself too much." It was also apparent that she needed to stop following him around and doting on him so much.

She really worked hard, and within about three months his rages had completely stopped. Within six months some of the OCD symptoms began to improve and he even began to tell her what was bothering him instead of staring stonily at the wall. The breakthrough moment for her came one morning when it was time to go to school and her son couldn't find his history book. For an anxious kid, this was unmitigated disaster. On this morning, his mother said, "C'mon, honey, it's time to go to school," and he walked up to her, scrunching up his face the way he did when he was about to fly into a rage. She was just bracing herself for the worst when he looked at her and said, "I can't find my history book. I don't know what to do." The mom told me that she was so flabbergasted by this, she didn't know what to say. She gets so blown away whenever he speaks to her and tells her what's bothering him that it's become a challenge for her to learn to think on her feet and respond.

I explained to her that in these situations—when he did something he hadn't been capable of doing before, such as walking into a room he'd totally avoided or putting something down on a table that previously had been off-limits—she needed to remain completely neutral. I've talked about how important it is to remain neutral in a variety of situations, but with anxious children this is particularly important. If you notice that your child has stopped doing something or has begun to do something he would never have done before, one of the biggest mistakes is to make a big deal of it.

Don't have a parade! That will only make the child anxious all over again because he'll worry that he can't keep it up and won't be able to repeat the performance. In addition, the improvements you notice may ebb and flow. A behavior may disappear for a while and then the child will become anxious about not doing it and it will reappear, only to disappear again as the anxiety diminishes. Over time, however, the more you mirror, the more resilient he becomes, and the less intense the ritualistic behaviors tend to be.

This particular child is speaking more and more now, although he is still struggling and his OCD will always be a part of him. Accepting that can be problematic for parents of special-needs children, who tend to say, "Okay, so now he can go into this one room, but he's still not going into those others," or "Well, great, she's not throwing tantrums every day, but she still loses it once a month." As a therapist, I find these changes exciting, but parents may not notice or be as excited about them because other struggles are still going on.

Mirroring and connecting aren't going to "cure" a child whose problems are related to a disorder rather than strictly behavioral, but whatever the child's problem, they will help him become more resilient and better able to function in the world. I can't emphasize enough that if you suspect your child has any of these disorders, you should first see your pediatrician to discuss the various options. What I am offering are supplemental techniques that will be extremely helpful but should not be used in place of proper professional guidance.

The Special Needs of the Gifted Child

When most parents learn that their child is "gifted," they almost always consider themselves lucky, if not extremely blessed. Who wouldn't want to have a child at the very top of the intellectual spectrum? But some—although certainly not all—gifted children also pose particular parenting challenges related to their intelligence. Being gifted is not always such a gift.

One reason for this, I believe (and this is an extremely simplified explanation), is that the left, logical, part of their brain may be so overdeveloped that, at an early age, they understand much more— concepts, similarities, patterns—than they are emotionally capable of handling. This then means that the right brain, which regulates emotions, may be overtaxed and may have a difficult time sorting through and coping with all the information the left brain is sending it. In addition to being funny, sensitive, entertaining, interesting, and loving, gifted kids can be challenging.

I have noticed in my practice that gifted children tend to be exquisitely sensitive, both emotionally, in terms of their feelings, and in their reactions to tastes and textures. They may also have extremely low pain thresholds and scream as if their arm were being amputated without anesthesia when a Band-Aid is removed. And because par-

ents know their child is gifted, these overreactions may be especially annoying. They tend to be gaggers (they throw up easily) and they
can be terribly dramatic. They fall into nosedives over seemingly
small things and overreact by announcing that they hate their life
and nothing ever goes right for them. They can give up easily when
trying new things and melt down over homework. Teaching them
how to ride a bike or to skate, for example, can be a nightmare, not
because they do not have the skill, but because they expect it to be
easy, and when it's not they often get very upset and quit in a huff.
Figuring out how to help these kids practice and stick to something
so they don't quit everything that doesn't come easily can be quite a
challenge. They also tend to be bossy and precocious, forgetful, and
easily distracted. Many experience social difficulties and have a hard
time regulating their emotions. Because they tend to be extremely
sensitive, they can also be emotionally needy and anxious. Oh, and
they can talk and talk and talk for a long time about everything. Not
all gifted children have all these traits; many have none. But many
of the traits they do have are simply a function of their understanding
too much, seeing patterns, and predicting events well beyond what
others see and worry about.

I remember when my son, Jacob, who happens to be gifted, was
four or five and got a splinter in his foot. He absolutely refused to let
us remove it, shrieking as if we were about to amputate his foot. So
we left it for a day, but when it appeared to be getting infected, we
knew it had to come out. We wound up taking him to the emergency
room of the local hospital, where you could hear him screaming at
the top of his lungs throughout the entire ER—"*I'm your only son!
How can you let them do this to me!*" And that was before they'd actually done anything more than look at his foot. It took several people
to hold him down when they were doing nothing more than putting the numbing cream on his foot. Then, when the doctor came

to remove the splinter, the screams rose to an even higher pitch. Truthfully, you would have thought they were sawing off his leg. Two seconds later, when the splinter was out, he said, "Oh, that wasn't so bad!"

Gifted kids' ability to see all the potential consequences of so many situations (I call them "horizon thinkers") leads them to worry more than most. *If I do this, then that might happen, and then if that happens, this might happen* . . . and on and on. At nine years old they might be worrying years into the future about things that are well beyond their age. *What if I don't marry a good person? What if I don't get a good job? What if I die? What happens when I die?* I call this "anticipatory anxiety."

In addition, when something does go wrong—let's say they get to hockey practice and suddenly realize they didn't bring their skates—instead of saying, *"Oh well, let's see what we can do to fix this. Maybe I can borrow a pair,"* they fall apart. They really worry about any minor glitch in any plan because they begin to imagine all the potential consequences in full living color with stereophonic sound, and that can paralyze them.

Even as babies, gifted children tend to have a very hard time settling themselves because their brain is so active. The kids themselves have explained this to me by saying, "I can't turn my brain off." They love all that intellectual activity, but it's also stressful. They worry and fret and "catastrophize," and more often than not we as parents simply don't understand what they're going through intellectually and emotionally, which means that we also aren't doing the mirroring that would help alleviate their anxiety.

In addition, gifted children tend to acquire language earlier than others, often at a year to eighteen months. Because of that, we, as parents, often begin talking to them as if they were little adults. As I've said, it's at the point when our children acquire language that we tend to give up or cut back on the mirroring we did instinctively when they were infants. With gifted children, that can happen even earlier than it would with other kids, and sometimes they're simply not capable, emotionally or physically, of responding as we expect them to. Our expectations can be unrealistic, and because of that, we may become increasingly annoyed and our child may become increasingly anxious. At the same time, the child becomes anxious and upset because she can't do what she knows she's supposed to.

I'm not suggesting that we shouldn't use complex language with our children. There are tremendous benefits to speaking in rich complex language to babies and young children, gifted or not, but I am saying that we shouldn't at the same time give up doing the emotionally nutritious baby stuff—the mirroring, soothing, playful baby talk, the cuddly, nurturing stuff. All children need both, and we're making a big mistake if we throw the baby out with the bath-water, so to speak.

Children who are artistically gifted—artistic or musical prodigies, for example—are often dealing with the opposite problem. It may be that their right brain, the sensitive and emotional side, is overdeveloped, and they may be extremely intuitive or supersensitive to other people's feelings. What this might mean is that if you're irritated or cranky they will absorb your emotional state and become cranky themselves.

Either way—left-brain- or right-brain-oriented—gifted children are more likely than most to get sucked into that vortex state we discussed in Chapter Two and sink into a pit of despair because their emotions are so overwhelming. Just having their Lego tower collapse can have them sobbing, "This is the worst day of my life! Nothing ever goes right for me! I shouldn't even be alive!" This can be either extremely frightening or extremely frustrating for parents when their children were fine just minutes before.

Some children, and not just those who are gifted, will simply pull out all the stops because they have tidal waves of emotions they just can't regulate. They may then say very worrisome things, like threatening to kill themselves or they may actually start banging their head on the wall. That's scary stuff, and what you as a parent need to do is stay calm but let your child know that hurting himself or talking about hurting himself simply isn't acceptable and will be taken seriously. Let him know there are other ways to let you know he's upset, and if the behavior continues more than once in the odd while, you should really discuss it with your pediatrician.

Often, behavior is cyclical, with long stretches of good behavior followed by tantrums and vortexes. Sometimes this is how children regulate. It's almost as if they were holding in their emotions to the point where they had to explode, and once they let it all out, they can once more remain calm for a fairly long period of time. This is not the healthiest way for children to regulate, and it important for us to be mindful of doing what we can to discourage their tantrums rather than inadvertently encouraging them.

What you always need to remember, however, is that when your child is in the throes of a vortex, the only thing you can do is disengage temporarily. The more you try to help, the more she will argue. The more you try to mirror, the deeper your gifted child may sink into the vortex of emotions. It is important to note that many gifted kids tend to respond this way to mirroring. They more than any other group often fight against the feeling of de-escalation, particularly if they are deeply upset. Continue to make at least three mirroring statements anyway; on some level the child will still register that experience, and it may be evident later that the child felt heard and listened to. Over time this will have a positive effect on your child in terms of ability to regulate big emotions. You just may not see evidence of this in the moment.

And if you are tempted (as we all are) to simply say, "Oh my God, it's just a Lego. It's not the end of the world!" you'll be invalidating her feelings, which isn't helpful either. I remember when my own son was four or five, and we were at the beach. He'd been collecting frogs in a pail, and after he'd kept them there for about twenty minutes, I thought it was time to release them, so I said, "You know, I think those frogs have been in that pail long enough. I think they want to go back to their families and you need to let them out of the pail," at which point he immediately start wailing, "I love those frogs! They're like family to me! My summer will be ruined if I have to say good-bye to those frogs!" It was all I could do to stop myself from laughing at the absurdity of it. But I knew I couldn't do that. Instead, I made three mirroring statements and then left him alone. Fifteen minutes later he was fine and couldn't have cared less about those frogs.

Remember to concentrate on mirroring when your gifted child is happy or only mildly upset. You will find that in the moment the child will respond much better to the technique and that consistent doses will eventually help the child react more positively when the child does enter a vortex.

Yet another problem gifted or highly intelligent kids may have is the fear of trying new things. Because they're so used to success, they often have a great deal of anxiety when they contemplate potential failure. (As I've said, they're very good at imagining every possible thing that could go wrong.) They tend to think that they should always be able to look at a task or a problem and be able to solve it or master it immediately. If someone needs to show them how or explain it, they see that as a sign that they're not smart enough—and being smart can be how they define themselves. Therefore, they tend not to like anything that can't be solved or mastered on a purely intellectual level. So if, for example, you hand a gifted kid a basketball for the first time, he may look at the hoop and figure, *Okay, I know exactly the arc I need to create to throw it and it will go right into the basket.* And if it doesn't, he may try two or three more times, and then he'll just stomp away disgusted, yelling that basketball is a stupid, impossible game. Whereas another type of child might keep trying and trying until he gets it, in the mind of a gifted child if something takes more than two or three tries to accomplish, it must be impossible. The way I try to explain this to them is that sometimes your brain knows how to do it, but your muscles need to learn. Your muscles need to practice what your brain is teaching them. If your brain could throw the ball directly into the basket, it would go in every time, but your muscles have to do it *for* your brain, and it's hard for them; those connections take time to grow in your brain. This seems to make a big difference because they are then able to see the distinction between execution and intelligence.

One reason I believe it's important to talk about and deal with this fear of failure is that, as children become adults, they may, in fact, not fulfill their intellectual potential because they don't want to put themselves on the line or tackle anything too challenging.

Finally, you may find that your child who was reading at the age of two and doing addition in his head at three may be incapable of tying his shoes or may walk around with his shirt on inside out and backward. I call this the absentminded-professor syndrome, but don't worry—he will catch up. It's just that he's so busy inventing wonderful things in his head that he doesn't have the time or the inclination to deal with the mundane. Try not to get so frustrated that you jump right in and do things for him, because that will just allow him to think that he doesn't need to master all those "dumb" things because someone's going to do them for him anyway.

Mirroring with gifted children can make an enormous difference in their ability to self-regulate and acquire social skills. It can be tough for them to deal with "ordinary" tasks and "ordinary" children, who may not be as quick as they are. They may become frustrated, condescending, or "braggy" when other kids don't follow their argument or get their sense of humor. They get bored easily and often have difficulty with the regular school curriculum for that reason. Gifted kids also tend to vortex easily and are one group for whom mirroring when they are upset only makes things worse. Keep mirroring; then follow the protocol dealing with a vortex. The challenge to us as parents, then, is to raise the whole child so that he or she grows up to become a whole person, not just a walking brain. What may be "cute" in a precocious little kid we don't want to become obnoxious in a short-tempered or intolerant or insensitive adult.

A Child Is Still a Child, Wherever She Falls on the Continuum

All kids, wherever they may fall on the intellectual/emotional spectrum, need the same things. They need to feel loved and understood, and they need to know what's expected of them. If they don't have that, they'll feel as if they're climbing the rock wall with no one at the other end of the rope. With it, they will feel less fragmented and more connected, and they'll be better able to organize and control their emotions, they'll be less anxious, and they'll be better able to navigate in the world. They won't all wind up perfect or even in that range we like to call the happy medium, but then again, we probably wouldn't want them to. What we do want is for each and every one of them to become the best they can be, which is what connected parenting is all about.

THIRTEEN

Troubleshooting Common Problems

I've found over the years that whatever problems their children may have, there are particular issues and situations that parents almost always bring up in the course of counseling. Since these appear to be universal concerns, it seemed like a good idea to list them here so that you can access the information easily, sort of like the quick-start guide for setting up your DVD player.

Sibling Rivalry

There was a wonderful article by Jeffrey Kluger in the July 10, 2006, issue of *Time* magazine that explored the impact our siblings have on the adults we become. In that article, Kluger cited a study done by Penn State University in 1996 showing that by the age of eleven, children have spent 33 percent of their time with their sisters and brothers. That's more than the time they've spent with their parents, teachers, and even their friends, suggesting that siblings have as much impact as parents, or more, on a child's personality and development. Kids learn a lot about social skills from their interactions with siblings, which means that we, as parents, need to pay attention (possibly more attention than we generally do) to how siblings act with one another.

On the one hand, parents generally can't stand it when their children are constantly fighting and, on the other hand, they often think it's just normal sibling behavior. Sometimes they're simply so fed up that they shut the door and try to ignore it altogether.

I've noticed that very often we will tolerate our children's behaving toward one another in ways that we would never tolerate if someone else's kid were treating our child the same way. That said, a certain amount of sibling fighting and arguing *is* normal; it's how children learn to negotiate, to be heard, to make a point, and when to back off. Interacting with siblings is how kids acquire and practice many skills. But research has also shown that the way we are treated as siblings significantly affects our self-esteem, how we perceive ourselves, what risks we are willing to take, and, in general, our emotional and behavioral health. For all those reasons it's important that parents foster healthy, empathic relationships among their children.

The first thing I tell parents is to take a good honest look at the way they treat not only their children, but also each other. If we tend to be sarcastic, for example, we may see that reflected in how our children respond. In addition, the more we mirror with our children, the more they'll mirror with one another. Without realizing it, we really do have a profound impact on the people our kids become. So, if your children are constantly battling, first try to ramp up the empathy and mirroring in the household. Then begin by addressing one behavior at a time, starting with the most offensive, which is generally hitting.

The program would go something like this. Hold a family meeting and announce that as parents you've let the hitting go on too long and you're no longer going to tolerate it. It isn't a question of who's done what to whom first. From now on your home is going to be a safe place. "We're still going to have fights and arguments sometimes, but we're going to be more respectful of one another, and hitting or hurting one another is just not happening anymore. Anytime anyone hits for any reason, there will be a consequence."

The point here is that you have to separate the behavior from its cause, and make it clear that there's never a cause to hit under any circumstance. You'll listen to their complaints, but if they choose to hit, they've chosen a consequence. It could be going to bed a half hour earlier or losing television or computer time, or whatever works for your household. You might even say that the person who hits has to do the other child's chore for a specified period of time. But you need to frontload the consequence and you need to follow through. You can also reward the child who got really mad and was about to swing but didn't. And do I need to remind you that you'll be mirroring and connecting while you're doing all this? If you're consistent, you'll find that within a week or two the hitting, if not totally gone, will be at least 50 percent better. What will happen, however, is that while you've fixed the hitting problem, they'll probably be verbally nastier to one another.

Think of it as water running through a pipe under very high pressure. If the pipe springs a leak and you plug it up, chances are that another leak will spring up in a different place because the pressure has to be relieved. That's why it's so important that the mirroring go along with the containing; it's the mirroring that's eventually going to turn off the tap and reduce the pressure.

You can't plug up all the leaks at once, so while you're dealing with the hitting you can't also be consequencing the nastiness, but once the pressure is off the hitting, you can move on to deal with the next behavior—making it clear, of course, that this doesn't mean hitting is once again acceptable. If you deal with each behavior one at a time, you'll find that after a while everyone will be treating each other better. And you'll also find that it takes less time to correct each subsequent behavior than it did the last. It won't be perfect, but it will be out of the red zone and into the normal zone. You may find that once the hitting gets better, the yelling or name-calling gets worse. This is common. Once the hitting gets better, you can target the screaming. One behavior or another might escalate after a while because you've slipped and left too much slack on the rope, but you can always tighten up, reinstate the consequences, and get the tension back to where it needs to be.

As parents, too many of us spend too much time acting as referees. There are times when we get too caught up in what happened and who is at fault. Sometimes we're so exhausted from running up and down the court that we just feel like blowing the whistle and yelling, "Stop it! Who cares? I don't want to hear another word!"

The best thing to do when two or more of your children are running up to you in hysterics, each blaming the other, is to divide and conquer. First, take the most compliant child and mirror his or her urgency as you ask him to think of everything you should know about what just happened. Ask him to wait for you in the next room and then deal with your most difficult child. Follow the CALM technique by saying something like, "You mean you were just sitting there minding your own business and your brother came in and took the TV remote right out of your hand?" You'll need to make at least three mirroring statements based on what your child says to you. Then present the problem and the solution. The solution may mean having the kids work it out, it may involve a consequence, or it may even mean a reward, depending on who did what to whom. Now, go back to the first child and repeat the strategy. If they won't separate or you're comfortable enough, you can mirror to each one right in front of the other. I call this mass mirroring. If one is being reasonable and the other is not, you can mirror indirectly by articulating what you think the unreasonable one might be feeling while he is in earshot. Then go back to mirroring the child you are talking too. Remember, you are not taking sides; you're just trying to understand both sides. Then get everyone to take ten minutes to calm down before coming back to see if they can work it out fairly. Remember to use friendship moves and blocks as discussed on page 139.

Favoritism—Real or Imagined

Parents tend to beat themselves up for a million reasons. Two issues many parents struggle with, but no one wants to discuss out loud, are (1) feeling that they love one child more than another, and (2) having their child tell them or let them know through action that he or she loves the other parent more (whether or not either of these scenarios is true).

If you think (or fear) that you favor one child over the other, you first need to take a good hard look at yourself. Examining your own agenda is almost always the first step toward changing behavior—both yours and your child's. Since every child is different, you might really have a simpler and easier relationship with one than the other. If one child is an angel, always good, loving, and helpful, and the other is constantly annoying and shrieking, it's perfectly natural to be drawn more easily to one than the other. Sometimes when a child tells you she's always the one who gets into trouble, she's right. And, paradoxically, if one is more demonstrative and loving while the other is more aloof, you may be taking the loving one for granted and trying extra hard to woo the one who's aloof.

Beyond that, however, it's also true that if you talk to any pair of siblings, each one will say that his or her parents love the other one more. I know that sounds odd, but it's very common. The reason is that it's as if every child had two drawers, a great big one with lots of room for storing every instance when her mother or father has been nicer to her sister or brother and a teeny-tiny one where she puts the memory of every time her parents were nicer to her. Very often her parents really are nicer to her, but the drawer is so small that in a very short time, there's no more room to store another memory. Once the drawer is full, nothing else goes in there. Meanwhile, the great big drawer still has plenty of space to put all the times her parents were nicer to her sibling.

So when a child comes wailing to you that you're always punishing her and "he" never gets into trouble, in that moment she honestly believes that to be true. You can stand there with a checklist or even a videotape to prove to her that she's wrong, but it's not going to feel that way to her. You'll just be invalidating her feelings. What you need to do is mirror: "You feel like you do something and you get punished and then your brother does the same thing but you're always the one who gets into trouble. And that feels horrible for you. I can't imagine what that must be like for you, and you feel like that a lot." Notice that you're not agreeing that the child is punished more than her sibling; you're just letting her know that you understand that that's the way she feels about it. If you do that, even though you're not agreeing with her, you'll notice that she stops saying it. What's happening is that she's actually making her "good memory" drawer bigger.

And this is also where you need to challenge yourself, because maybe the child is right. Maybe one child does get on your nerves more than the other. Often one child is more reactive than the other, and what you miss is the subtle other child who knows just how to get the reactive one going and then smile like the Cheshire cat and come out smelling like a rose.

But if it's true that you may bond more easily with one child than another, it's also true that a child, for whatever reason, may become more attached to one parent than another, and this can be equally hard on both parents. It's common for a child to be more attached to the mother. When that happens, he or she may go to the mother for nurturing and caring and, if the father tries to provide it, protest, "No, no Daddy. I don't want Daddy." This can, of course, be tough on Daddy, who may then try even harder to win the child over. But, ironically, if he tries too hard the child may reject him all the more, in part because it's human nature to reject people who seem too needy and in part because the child becomes a bit puffed up with his or her sense of power.

The deeper you get involved in that dynamic, the more entrenched it will become. The more hurt and upset you are that your child is rejecting you, the more likely it is that your child will continue to reject you. The best and surest way to reconnect is to mirror and use baby play. But again—and this may seem counterintuitive or paradoxical—it's important that you not appear to be trying too hard. Sometimes if the parent who is being rejected tries to pick up or hug the child (and I'm assuming here for simplicity's sake that it's Daddy, although, as I've said, it might also be Mommy), the child will say, "No, don't touch me. I want Mommy." So what you need to do is mirror over little things and perhaps use a picture or a toy for your baby play, pretending that it's the child.

You can also join with what the child is feeling. If he whines, "No, I want Mommy," you can simply say, "I know you love your mommy, I understand why you want your mommy. Of course you want her: she's wonderful," which immediately makes you an ally rather than an opponent, and more often than not, at that point the child will simply stop asking for Mommy. When you're non-defensive you'll find that you have not only more choices but also much more power.

Another mirroring approach, if you get too close and the child rejects you, is simply to say, "You know what, I love you, and when you're ready, I'll come back." Just be nondefensive, and when you've said that much, walk away. Interestingly, this will leave your child wanting more and thinking that *he'll* have to work harder to win *you* back. In other words, it totally turns the dynamic on its ear. What you're doing here is giving the child enough time and space to feel safe enough and comfortable enough to take that step toward you.

Still another nonintrusive, nonthreatening way to reconnect is to purchase an erasable whiteboard, put it up on the back of your child's closet door, and leave her a note each day. Your message might say something like, "I love the way you [did whatever]," or "My favorite thing about you is . . ." and sign it. This is a great thing to do with older kids, too, and even though you might think they'd consider it corny and embarrassing, I guarantee you they won't. One of the things I enjoy most is having parents who were skeptical of something I'd suggested coming back to tell me—the surprise evident in their voice—how much their child loved it.

The reconnection may happen quickly or take more time, but when it does, the parent who had previously been favored may be thrilled or become a bit jealous. I know you might think that's crazy and that it won't happen to you, but, crazy or not, it does sometimes happen, and the more aware of it you are, the better you'll be able to deal with it.

By way of fair warning, I should also say that when a child prefers one parent over the other, the one to whom she is most attached will almost certainly, ironically, become the recipient of most of the child's bad behavior simply because she feels safer with that parent. When that occurs, the closer or favored relationship may begin to unravel, and that really leaves the child twisting in the wind with nothing to hold on to or to anchor him.

It's also true that the bond with one parent can become frayed for a variety of legitimate reasons that may be frightening to a small child—if one parent travels a lot for business, if a parent is ill or in the hospital for an extended period of time, or simply if a parent is very busy with work and becomes extra crabby for a few weeks or months. In any of these instances it's easy for a child to feel threatened and/or abandoned and to withhold or withdraw attachment for fear that he or she will be hurt. These feelings can be particularly exacerbated either when the child is adopted or when parents are going through a divorce.

The Special Challenges of Adoption and Attachment

Most adoptive parents—especially those who adopt babies at birth— believe quite naturally that when they bring their babies home and love them, that will be "enough." And in many, many cases, of course, it is. But more recently it has been recognized that babies do have a visceral or neurological "memory" of their connection with their birth mother in the womb. Even in the womb a baby's brain is beginning to organize around predictable sounds and rhythms, and the baby is beginning to self-regulate around the signals coming to it from the mother. In her book *The Primal Wound*, Nancy Verrier describes what it is like for a baby to then be separated from his birth mother and to remember that separation.

What may happen then is that the baby might resist attaching to his or her adoptive parents because he or she fears being abandoned again. Already that infant brain has organized itself to cope with abandonment. Self-protection is human instinct, and it's at work even in the tiniest baby. This means that adoptive parents must work extra hard at mirroring, attaching, and strengthening that bond. And if the baby is older—say twelve to eighteen months, as is often the case if you're adopting a baby from overseas—this may be even more important.

If she was in an orphanage where there wasn't much mirroring or physical contact, the baby may have trouble forming attachments. And if she *was* mirrored to and nurtured, she may feel once more abandoned. Either way, it can make it even more critical for the adoptive parents to constantly mirror and engage in baby play.

If, however, your baby isn't responding as you assumed he would to all your loving attention, you may instinctively feel rejected and disappointed—especially if you've been waiting a long time and are overjoyed to finally have your baby home with you. Then—as is also the case with parents of babies who have an underlying disorder or neurological problem that makes it harder for them to attach—you may begin to mirror less when you actually should be mirroring more.

I do want to emphasize here that there's no blame attached to any of these reactions; they are totally human and totally instinctive, and they can also occur with birth parents. We believe (because society tells us so) that the moment we hold our baby for the first time, we will fall in love, and most often that happens, but sometimes it doesn't. Attachment is something we have to work at, and it comes more naturally to some people than to others. When it doesn't, parents may begin to think there's something wrong with *them*, but there isn't. And this may be particularly true of new dads, who often need more time to develop the attachment that generally comes more naturally to mothers.

Furthermore, I should say that not all adoptive parents and babies will experience attachment problems. If the baby is naturally resilient, the primal wound may have less effect than it does on a baby who is more reactive. Again, it's about how one human being differs from another, and I don't want adoptive parents to go looking for trouble. That said, the connected-parenting program is particularly important for forming a bond with adopted children. Furthermore, if you as an adoptive parent do sense that the bonding experience isn't occurring quite the way you thought it would, being aware of the attachment dynamic and knowing that you have the ability to make changes will be both reassuring and empowering.

When Attachment Is Frayed by Divorce

The withdrawal and instinctive self-protection that results from fear of abandonment can also be triggered when parents are divorced or in the process of being divorced. This is also when a child might reject one parent in favor of the other.

Most often the child will be closer to the custodial parent simply because that's the person with whom he spends the most time. However, the custodial parent is also the one who does most of the hard parenting and is, therefore, most likely to bear the brunt of the child's bad behavior. Because his time with the noncustodial parent is limited, he's more likely to avoid challenging that parent, to be a bit more protective of him or her, simply because he doesn't want to spend his limited time fighting. Instead, he'll bring his anger or resentment home to the one where he feels safer and more comfortable.

In addition, the noncustodial parent may often take on the role of "Disney Parent" and make the child's visit all about breaking the rules and having fun. For the same reasons that the child doesn't want to make waves, that parent will have a harder time doing the hard parenting. And again, this will make it harder for the custodial parent when the child returns home complaining,"You're mean! This is how it is at Daddy's [or Mommy's] house." Don't let that fool you, or lure you into becoming more lenient.

If you do send your child off to spend a weekend with Dad (or Mom, because certainly it can go either way), where there are no rules, and where jumping on the sofa is standard procedure, so long as you've been mirroring and limit-setting while he's with you the foundation will be laid, and it will hold. He may be exhausted or hyperactive for a day or two when he comes back, and there may be a transition phase when you feel as if all the work you've been doing has been undone, but if you continue to use the techniques you've been using, you'll see that quite quickly things will return to normal. You just have to trust that what you do will be sufficient, and it will be.

In fact, one of the most interesting and gratifying results when parents share custody is that after a while the child begins to take the CALM confidence he's acquired from one into the home of the other because he's been taught a different way of being in the world.

In one extreme case, Jason, the nine-year-old son of divorced parents, lived with his father but spent weekends with his mother. At his mom's, he had no regular mealtimes and generally stayed up all night with her, eating pizza and watching TV. When he got back to his dad's house he was often physically ill and always out of control for a few days. He was angry to the point of being physically violent, and found himself so unlovable that his behavior with his father was simply horrible. Interestingly, Jason's younger sister, who kept the same schedule, didn't seem to be bothered by the differences between the two households.

After coming to see me, the dad began to work on mirroring and containing to get his relationship with his son back on track. He'd been reluctant to try to set limits with Jason because he was afraid that it would only make him angrier, but exactly the opposite happened.

The dad began to see some behavioral changes right away as Jason's moods evened out and he became more settled and generally more pleasant, but Dad still didn't know what to do about Mom. In the beginning, Jason was very protective of his mother and would never criticize her. What happened, however, was that as he began to feel safer with his dad he also started to open up with him. Whereas initially he'd wanted his parents to get back together, after a while he began to articulate the fact that he really wasn't comfortable with what was going on at his mother's house and even admitted that he really thought it would be better if they didn't reconcile because, as he put it, "I really like the way things are in our house."

After three or four months, he also started to behave differently with his mother, saying that he wanted to go home when he felt sick. His father's mirroring was having a global impact on his behavior even though his mother wasn't mirroring—wasn't, in fact, doing anything different from what she'd been doing all along.

What happened is that his father's home had become an oasis where things were predictable and made sense. Jason felt safe there and, because of that, he also became more confident and resilient in his relationship with his mother. The fact is that in such unsettled times children need and crave more, not less, structure.

Ideally, of course, both parents would be mirroring and setting limits because that would make it easier for the child, and even if the rules were not exactly the same in both households, he would know what was expected of him in each place and would, therefore, feel safer with both parents. But no matter how in sync the parents are, the child will need some transition whenever he goes from one place to another, and both parents will have to be extra careful to use their connected-parenting techniques for the first twenty-four to forty-eight hours to reestablish the pattern.

Aside from dealing with two sets of rules, what can make it difficult for a child to deal with divorce is that by the time a couple decides to separate or divorce, a lot of damage may already have been done. There may have been a lot of yelling or arguing or downright hostility in the home, and that is always extremely painful for children, whether or not the family remains intact. I know that when you're under emotional strain it may be difficult to always be thinking about the children.

The same is also true when we criticize the other parent in front of or to our children. If you're constantly complaining that "Daddy never picks you up on time" or "Mommy never calls when she says she's going to," you're hurting your child just as much as if you had slapped him in the face, if not more. All I can say is, don't do it. It can be damaging to the child and destructive for everyone. Find a friend or a therapist to whom you can vent—anyone other than your child.

There are several scenarios that can ensue when you complain to your child about her other parent. She might come home and say, "Daddy says you're [fill in the blank]," which is bound to offend you so much that your own agenda will take over and you'll start fighting with your child. Or she might come home and you'll ask her, "What did Mommy say about me?" Then, because she's trying to protect both of you, she might say, "She didn't say anything," whether that's true or not. And even if she does tell you, it could be because she agrees with the other parent or because she doesn't (as in, "You won't believe what Mommy said about you!"). However it plays out, you're putting your child in an untenable and extremely painful position.

If she does come home and report, what you need to do is take a nondefensive stance. Don't argue; don't try to correct the child. Simply say, "I'm sorry your daddy—or mommy—feels that way. It's got to be awful for you to hear that. You know in your heart what kind of mommy—or daddy—I am." If the other person continues to demean or complain about you to your child, so be it. That doesn't mean you have to do it.

In a best-case scenario, of course, you will be working together, but, again, you can't control what happens in someone else's home. What I tell my clients is that the other parent's house is a black box. You don't have entry there and you can't worry about what's happening there. Assuming that there's nothing actually dangerous to your child going on, there isn't anything you can do. The only thing you *can* do is to make your own home an oasis so that it becomes your child's "true north." Be sure that it is safe and predictable, that it makes sense, and that it is loving.

Not only will you be protecting your child from harm, but you will also appear to be much more reliable and trustworthy, which, in the end, will draw your child closer because she will feel safer when she's with you. And if you're having a problem, stop and remind yourself that your child didn't want this divorce—you did. And ask yourself how you would feel if someone told you that you could live with only one of your children. Which one would you choose?

When Parents Can't Always Be There

When you work long hours and get home late or travel often for business, it can be very hard to connect with your children and feel part of their lives. You may feel left out of the rhythm and flow of the family, or you may just be too tired and pressured to have the energy it takes to follow the strategies in this book.

Once again, all I can say is that you can't afford not to, and you can make the most of the few hours you have by mirroring and using baby-play techniques. If you are a parent of young children, you may find that you are attacked joyfully when you walk in the door feeling exhausted and still thinking about your day. Your wife or husband may say, "Thank God you're here, I need a break," and hand you the kids. Here are a few tips to help you make the precious hours you have as positive as you can.

- Take a minute to unwind in the car or on the subway on the way home. Don't check your BlackBerry or make calls. Listen to music, talk to a friend on the phone, and relax.
- Tell yourself that your family needs you, and know that you are going to be "on" when you walk in the door.
- If it's late and close to bedtime, resist the urge to wind up the kids just when the person who was home with them has no doubt gotten them settled. This is not the time for adrenaline play.
- Instead, get down on the floor and cuddle with your kids. Sit down with your teen and tell him you're all his for thirty minutes.
- Then, when you're done, get changed, look at the paper, check the mail, and take a few minutes for yourself.

- Be present for your kids' bedtimes. This is as important for you as it is for them.
- After they're in bed you can turn your BlackBerry back on or go to the computer to check your e-mail.
- Don't forget how important it is to connect with your spouse or partner as well. Remember to mirror with your partner; it is a powerful way to reconnect and stay strong.

Bullies and Bullying

You can do everything in your power to build your child's confidence and resilience, but there's not much you can do about other people's children. Despite your best efforts, your child may still become the target of a bully, and if that happens it will rip your heart out. There are few things more painful for a parent than knowing her child is being hurt emotionally or physically and believing there's nothing she can do about it. But there are some things you can do.

First of all, you need to know when your child is being bullied, and you can't necessarily count on him or her to tell you. Look for changes in mood, a drop in grades, irritability or suddenly picking on siblings, being oversensitive, taking things more personally than in the past, suddenly not wanting to go to school, headaches, or stomachaches that can't be explained. And if you notice any of these changes, be a good listener. You'll need to mirror first, saying something like, "You know, sweetie, you're an amazing kid and you're usually very happy. I know you, and something must be really bugging you. I want you to know that I'm not going to pressure you; I'm not going to make you tell me. I just want you to know that whatever it is must be really bad because I can see it in your face." And then walk away. Walking away instead of going into interrogation mode or what I call going on a fishing expedition is really important because it will make it much more likely that your child will let you in on what's going on. Think of it as if you and your child were on opposite sides of a swinging door. He's pushing on one side to keep you out and you're pushing on the other to get in. If you stop pushing (or badgering him), he'll push the door open and come to you.

Boys may be more physical, but they also tend to get it out and get it over with. Girls can be physical, but they're much more likely to be mean and demeaning. They may, for example, shut a particular girl out by closing ranks and not letting her sit with them in the lunchroom, they may make nasty remarks about her hair or her clothing, or they might start rumors about her. Emotional bullying can be even more damaging than physical bullying and also harder to spot.

Particularly among girls there is often one, whom Rosalind Wiseman, educator and author of *Queen Bees & Wannabes*, has termed a "Queen Bee," who is surrounded by a "court" of acolytes currying favor. These acolytes may or may not agree with her opinions or her behavior, but they're afraid to cross her and be shut out themselves. What this means for the child being bullied is that she falls prey to "social contagion." Once the Queen Bee decides a particular child should be shunned and tells her friends, the entire group will begin to treat her differently. What's interesting from a psychological standpoint is that in this kind of situation the Queen Bee is really bullying her friends as much as the one she's decided to ostracize. All it would take is for three members of her court to say, "Why are you doing that? I'm not going to go along with it," for her to stop. Her power resides in their fear.

Social contagion can be passed on even to parents. Let's say, for example, that you as a mother notice you haven't seen your child's friend Suzy for a while and ask why she's not invited over anymore. Your child might shrug and say, "Oh, Suzy, she's a loser," or "She's really weird and annoying," and you then might think, *Oh, well, I don't want my child being friends with someone like that.* Parents want their kids to be well liked—many want their child to be in the popular group—and they may, therefore, inadvertently encourage bad behavior. If you find yourself thinking that way, you probably need to check your own agenda. Your child doesn't have to be friends with Suzy if she's annoying, but she does need to be respectful. It is rare for parents to recognize "bullying behavior" in their own child. It is important to be open and aware of your child's attitude toward others.

Kids are always told that if they're being bullied in school they should tell a teacher, but that will only work if there is a system in place to support them. Teachers constantly have kids complaining to them about other kids being mean, and sometimes they tell the children to deal with it themselves. But that doesn't mean the school shouldn't be held responsible—it should.

If you, as a parent, are aware that your child is being bullied, you first need to find out what the school's policy is with regard to bullying. It should be the same for emotional bullying as it is for physical, and the bully needs to be held responsible for his or her actions. Above all, don't be afraid to take your complaint to the teacher (or the principal if you're not getting satisfaction from the teacher) because you think that will only make it worse for your child. You can also suggest that the school have a bullying expert come in to assess the situation. School boards often have such resources to offer. You might also suggest that the teacher keep a bully box on her desk so that children who are being bullied can let her know without having to actually talk about it. Many kids don't want to tell their parents or their teacher, but they can write their problem on a piece of paper and the teacher can check the box at the end of each day.

You can never change another child's behavior, but if, as I said, you've been mirroring with your child, you'll have been building the resilience your child needs to stand up for himself and withstand bullies. To provide a child with the tools to do that more effectively, I suggest arming him with what I call "stand-up-for-yourself statements." The point here is that if a child is able to very strongly stand up for himself, the bully won't be getting what he's looking for and will more than likely stop.

I explain this to kids in terms of a video game. Almost all video games have some kind of power bar or icon that lets the player know what level of power he's on. When someone is being a bully or says something mean, if you get upset or even try to ignore him, the bully's power bar goes up and the victim's power goes down. So I tell kids that they can't hand over their power to the bully, and every time they get upset or cry or get very angry that's what they're doing.

Making a stand-up-for-yourself statement is not the same thing as bullying back. To do that would be to encourage it to continue and/or to become a bully yourself. One of my favorite stand-up-for-yourself statements was made by a little third grader who was wearing a pair of "light-up" shoes that one of her classmates obviously thought were too babyish for third grade and decided to make this a reason to torment her. Because we'd already talked about stand-up-for-yourself statements, my client just looked the bully in the face and said, "Why are you so interested in my shoes? I happen to like these shoes and I don't care what you think." And then she turned and walked away. Walking away is very important here, too, because it leaves the bully with absolutely nothing to say. In this case, she might also have said, "Oh, right, this is where you make fun of my shoes. Can you think of something else, because this is getting old." Or, if the child is really at a loss for a response, "What *is* your problem?" or "So? Whatever!" also works just fine so long as it's said with confidence. The point is to not give the bully any further ammunition. Kids need to understand that bullies pick on people who are fun to pick on, and if you show them that you're not upset, it won't be fun anymore.

You can practice role-playing stand-up-for-yourself statements with your child. Just be sure that when you're doing this you make it clear that what you're doing is meant to be empowering and that you're not blaming your child for being bullied. You can have your child play the role of the bullier while you're the one making the stand-up-for-yourself statements, using all your body language and tone of voice to get across the fact that you're not being intimidated or bothered. This will let him see and hear what standing up for himself looks and sounds like so that he can think about how he'd feel if he were the bullier and someone was making these statements to him.

The sad truth is that there will always be bullies and there will always be children who attract them. And the more competitive (and, consequently, the less empathic) our culture becomes, the more bullying there will be. Many adults appear to believe that bullying and/or being bullied is just a "normal" part of growing up. If you think that, consider how you would feel if you walked into your office or a party and suddenly everyone started whispering about you. How would you feel if you walked into the company cafeteria and everyone told you that you couldn't sit with them? We sometimes forget that children feel things every bit as much as we do, and that they often have fewer tools to deal with their feelings than we do.

In fact, I've found that there are some parents who actually admire their children for being bullies. They seem to think this is a sign of strength and leadership ability. I would beg to differ, and I would assure you that teaching your child to be empathic is not preventing him from becoming successful. On the contrary, it is more likely to make him a really great leader, not to mention a happy and full-filled adult.

Being a bully, on the other hand, is likely to haunt kids into adulthood. It's a negative behavior that's as detrimental to the bullied as to the bully. Many kids who are bullies grow up to be bigger bullies, and those who don't often feel so bad about their bullying that they carry the shame with them for years. One friend told me recently that he still felt so bad about being a bully as a child that he'd tracked down one of his victims more than twenty years later to apologize.

If you suspect that your child might be a bully, what you need to do is to empathize more about other things, increase your mirroring, and adjust the tension on the rope. If you do, your child won't feel the need to use her power in negative ways because she'll be receiving powerful rewards for doing other things. In the end, mirroring and connecting not only give children the resilience to withstand bullying, but also give those who seek power by bullying a better sense of their own power so that they won't need to bully. Any way you look at it, it's a win-win strategy.

When Your Child Won't Go to School

This is a tough one. When a child—particularly an older child or teenager—doesn't want to go to school (or day camp or an after-school program) getting him or her to comply can seem like an impossible task. The anxiety and stress this causes parents can be very overwhelming. And it leaves them swinging between anger at their child for being so resistant, defiant, and impossible, and terror that he or she will be missing out on life and falling into a pattern of quitting and avoiding.

To understand how your child might be feeling, go back to the discussion of anxious children in Chapter Twelve. Then you must go about the very difficult task of trying to figure out how much is behavior and how much is genuine panic. Once again, mirroring as much as possible not only about school but also about unrelated issues—both the good things and the bad—is very important because it tightens that rope, helps build resilience, and encourages risk-taking. Frontloading is also critical here, as are messages of competence such as, "I know you can also do this. I wouldn't ask you to go anywhere I didn't think you would be safe." You can also try having the child write a letter from his left brain to his right brain reassuring himself that once he is at school he will be all right.

It is very important that your child not get in the habit of staying home. The problem is that her decision not to go to school is based on the fight-or-flight mechanism that's telling her to retreat and hide until the tiger padding outside her cave goes away. School, however, does not go away, and the longer she hides and avoids it, the more unmanageable the problem will become. So even if you have to sit in the car or in the school office with her all day, that's better than letting her stay home.

I realize that many parents can't stay home, but if you can take a day off, I advise that you do so to reinforce the plan. If you can't, see if there is a trusted relative who is willing and able to carry it out properly. And if neither of these scenarios is possible, go to work and enforce it in the evening when you get home.

Keep in mind that this is a last resort. Often a trusted teacher or a caring principal will be willing to talk to your child on the phone.

This takes love, patience, and determination as well as a willingness to follow the strategies for anxiety suggested in Chapter Twelve.

With children who may not be anxious but who just want a day off, parents will be faced with the "Are they really sick?" dilemma. For this, frontload your child and tell him that if he stays home from school there will be no TV, no computer, and no screen time of any kind. He will have to stay in bed for most of the morning and he's going to be very bored. If he's really sick, you'll know it because he won't care. If he's faking it, he'll only do it once because his day will be so long and boring that staying home will have lost its appeal. I must add that once this was implemented in my house it became very easy to tell who was sick, and my days of getting duped dropped dramatically.

When You Think Your Child Is Lying

Lying is a tricky issue. We tend to give our children very black-and-white messages about it, but it is anything but a black-and-white issue. We tell them that lying is wrong, that no one will trust them if they don't tell the truth, and that honesty is the best policy. But we don't always practice what we preach.

As parents, it is important to examine our own behavior in order to fully understand our children's. Do we always practice the truth? Do we tell our kids to say they're ten so we can pay less for a ticket to the movies? Do they hear us using lies to get out of plans or commitments we don't want to keep? Do they see us using lying as a coping mechanism to avoid offending someone or to avoid conflict? We must consider these issues when we look at how and why a child lies. We also need to practice the truth and model it whenever possible. If we have to tell a white lie for situational or ethical reasons, we need to discuss our decision with our child and take responsibility for it.

Children lie for many reasons (many of which are the same reasons we do): to avoid getting into trouble, to make themselves sound more interesting, to get back at people, to avoid feeling anxious, to fit in with peers. It is important to remember that all kids tell stories or lie occasionally. It is when this behavior becomes a consistent pattern or coping style or when it seems to preoccupy the child that parents should worry. If lying occurs everywhere in all settings and comes back to you from multiple sources, there could be a problem.

How we react to our child's lying can determine whether the behavior improves or becomes a bigger problem. Getting angry, threatening, or shaming the child can and most often does cause him to shut down communication and ensure that he remains defensive and committed to telling a better lie the next time. It is very important to remember that children get just as upset if you don't believe their lies as if you don't believe their truth. The experience of someone not believing them can be so upsetting it can override any desire to tell the truth and cause them to get very stuck.

If you know your child is lying, first use the CALM technique. Hear what he has to say without commenting, guiding, reprimanding, or teaching. Then reflect that without any hint of sarcasm or judgment. By doing that you will create safety in the conversation. Once he feels safe, your child will be able to hear how his story sounds without becoming defensive and will often, all by himself, adjust the story to tell the truth. When he does that, praise him for being truthful and then use the opportunity to talk to him about why lying is a problem. This is where you correct, guide, and, if necessary, impose a consequence. Just make sure the child understands that the consequence would be worse if he hadn't told the truth. Your child should remember the experience as being relatively positive so that he will be more likely to tell you the truth in the first place the next time.

If he doesn't change his tune but sticks with his original story, you need to tell him that you love him, that he is a good person, but that you're having trouble believing him, and why. Then simply state that you'll talk about it later and give him some time to make the right decision. Sometimes when a child—or anyone—feels cornered, he can't think clearly and will get stuck—even if he wants to do the right thing. But even if the truth never comes out, the child will probably remember how this conversation felt (not so good) and will also be more likely to tell the truth the next time.

Children remember not *what* you said in a conversation but *how you made them feel*. Make them feel like telling the truth.

Vacations the Whole Family Can Enjoy

Family vacations can be problematic mainly because we parents mistakenly believe that because we're going on a fun trip, our children should all be especially "good" and we, as parents, should be on vacation. If that doesn't happen, our own agenda is likely to kick in so that we start screaming, "We spent all this money to take you on a great vacation! Not everyone gets to go on such a great vacation." And that's when all hell is likely to break loose. So here's my first and most important piece of advice for parents: when you have kids, you're *never* on vacation. You're not taking a vacation from parenting; you're merely changing the venue—hopefully to someplace warmer and nicer, but whatever problems you may have are going on vacation with you.

One of the best things you can do to head off trouble before you even leave home is to tighten up on all your techniques: mirror more, baby-play more, but also set more limits, remain really firm, and make sure you are frontloading. Mean what you say and say what you mean. If you're going to be eating in restaurants, frontload the behavior you'll be expecting; remind your children about friendship moves and friendship blocks. Then, start to issue consequences as soon as the vacation starts. If someone acts up at the airport, you can say, "Okay, you sit here and you sit there and your iPod is now my iPod. You've made the choice and you've just lost it for the next half hour." Don't be nasty about it, don't yell; remain neutral but let your children know you really mean it. They'll remember that, hopefully for the rest of the vacation. If, on the other hand, you loosen up because you think it's vacation time, and if your kids are taking advantage of that, you'll have a hard time reining them in as things get worse instead of better—which they will.

As a rule, especially if you have younger children or those who are particularly sensitive to eating and sleeping disturbances, you'd be best off sticking as close as possible to their normal meal- and bedtime routines. You don't want to be too rigid, but if you extend their bedtime or skip a meal one day, it's best not to do it two days in a row.

Another tip, which probably sounds logical when you're at home reading this but might fall by the wayside when you're actually at your vacation destination, is to give your kids some downtime. Don't think that you can drag them from one activity to another from breakfast until dinner without having them become cranky or wild-eyed, or worse. Children get both tired and overstimulated, and the combination is a prescription for acting up and acting out. If you keep dragging them around and filling them with junk food or quick snacks to stop their whining, you're going to pay the price. If you know you're going to be missing a meal, or if you're not sure what kind of food will be available, try to carry snacks with you—some children need to eat as often as every one and a half to two hours.

Also, try to structure your days. Sometimes writing down what you're going to be doing and giving your kids a schedule helps them know what to expect. As I've said before, we adults are constantly expecting our children to follow our agenda, pulling them away from one thing to do something else without any warning. How do you feel when you're in the middle of doing something and someone comes along and tells you to stop because you have to do something else? Kids feel the same way, only more so, because they generally have much less say in what they're going to be doing. When you're making up your schedule, try to let your children have some input. You don't have to say, "What would you like to do today?" That's actually giving them *too much* choice. But you can say, "This morning we'll be going to the beach. Then we're coming back to the hotel for lunch. After lunch, we can either go to the water park or we can go to see the seals. Which would you rather do?" This is called perceived choice, and it's a great strategy that allows kids to feel they have a choice while at the same time keeping their choice within the structure you've decided is best for them. If you have children of different ages, you and your spouse or partner can split up so that each child gets to do something he or she wants to do. Of course, there will have to be compromises; no one (including you) is going to get to do everything he or she wants to do. You can frontload that in advance, but also understand that you may have to skip something on your own agenda if, for example, you have a small child for whom the activity would be totally inappropriate and, therefore, virtually guaranteed to trigger a meltdown. Keep in mind that if you don't plan a trip that includes activities both you and your children will enjoy, no one is going to have a good time.

But what about the travel itself—getting to where you're going?

Plane trips can be difficult. Try to head off trouble at the pass by taking along lots of snacks. Also, take along several brand-new toys and/or games—things your child has never seen before—and bring them out one by one. Is this appeasement? Maybe. But if you're in a small, enclosed space for several hours, sometimes appeasement is your best course of action. It can be extremely stressful if your child is screaming or kicking the seat in front of him and the people all around you are sending you death stares. That anxiety can easily get in the way of your remaining neutral, and your child will then pick up on how nervous you are, which will either add to her anxiety or give her the bright idea that she can really get to you. If your child has a meltdown, all you can do is mirror, set your limits, and try distraction. And if your fellow passengers see that you're taking charge and doing everything you can to control the situation, they'll usually cut you some slack—and maybe even admire you for it.

Car trips are similar, if less public. Take along books, games, videos, snacks, and—if you're traveling with more than one child—remember to teach them to use their friendship moves and blocks (see page 139).

Bottom line: When you go on a family vacation, make sure that you pack your bag of tricks.

Planning Successful Playdates

When children have problems with social skills, it can be difficult for them to "play nicely together." There are, however, things you can do to make playdates go more smoothly, which will help build your child's social skills, which will then make it more likely that future playdates will also go smoothly.

One of the best things you can do to ensure a successful experience is to keep it short and sweet. For younger children, those who have difficulty socializing, or those who are easily overstimulated, about an hour and a half is a good time frame. The mistake so many of us make is that when things are going well, we're seduced into letting them go on too long. Rather than let the date end with the children fighting, end it when everyone is happy, feels good about the experience, and wants to do it again.

Sometimes all goes smoothly until it's time to leave, and this is often because small children just don't know what to say or how to end it. I've found that scripting a good-bye for them can make it a lot easier. Let's assume that you've already let your child know that he'll be playing with Josh but that when you say it's time to go, he'll have to say good-bye and come along. When that time comes, however, he may start to whine and complain that he doesn't want to leave. What you can do then is help him by saying, "Okay, it's time to leave. Tell Josh, 'Oh, I'm so sorry. I had a really good time, but I have to go now.'" And, just as when you're mirroring, use the tone and inflection your child will be using when he says those words. This is called scripting. It can be difficult for little kids to know what to say, and by giving them the words, you're actually giving them the tools to master a new social skill.

If your child struggles with positive social interaction it's also a good idea, particularly if he or she is very active, to create structured activities and let your child know what he or she is going to be doing. You can even write it down; kids actually love that. So, you might say, "First we're going to be doing this activity for this amount of time, then we're going to have a snack, and then we're going to do this." For children who are five or six, board games, baking, and imaginative play generally work well. Bowling is also a good, structured activity, or going to a playground, or even going to a movie.

Before the playdate begins, you'll need to frontload your child, basically telling her what kind of behavior you're going to expect and letting her know that if she is rude or mean or hits the other child, the playdate will be over.

Remember to talk about the expected behavior in narrative terms. With young children you can say things like, "I don't want to see the No Monster or the Cranky Bug." You can make a game out of locking the No Monster out of the car, rolling up the windows so that the imaginary monster can't get back in, and driving away. Or have some fun pretending to lock the No Monster in the closet so he doesn't wreck the game your child is playing with his friend. Tell your child the No Monster or the Cranky Bug or whatever you call it isn't allowed to come to that playdate or the zoo, and work with him to ensure success by offering help and strategies like using the volcano discussed in Chapter Twelve. As a parent you have to have many tools in your toolbox and use them all.

You can also talk about frustration, and make a plan together about how to keep the behavior from ruining the play. Use these moments to point out the connection between choosing, good behaviors and seeing good outcomes; when we make good choices, good things and happy faces are more likely to follow. Remember that these strategies can work in all kinds of situations, not just playdates.

When you're planning your strategies you'll also have to explain to the other child's parent or nanny or whoever is bringing her over that your child is a little bit cranky, so this or that might happen, and if it does, it's not her child's fault. I also suggest that you have some kind of "door prize" to give the visitor if she has to leave before the playdate is officially over, because you don't want her to feel blamed for your child's bad behavior.

Make sure you're comfortable enough with the other child's parent to do this. You probably don't want to do it with someone you don't know very well or someone who's going to say, "Well, if your child is so terrible why would I bring my child to play with her at all!" And if something does go wrong, remember that there are times when it is not your child's fault.

Most important of all, if your child does misbehave, make sure that you follow through with what you've told her is going to happen. Following through, letting her know that by behaving as she did she was making a choice and that her choice has a consequence, is what's going to lead to her making better choices for playdates in the future.

Equally important, do praise your child if the playdate goes well, and also point out how much better it is when things go well. To do this, I like to use the "Good brings good" formula. Point out that when your child makes a good choice something good will follow, and that if he makes a bad choice (or, if you're uncomfortable with the work "bad," an icky or yucky choice, or whatever other term you prefer), something negative will happen. For example, you might explain that if another child grabs your child's toy and your child pushes the other child or tries to grab it back, the child who was pushed will push back or your child will get into trouble, so two bad things will have happened. Your child still won't have his toy and he'll be facing a negative consequence. On the other hand, if another child grabs his toy and he asks you to help him get it back, you'll no doubt praise him for doing that, you'll help him get his toy back, and he'll receive a reward for making a good choice. This is a good way to explain the notion that behaviors have consequences. You'll probably have to repeat the idea over and over, but eventually your child will get it.

If your child is a bit of an outsider at school or if there's another child he's not getting along with very well (assuming it's not the class bully), inviting someone into your home and letting him or her have a positive experience is a way of helping your own child become part of the group or get over whatever has been going on between him and another child in the class. The bond that's formed during the playdate can then carry over into the school environment and make your child more confident.

Of course, the trick is to be sure that it *is* a positive experience for both children. So, again, letting your child know what's expected of him before the playdate begins is absolutely key. Explain, for example, that if his friend wants to do something and he doesn't want to, he can do what his friend wants for a little while and then they can both do what he wants. You can also talk about what toys she might not want to share and put them away ahead of time to avoid any problems.

Then try not to hover. Certainly you need to keep your ears open and be aware of what's going on, but try to let the children work things out for themselves as much as possible. And don't reprimand your child in front of his guest. You can make global statements in front of both children, such as, "Sometimes it's really hard to share the toys you love, so what can we do to make it easier for you to play together?" Otherwise, if you see or hear something you don't like, take your child aside into another room and speak to her privately. You can remind her about friendship moves and friendship blocks (see page 139) and of the consequence you discussed if the behavior continues.

The same rules generally apply—with age-appropriate adjustments—for children up to the age of about eleven. You know your own child. You know how much supervision he or she needs.

Not so long ago, probably when you were growing up, kids had a lot more freedom. Personally, I remember going outside, finding the neighborhood kids, and staying out all morning until it was time for lunch. Some kids were mean and some kids were nice, and we worked it out. It's through that kind of unstructured play (with friends as well as siblings) that children learn how to advocate for themselves, how to be flexible, how to make a point, and how to negotiate— among other important skills they'll need as adults. Now, however, children's activities are much more structured and are generally supervised by an adult who is in charge and making the rules. When there's a conflict, the adult will say, "Okay, now you go over and apologize to so-and-so . . ." An adult is always telling them what to do. Because of that, it's important for parents to find the delicate balance between constantly hovering and acting as the referee and being so permissive that their children think it's okay to behave in ways that are simply not acceptable.

Another aspect of learning when to let go and let be is recognizing when it's time for your child to start making his or her own social arrangements. By the time your child is in about fourth or fifth grade it's no longer appropriate for you to be making his playdates. If you do that, there's the danger of your child's falling into the trap of learned helplessness. Not only that, but if you continue to accost moms in the school yard to make a date for your child (and it's often the mothers of kids who don't do particularly well socially who do this) you run the risk of having them run away from you and, thus, becoming part of the problem instead of the solution. If other mothers come to view you as aggressive and obtrusive, they're more likely to stay away from your child because they don't want to deal with you. This is a tough thing to hear, I know, but it's important to understand that you can and do impact your child's social world.

At first, you might suggest that your child call his or her friend to make plans and then you'll speak to the mother to be sure that the plans they've made are appropriate and acceptable to her. You may also want to make the transition easier by reminding your child that if she doesn't want to be bored she should make some plans for the weekend, and you can discuss what she might want to do or whom she might want to invite over. You can even rehearse the call, but then you need to step back and let her follow through. If you feel it is as simple as her not getting around to it, well then, if she winds up with nothing to do for a weekend or two, she might learn from that experience and do what it takes to make sure it doesn't happen again. If she appears to have trouble making plans for other reasons, you can work with her to come up with plan-making strategies and talk to her about why it's so difficult for her.

One thing parents often ask me is what to do if they don't like one or more of their child's friends, and my answer to that is, "It depends." If it's simply your personal agenda—and there will always be some children you like better than others—it's tough, particularly once your child is ten or eleven years old, to pick his friends. If, on the other hand, you have a genuine and valid reason—if your child is misbehaving whenever a particular child is around or if she's being rude at home after playing with this child, or if the other child is acting like a bully or using poor judgment in his or her choice of activities—you can intervene. Limit playdates to your own home, where you can supervise them, and let your child know in advance that if his behavior changes during or after the date, there will be no more playdates with this child until he shows that he can make better choices. But also bear in mind that the Romeo and Juliet syndrome applies here, and the more you forbid your child to see someone, the more attractive that person can become. If you're the obstacle, they'll bond over that, whereas if you choose not to become the obstacle, your child is more likely to see the other person more clearly. Encouraging her to play with other children and mirroring to strengthen her from the inside out will help her make better choices on her own.

The one thing you need to be sure of is that wherever your child is going and whatever he's doing, you can be reasonably certain that he's safe. The older the child is, the more important this becomes.

Do You Think Your Kid's a Quitter?

Children can be fickle. They may be brimming with enthusiasm about a particular activity and then, a few weeks later, they don't want to do it anymore. Many of my clients want to know if it's okay to allow their kid to quit an activity he doesn't like or in which she's lost interest, or whether that's going to mean he or she becomes a quitter. I say, as with just about everything, you need to find some kind of balance.

You certainly don't want to let your child think he or she can drop in and out of activities at whim. But you also need to take a good look at your own agenda and decide whether you want your child to stick to something because it's important to *you*, and, if so, why? Perhaps you think swimming lessons are important for safety reasons. Perhaps you believe karate will build self-confidence. On the other hand, you may sending your daughter for ballet lessons because you always wanted to be a dancer or insisting your son take piano because you wish you could play. But even if your child asked—even begged—to do something and then changed his mind, you need to be a bit flexible.

I believe that when a child asks to participate in an activity, she ought to stick with it for a period of time, but I also think that if she gives it a fair chance and continues not to enjoy it, she should, in most instances, be allowed to drop out. There may be a couple of activities you consider nonnegotiable, and, if so, you need to make that clear from the beginning. (My children, for example, know that karate is nonnegotiable. That's the sport to which we've chosen to commit for the long term.) With others you should try to be more flexible. It seems counterproductive to me to force a child to continue an activity he or she clearly doesn't enjoy.

Beyond participating, however, there's the question of your wanting your child to make a genuine effort to excel. To some degree, this can be a two-edged sword. It's perfectly okay to motivate a child to try harder—so long as you don't do it by nagging, which virtually never works in any case. What you need to do is make positive statements like, "I know you can do this," or "This is what I know you're capable of," and then stop. You can also offer a positive reward, so long as it's for something the child has really worked to accomplish.

The potential pitfalls are that you may be asking your child to do something that's beyond his capabilities or, because he has a particular talent, you'll be praising the talent instead of the effort and, thereby, sending the false message that you love him *because of* the talent. It's great for a child to excel at something. In fact, studies have shown that for children who've had difficult lives, having a special talent is extremely protective emotionally and psychologically. But constantly praising your child for a talent or achievement puts an enormous amount of pressure on him. And it's also important to remember the study cited earlier in which children who were praised for trying hard rather than for their intelligence were more likely to persevere and do better over time. I believe the same applies to praising them for a particular skill.

No two children are alike, so you may have one child who's particularly talented in one area and another who is less—or differently—talented. What's important, then, is that they each have an activity that's all their own. They shouldn't have to compete against each other, and you shouldn't be comparing them either to each other or to their friends or your friends' children. What you always need to do is praise and celebrate each child's own efforts and abilities. All children are special in some way, and as parents we need to let them know that.

At the same time, however, I believe that you'll have a happier, less anxious child if you can just give him some time to play, chase butterflies (literally or figuratively), and simply be a child. Children these days tend to be as overscheduled as we are, and for the most part, they don't get to say much about whether or not they want to go to kiddie swim or toddler gymnastics or peewee soccer. Partly, I believe, this has to do with parents' feeling pressured to provide their kids with as many good experiences as possible and to help them get ahead. With every activity they put their children into, parents are thinking, *This is going to help him later in life,* or *This is going to help her be successful.* What it means, however, particularly if we have more than one child, is that the entire family is in a state of frantic movement all the time.

Children are in situations where they're being controlled by an adult virtually every minute of the day.

It's when they have unstructured playtime that children get the opportunity to figure these things out for themselves and acquire all kinds of critical life skills. They learn how to negotiate, how to be heard, how to take turns, how to wait, how to listen, how to make a point without hurting anyone's feelings, when to talk and when to be quiet, when something is funny and when it's not. They learn that these are important skills and that the better they learn them, the more fun they'll have playing with their friends. The brain does a lot of growing and pruning during these play experiences, which are an extremely important part of childhood. Playing also helps kids acquire academic skills like math and logic, and storytelling and language skills, and they have much more fun learning them that way than if you were sitting with them turning over a stack of flash cards.

As always, it is about balance. Various types of structured activity are certainly important, but there is also a time and an appropriate place for play. These are important, special moments between kids that we all remember from our own childhoods. I can remember, as I'm sure you can, running outside to play after school or on the weekend and feeling wonderful and free. There were no playdates; we just walked out the door to a neighborhood full of kids. Now the streets are empty; kids are busy with programs, lessons, and tutoring. That doesn't mean they're better off, though, and I think deep down we all know this.

In addition, some children need more quiet time than others. They need to be left alone to read or play with their Legos or their Barbies between events that involve a lot of social interaction. Others, particularly those who have any tendency toward hyperactivity or attention-deficit problems, need a great deal of stimulation. These kids don't do well with a lot of downtime, and boredom can be excruciating for them. Children have triggers just as you do, which also means that there are situations in which they are more or less likely to act out or melt down. As a parent you know your own child; you know how much downtime he needs or prefers and how much stimulation, social interaction, and structured activity he can tolerate or thrive on.

Living Safely in a Virtual World

In a world where we're all plugged in and able to communicate with anybody anytime, our children are privy to information and resources we'd never have been able to access at their age. The virtual world presents kids with many opportunities and, at the same time, presents us as parents with even more challenges.

Television and video games, as well as computers, expose kids to images and ideas they simply shouldn't be seeing. Just because you walk into the room and find your child watching a cartoon, don't assume it's age-appropriate. There are adult cartoons shown in prime time that no one's child should be watching. Some video games really are not only violent, but also antisocial in their content. So monitor the games you buy and activate the child controls on your TV.

The parents I talk to in my practice always seem surprised when they learn that their children are doing or viewing inappropriate things on the computer, but sometimes they just happen upon websites they never intended to access. If you doubt that this could happen, try typing "X Men" into your search engine and see what comes up. Not only are some of these sites inappropriate for kids, they can also be traumatic—whether the children do or don't understand what they're seeing.

So what can you do? Not only should you make sure that the child-safety devices on your computer are activated, but you also need to know your administrative password. If you don't, an enterprising child can easily undo whatever you've done to protect her and you'll never know it. Make sure you know her personal password and check it. If you know it, however, your child can and will change it, so your motto should be, "No password, no computer." Beyond that, you should find out from your Internet service provider how to obtain a history of the sites your child has visited and the e-mails she's sent. Not only does this allow you to find out where she's been going and what she's been doing on the computer, but also by having a record of her "conversations" you'll know and have hard evidence if she's been bullied (or bullying) online.

Protecting our children, however, goes beyond blocking what they shouldn't be seeing. It also means helping them to understand what's private and what's public. Because our kids have always lived in a world where computers are as common as telephones, they often think that "talking" to their friends on the computer via MySpace or Facebook, for example, is as private as having a phone conversation—but it isn't. As parents, we need to help our kids understand that in the virtual world virtually nothing is private. What I tell parents is that they should teach their children to think before they post a message on any website, "Would I say this if I were standing in the middle of a room full of people?" If the answer is no, they shouldn't "say" it online, either.

Because our kids are so computer savvy, we need to be savvy as well. We parents need to make it our business to understand the lingo (POS for "parent over shoulder," to name just one of the most obvious examples) and learn the tricks of the computer trade. (Websites such as http://www.indoindians.com/computerlingo.htm and http://www.netlingo.com will help to educate you.) We also need to listen to the advice of professionals and law enforcement officials about keeping the family computer in a public space and monitoring what our kids are doing. That's particularly true if the computer is equipped with a webcam. It's possible for the person with whom you're communicating to zoom in on a webcam image in order to obtain identifying information, including a name and address. Although your child may be more computer-literate than you, he or she is also more naïve and trusting, so it's up to you to protect your child and keep him or her safe from Internet predators.

You may meet with a fair amount of resentment and resistance, but again, this is where you need to use all the tools you've been acquiring: mirror, present the problem, and come up with a solution. Where our children's safety is concerned, no effort can be too great.

This is where you can use the line, "I love you enough for you to be mad at me."

The issues discussed in this chapter are, as I've said, those most frequently cited by my clients. You, of course, may have a different problem you'd like to resolve with and for your child. If so, just remember that all the techniques I offer throughout this book are adaptable to and will bring equally positive results in virtually any situation.

Managing
Through Mirroring

Any child, no matter how young or old, no matter his or her level of intelligence or behavior, will thrive with this model of connected parenting. It's worth repeating that even though we've been examining the behavioral or emotional issues of challenging children, it's equally important to practice mirroring and containing with every child. The so-called good kid will benefit from it as much as the anxious, angry, and acting-out child.

What you need to remember is that the tools I've been giving you are not a short-term cure or something you do until the problem goes away and then stop. Nor are they meant to replace any other tools or therapies you already have at your disposal. Connecting with your child through mirroring and containing is not an either/ or proposition. It doesn't require that you forget whatever else you have been told or have learned about your child up until now.

Nor is it a miracle. This is something I tell parents over and over again. Once you begin to mirror with your child, she will start to behave better. But then, I can almost guarantee, you will start to relax; maybe you'll let down your guard and not mirror as frequently. Or perhaps you'll become lax about imposing or enforcing consequences. If so, your child will then regress, and you will be surprised by the intensity of your reaction. You might think that after this respite from negative behavior you'd have developed more patience for coping with bad behavior, but you may find that you actually have less.

Over and over parents tell me that "Sophie did such-and-such, and I can't believe how I flipped out!" It's almost as though they were thinking, *I thought we were through with this. I can't go back!* In short, they panic.

Use your child's behavior as a barometer for how you're parenting. If the behavior seems to be deteriorating, you'll need to tighten up on the rope and increase your mirroring because the connection may have weakened for some reason, and your child is trying to re-establish a sense of where the boundaries are set. You won't be able to apply the same tension at all times, but you need to be aware of when there's too much slack. Your child's behavior is a kind of communication that will let you know how he's feeling.

What you need to remember is that this isn't like the movies; there's no perfect arc. Instead, things will get better, then worse, then better again. The more you mirror and contain, the less frequent and less intense the tantrums will become, and the quicker your child will recover. When you see your child every day, you may not notice how much he's growing until you realize that his pants are suddenly too short. In the same way, you may not realize how much he's growing emotionally. You may need to remind yourself of where you were and how far you've come. Try to notice the changes: *Hmm, he only had two blowups this week and they only lasted twenty minutes instead of an hour and a half.* Buy a notebook and write it down; keep a journal. I know it's difficult for many people, but doing that will help you begin to see your child differently. Also, take the time to discuss with your spouse or partner the changes each of you has noticed. This can be a great reality check when one or the other of you has come to take for granted or failed to notice something that would have seemed miraculous just a short time before.

That said, sometimes feeling better doesn't feel that much better for any one of a variety of reasons. Some behaviors may change very quickly, but others that are a bit stickier will tend to hang around. You may think your child is still having meltdowns, whining, hitting, saying no, or flying off the handle, but then you will notice that these episodes are occurring less frequently or that your child is recovering more quickly and moving on. Finally you will notice that the behaviors are less intense, and eventually you'll be enjoying longer and longer stretches when you say to yourself, "Wow, she's been great the last few days."

Do not be alarmed if your child appears to be crying more. I believe that underneath a lot of anger is sadness, and sometimes when a child feels safer he is able to cry more easily. This does not mean he is getting worse; often it means he is getting better. It means he now trusts the connection between you enough to show you how he really feels. In other words, it is coming out in tears instead of tantrums. Continue to mirror and show that you can tolerate his sadness. It will pass and the crying will ease up. Eventually you will find that your child no longer needs to show you what is wrong by using his behavior. You will have proven yourself as a listener so that he can tell you with words.

While all this is still a bit new, you may be unconsciously waiting for the other shoe to drop, anticipating that phone call from school, or waiting for the next tantrum. It can take a few months for you to accept that the changes you see have really taken hold. In addition, now that your child is better, you may be noticing all the little things you'd been letting slide because you were dealing with the big issues. It's not that different from when you decide to repaint the living room, and once the big job is done you first admire the fresh paint and then you start to notice that the sofa cushions are looking a bit frayed or the carpet could use a good cleaning.

And then, of course, there's the "other" child—the one who was easy and who had to take a backseat while you were preoccupied with the problems of the difficult one. Once the difficult one is no longer so difficult the easy child very often steps up and starts acting out. Again, you may not believe that this is going to happen in your home, but it happens more frequently than you would think.

A family functions like a system, and if you change something within the system, it triggers something else. If the child who was always in trouble is no longer in trouble, the good one often loses his self-definition. *If I'm not the good one, then who am I?* That can be quite upsetting for a child, so he will start to test the waters and may try out different tactics to discover his new place. Or perhaps you've been neglecting to mirror and connect with your easy child as much as you could because you've been devoting all your energy to her problem sibling; if so, just stepping up your mirroring and setting more limits will very quickly get her back on track.

In some situations, the easier child may have been trying to be the best little child in the world because he or she was so aware of how stressed you were from dealing with his or her sibling, and now that the crisis has eased he sees an opportunity to let loose a little bit. And, finally, it may be that the "good" child isn't acting any differently at all, but because you're no longer so focused on your other child you are now noticing these behaviors.

If you have been dealing with a particularly difficult child, it's important for you to acknowledge to his or her siblings that you understand how hard it has been for them to live with all that tension in the home.

And, finally, remember that you will not always feel like mirroring and empathizing. If you wait to feel like it, it may not happen. It is something you must consciously think about even when you've become really good at it. Above all, remember that your child *is* still a child and she *will* misbehave. All children misbehave. It's their job. What matters is how you react. This book will not give you a perfect child, but it will give you more tools to deal with those times when your child's behavior is, inevitably, less than perfect.

If you still have any doubts about the power of mirroring and connecting, consider this story.

More than twenty years ago, while I was still working toward my master's degree, I worked at a group home for children in trouble. Most of them were twelve to fourteen years old, and they were smart, tough, and adept at running rings around their social workers. At first, they treated me the same way they did the rest of the staff. When they went to bed clutching their stuffed animals, however, they were just children, and they were afraid. They looked so small and vulnerable then that I couldn't help thinking how different their lives were from my own at that age, and my heart ached for them.

As part of their bedtime routine, I started to sing them lullabies and tell them stories. They loved listening, and their tough exterior melted away as I sang and told them stories about faraway places. Other staff members told me I was crazy, these kids were too tough and too hard, and I shouldn't get so close to them. But I felt a strong need to nurture them. They spoke like younger children and quietly cried as I sang and rubbed their backs. They were alone and hurting and in tremendous emotional pain. I remember one child in particular, who, when she was scheduled to leave the next day, put her hands on my cheeks and said, "I just want to remember this face, the face of someone who cares about me."

After just a few days, I began to notice changes in the way the children—because they were children—behaved with me. They started to listen instead of always ignoring or arguing with me. The other staff members decided it was because I was too soft and I was letting them get away with things, but it wasn't. The difference was that I had established a relationship with them, and they wanted to listen to me because I cared about them. Those kids taught me how critical it is to show compassion and how essential it is to help children be their best. They showed me that this is at the core of what we must be to one another. It's what connected parenting is all about.

Being a mother or a father is probably the hardest job you'll ever have, but also the most important and the most rewarding. Although at times it may seem endless, the time you have with your children is really very short. Before you know it, they're grown up and gone. Before that happens, every parent should ask him or herself three questions: *What do I want my children to remember about their childhood? What will I feel when my children are gone and I look back upon myself as a parent? What do I want my children to remember about me?* In the end, when they're adults and out of the house, I believe that what we want them to remember is how special they were to us and how deeply loved they felt. This is a gift that will last them a lifetime and one that they will then pass on to their own children.

Suggested Reading

Brown, Thomas E. *Attention Deficit Disorder*. New Haven, CT: Yale University Press, 2005.

Cox, Adam J. *No Mind Left Behind: Understanding and Fostering Executive Control—The Eight Essential Brain Skills Every Child Needs to Thrive*. New York: Penguin, 2007.

Doidge, Norman. *The Brain That Changes Itself*. New York: Penguin, 2007.

Faber, Adele and Elaine Mazlish. *How to Talk So Kids Will Listen and Listen So Kids Will Talk*. New York: Collins Living, 1999.

Glasser, Howard and Jennifer Easley. *Transforming the Difficult Child*. Tucson, AZ: Nurtured Heart Publications, 1999.

Greene, Ross. *The Explosive Child*. New York: Harper, 2005.

Huebner, Dawn. *What to Do When You Worry Too Much*. Washington, DC: Magination Press, 2005.

Hughes, Daniel. *Building the Bonds of Attachment*. Northvale, NJ: Jason Aronson, 2006.

Jackson, Marsha. *Boom . . . Boom . . . Boom: A Story to Raise Your Child's Emotional Inteligence*. Full of Ideas Publishing, 2008.

Kendall, Philip C. *Child and Adolescent Therapy*. New York: Guilford Press, 2005.

———. *Cognitive-Behavioral Therapy for Anxious Children*. New York: Guilford Press, 2006.

———. *Coping Cat Workbook*. New York: Guilford Press, 2006.

Kutscher, Martin. *ADHD Book*. Self-published, 2002.

———, et al. *Kids in the Syndrome Mix of ADHD, LD, Asperger's, Tourette's, Bipolar and More!* London: Jessica Kingsley, 2007.

Levine, Mel. *The Myth of Laziness*. New York: Simon & Schuster, 2003.

Mamen, Maggie. *The Pampered Child Syndrome*. London: Jessica Kingsley, 2005.

Manassis, Katharina. *Keys to Parenting Your Anxious Child*. Hauppauge, NY: Barron's Educational Series, 1996.

Maté, Gabor. *Scattered*. New York: Plume, 2000.

———. *When the Body Says No*. Hoboken, NJ: Wiley, 2003.

Neufeld, Gordon, and Gabor Maté. *Hold On to Your Kids*. New York: Ballantine, 2006.

Papolos, Demitri and Janice. *The Bipolar Child*. New York: Broadway, 2007.

Polis, Ben. *Only a Mother Could Love Him*. London: Hodder Mobius, 2005.

Sears, William and Martha. *The Attachment Parenting Book*. New York: Little Brown, 2001.

Tanguay, Pamela B. *Nonverbal Learning Disabilities at Home*. London: Jessica Kingsley, 2001.

———. *Nonverbal Learning Disabilities at School*. London: Jessica Kingsley, 2002.

Webster-Stratton, Carolyn. *How to Promote Children's Social and Emotional Competence*. London: Paul Chapman Educational Publishing, 2000.

Index

"Sometimes we try so hard to be the perfect parent, and put so much effort into it that we can't get out of our own way. Jennifer Kolari shows us ways to deal with our children that are so simple and yet so brilliant it's like magic. If you are a parent, know a parent, or are planning to become a parent, you need this book. As a pediatrician for nearly twenty years and the mother of four children, I can honestly say I wish I'd had this book before my first child was born, it would have made life so much easier. The techniques in this book can be effectively applied to a two-year-old or a twenty-year-old, and that's the beauty of *Connected Parenting*."

—Debra DeBiasse, M.D., FAAP, Salina Regional Health Center, Salina, Kansas

"With *Connected Parenting*, Jennifer Kolari provides a novel approach to parenting the challenging child. Her CALM approach (connect, *affect*, *listen*, *mirror*) is not necessarily instinctive for most parents. Instead of starting with advice on changing behavior, she begins with the more fundamental task of rebuilding frayed relationships and understanding the emotions behind the unwanted behaviors. Ms. Kolari uses mirroring, a therapy technique, as a strategic form of parental communication. The mirroring approach takes practice but accomplishes several important goals; it makes the child feel understood, diffuses emotions, and leads to opportunities for repair. Incorporated into the relationship with one's child, the technique has long-lasting effects on the child's behavior. Although Ms. Kolari directs her work toward the relationship with the challenging child, the lessons learned can be applied to all relationships. *Connected Parenting* is compelling reading for any parent who has been challenged by the relationship with his or her child."

—John T. Kanegaye, M.D., FAAP, FACEP, Division of Emergency Medicine,
Rady Children's Hospital–San Diego, Associate Clinical Professor,
Department of Pediatrics, University of California,
San Diego School of Medicine

"All the secrets are revealed in *Connected Parenting*. These are the keys to unlock the barriers that exist between parents and children. For parents, educators and Family Medicine residents, Jennifer Kolari's first book should be required reading. The tools are invaluable, but most important, they are effective and behavioral change will successfully occur."

—Dr. Marvin Gelkopf, M.D., CCF, FCFP, Assistant Professor, University of Toronto

"As a practicing pediatrician, I have had the privilege of observing the success of Jennifer Kolari's therapeutic techniques over many years. Now that these techniques are available in this book, I will be recommending *Connected Parenting* to every parent who brings their infant to my office."

—Dr. Till Davy, FRCP(C), FAAP, Honorary Consultant,
The Hospital for Sick Children, Toronto,
Associate Professor of Pediatrics, University of Toronto

"Reading this book is like being in a private therapy session with Jennifer Kolari. Real-life scenarios are described. We are given the words to use when we face typical difficult parenting situations. Staying calm and using the CALM technique truly make a difference in the life of the child and the life of the family. The mirroring method that is taught by *Connected Parenting* and is described in this book is very powerful and very effective. Now parents can have unlimited access to the excellent Connected Parenting techniques described in this book."

—Dr. Daphna Grossman, M.D., CCFP(EM), FCFP

"*Connected Parenting* has changed how I interact with my son in such a positive way. More important, I see how mirroring is a lifelong tool that is essential in every relationship."

—Sarah Stirtz, Registered Nurse, Salina, Kansas

"Jennifer Kolari has taken her exceptional gifts as a child therapist and made them accessible to a wider audience. More than any other parenting book I have read, *Connected Parenting* offers parents a framework by which they can demonstrate and communicate a deep understanding of their child's inner emotional life. Calming your child and in particular mirroring are much more than mere techniques. These are the building blocks of loving, enduring relationships."

—Pauline Pariser, MASc, M.D., CCFP, FCFP